Lecture Notes in Computer Science 5413

Commenced Publication in 1973
Founding and Former Series Editors:
Gerhard Goos, Juris Hartmanis, and Jan van Leeuwen

Editorial Board

Andrea De Lucia   Filomena Ferrucci (Eds.)

Software Engineering

International Summer Schools
ISSSE 2006-2008, Salerno, Italy
Revised Tutorial Lectures

 Springer

Volume Editors

Andrea De Lucia
Filomena Ferrucci
Università di Salerno
Dipartimento di Matematica e Informatica
Via Ponte Don Melillo, 84084, Fisciano, SA, Italy
E-mail: {adelucia,fferrucci}@unisa.it

Library of Congress Control Number: Applied for

CR Subject Classification (1998): D.2, D.1, F.3, K.6.3

LNCS Sublibrary: SL 2 – Programming and Software Engineering

ISSN   0302-9743
ISBN-10   3-540-95887-8 Springer Berlin Heidelberg New York
ISBN-13   978-3-540-95887-1 Springer Berlin Heidelberg New York

springer.com

© Springer-Verlag Berlin Heidelberg 2009
Printed in Germany

Typesetting: Camera-ready by author, data conversion by Scientific Publishing Services, Chennai, India
Printed on acid-free paper   SPIN: 12605804   06/3180   5 4 3 2 1 0

Preface

Software Engineering is widely recognized as one of the most exciting, stimulating, and profitable research areas with significant practical impacts on the software industry. Thus, training the future generations of software engineering researchers and bridging the gap between academia and industry are especially important. The International Summer School on Software Engineering (ISSSE) aims to contribute both to training future researchers and to facilitating knowledge exchange between academia and industry. Beginning in 2003, it has become an annual meeting point that is now in its fifth edition (2003, 2005, 2006, 2007, and 2008).

ISSSE is intended for PhD students, university researchers, and professionals from industry. Attracting more than 60 participants each year, the program of the school includes six state-of-the-art tutorials given by internationally recognized research leaders on very relevant topics for the scientific community. Each tutorial provides a general introduction to the chosen topic, while also covering the most important contributions in depth and identifying the main research challenges for software engineers. The focus is on methods, techniques, and tools; in some cases theory is required to provide a solid basis.

The format of the school aims at creating extensive discussion forums between lecturers and industrial and academic attendees. Besides traditional tutorials, lab sessions are also included in the program together with student talks and tool demos to further stimulate the interaction. The school is held on the campus of the University of Salerno and benefits from the facilities of the university (e.g., laboratories) and from its location, very close to some of the most beautiful and historical places of Italy, such as the Amalfi Coast, Capri, Pompei, and Paestum.

This volume collects chapters originating from some tutorial lectures given at the last three editions of the school (2006, 2007, and 2008) and aims to provide a contribution on some of the latest findings in the field of software engineering. Several interesting topics are covered including software adaptability and dependability, autonomic computing, usability in requirements engineering, testing of service-oriented architectures, reverse engineering, collaborative development, web cost estimation and productivity assessment, empirical software engineering, and experience factory. The volume is organized in three parts, collecting chapters focused on software requirements and design, software testing and reverse engineering, and management.

In the first chapter, Paola Inverardi and Massimo Tivoli take into account two of the key requirements that software in the near ubiquitous future (Softure) will need to satisfy, namely, adaptation and dependability. Software systems need to be adaptable according to the context changes determined by the diversity of computing platforms where software systems are to get deployed and the different execution environments where they have to operate. Moreover, the pervasiveness of software systems and the highly dynamic nature of service provision make Softure dependability more complex. Thus, ensuring the dependability of self-adaptive systems poses numerous challenges to software engineers. In the chapter, the authors analyze some of these challenges and describe possible solutions.

In the second chapter, Hausi A. Müller et al. focus on autonomic computing, an approach to building self-managing computing systems with the aim of addressing the management complexity of dynamic computing systems through technology simplification and automation. Autonomic computing is inspired by the autonomic nervous system of the human body that controls important bodily functions without any conscious intervention. It includes a broad range of technologies, models, architecture patterns, standards, and processes and is based on some key aspects, such as feedback control, adaptation, and self-management. In particular, at the core of an autonomic system are the feedback control loops that constantly monitor the system and its environment looking for events to handle. The authors address the problem of designing such highly dynamical systems, arguing that both a software architecture perspective and a feedback control perspective need to be taken into account. Moreover, they show how autonomic computing technology can solve continuous evolution problems of software-intensive systems. Finally, they illustrate some lessons learned and outline some challenges for the future.

In chap. 3, Natalia Juristo focuses on usability, which represents one of the most important quality factors of a software product but it is often insufficient in most software systems. In particular, the author proposes an approach to build software with higher usability. According to such an approach usability features need to be considered from a functional viewpoint at requirements stage, because as some empirical studies show, software design and usability are related. To address the difficulties of usability features elicitation and specification, the author proposes specific guidelines that support face-to-face communication among the different stakeholders and lead software developers to ask the appropriate questions so as to capture usability requirements information and cut down ambiguous usability details as early as possible.

Chapters 4 and 5 focus on software testing of service-oriented architectures. In the life-cycle of any software system, testing is a crucial activity to ensure adequate software dependability but it is also one of the most expensive. This is especially true with service-oriented architectures. Indeed, this emerging paradigm for distributed computing is radically changing the way in which software applications are developed and posing several new challenges for software testing. These mainly originate from the high flexibility and dynamic nature of service-oriented architectures and the use of some unique features such as service discovery and composition, ultra-late binding, automated negotiation, autonomic system reconfiguration, and so on. In chap. 4, Gerardo Canfora and Massimiliano Di Penta provide a broad survey of the recent research carried out on the topics of testing of service-oriented architectures. The authors analyze several challenges from the viewpoints of different stakeholders and present solutions for different levels of testing (unit, integration, and regression testing) and for both functional and non-functional testing. The authors conclude the chapter by exploring ways to improve the testability of service-oriented architectures. In chap. 5, Antonia Bertolino et al. deepen the discussion to challenges and solutions concerning testing activities by focusing on the validation framework developed in the European Project PLASTIC. In the framework, different techniques can be combined for the verification of functional and non-functional properties for both development time testing and service live usage monitoring. The authors also describe some techniques and tools that fit within the proposed framework.

Chapter 6 focuses on software architecture reconstruction, i.e., the kind of reverse engineering where architectural information is reconstructed for an existing system. Software architectures are able to provide a global understanding of a software system that is essential to effectively carry out many maintenance and migration tasks. Nevertheless, frequently software architecture is not sufficiently described, or it is outdated and inappropriate for the task at hand. Thus, it is necessary to reconstruct it gathering information from several sources (source code, system's execution, available documentation, stakeholder interviews, and domain knowledge), applying appropriate abstraction techniques, and suitably presenting the obtained information. In this chapter, Rainer Koschke introduces a conceptual framework for architecture reconstruction that represents a combination of common patterns and best practices reported in the reverse engineering literature. The current state of the art of techniques and methods for software architecture reconstruction is also summarized here. Finally, the author discusses a number of research challenges that should be tackled in the future.

In chap. 7, Filippo Lanubile focuses on the globalization of software development that represents a trend in today's software industry. Indeed, developing software using teams geographically distributed in different sites can provide an important competitive advantage for software companies but at the same time it presents challenges that affect all aspects of a project. The author focuses on the collaboration issues that arise from the negative effects of distance, illustrates a taxonomy of software engineering tools that support distributed projects, and presents several collaborative development environments. Computer-mediated communication theories that can be useful to address the development of more effective tools supporting collaboration in distributed software development are also discussed. Finally, the author summarizes a family of empirical studies which have been carried out to build an evidence-based model of task–technology fit for distributed requirements engineering.

Web applications are constantly increasing both in complexity and number of features. As a result, Web effort estimation and productivity analysis are becoming crucial activities for software companies to develop projects that are finished on time and within budget. Indeed, they are essential elements for project managers to suitably plan the development activities, allocate resources adequately, and control costs and schedule. In chap. 8 Emilia Mendes introduces the main concepts and techniques for Web effort estimation and reports on a case study where the process for the construction and validation of a Web effort estimation model is illustrated step-by-step. Moreover, the author introduces the main concepts related to Web productivity measurement and benchmarking and describes a case study on productivity benchmarking.

In the final chapter, Giuseppe Visaggio addresses the relevant challenge of transferring research results in production processes and exchanging results between researchers and enterprises. Indeed, competition requires continuous innovation of processes and products and a critical issue for organizations is how to speed up knowledge creation and sharing. Knowledge management aims to provide an answer to this issue by managing the processes of knowledge creation, storage, and sharing. The author presents a widely known model of knowledge management, namely, the experience factory, that collects empirical knowledge in an experience package with the aim of mitigating the consequences of knowledge loss due to staff turnover, improving products and processes, and assuring near-the-job learning. Based on previous technology transfer experiences, the author proposes a model for systematically structuring the content of a package and allowing for an incremental and cooperative production of packages. A platform that supports the collection and distribution of knowledge-experience packages is also described.

We wish to conclude by expressing our gratitude to the many people who supported the publication of this volume with their time and energy. First of all, we wish to thank the lecturers and all the authors for their valuable contribution. We also gratefully acknowledge the Scientific Committee Members, for their work and for promoting the International Summer School on Software Engineering. Thanks are due to our department (Dipartimento di Matematica e Informatica, Università di Salerno) for the administrative and organizational support we received every day. We are also grateful to Vincenzo Deufemia, Sergio Di Martino, Fausto Fasano, Rita Francese, Carmine Gravino, Rocco Oliveto, Ignazio Passero, Michele Risi, and Giuseppe Scanniello, who were of great help in organizing the school. Finally, we want to thank Springer for providing us with the opportunity to publish this volume.

We hope you will enjoy reading the chapters and find them relevant and fruitful for your work. We also hope that the tackled topics will encourage your research in the software engineering field and your participation in the International Summer School on Software Engineering.

October 2008

Andrea De Lucia
Filomena Ferrucci

Table of Contents

The Future of Software: Adaptation and Dependability[*]

Paola Inverardi and Massimo Tivoli

University of L'Aquila
Dip. Informatica
via Vetoio, 67100 L'Aquila
Fax: +390862433131
{inverard,tivoli}@di.univaq.it

Abstract. Software in the near ubiquitous future (Softure) will need to cope with variability, as software systems get deployed on an increasingly large diversity of computing platforms and operates in different execution environments. Heterogeneity of the underlying communication and computing infrastructure, mobility inducing changes to the execution environments and therefore changes to the availability of resources and continuously evolving requirements require software systems to be adaptable according to the context changes. Softure should also be reliable and meet the users performance requirements and needs. Moreover, due to its pervasiveness and in order to make adaptation effective and successful, adaptation must be considered in conjunction with dependability, i.e., no matter what adaptation is performed, the system must continue to guarantee a certain degree of Quality of Service (QoS). Hence, Softure must also be dependable, which is made more complex given the highly dynamic nature of service provision. Supporting the development and execution of Softure systems raises numerous challenges that involve languages, methods and tools for the systems thorough design and validation in order to ensure dependability of the self-adaptive systems that are targeted. However these challenges, taken in isolation are not new in the software domain. In this paper we will discuss some of these challenges and possible solutions making reference to the approach undertaken in the IST PLASTIC project for a specific instance of Softure focused on software for Beyond 3G (B3G) networks.

1 Introduction

The design and the development of dependable and adaptable software applications in the near ubiquitous future (Softure) cannot rely on the classical desktop-centric assumption that the system execution environment is known a priori at

---

[*] This work is a revised and extended version of [6]. It has been partially supported by the IST project PLASTIC. We acknowledge all the members of the PLASTIC Consortium and of the SEALab at University of L'Aquila for joint efforts on all the research efforts reported in this paper.

A. De Lucia and F. Ferrucci (Eds.): ISSSE 2006–2008, LNCS 5413, pp. 1–31, 2009.

design time and, hence, the application environment of a Softure cannot be statically anticipated. Softure will need to cope with variability, as software systems get deployed on an increasingly large diversity of computing platforms and operates in different execution environments. Heterogeneity of the underlying communication and computing infrastructure, mobility inducing changes to the execution environments and therefore changes to the availability of resources and continuously evolving requirements require software systems to be adaptable according to the context changes. At the same time, Softure should be reliable and meet the users performance requirements and needs. Moreover, due to its pervasiveness and in order to make adaptation effective and successful, adaptation must be considered in conjunction with dependability, i.e., no matter what adaptation is performed, the system must continue to guarantee a certain degree of Quality of Service (QoS). Hence, Softure must also be dependable, which is made more complex given the highly dynamic nature of service provision.

Supporting the development and execution of Softure systems raises numerous challenges that involve languages, methods and tools for the systems through design and validation in order to ensure dependability of the self-adaptive systems that are targeted.

However these challenges, taken in isolation are not new in the software domain. Adaptable and re-configurable systems do exist in many software application domains from tele-communication to the software domain itself, e.g., operating systems. Dependable systems have been intensively investigated and methods and tools exist to develop them. Hence what are the new challenges for Softure? In the following we will discuss some of these challenges and possible solutions making reference to the approach undertaken in the IST PLASTIC [13] project for the specific instance of Softure as software for Beyond 3G (B3G) networks. Our thesis is that Softure requires to rethink the whole software engineering process and, in particular, it needs to reconcile the static view with the dynamic view by breaking the traditional division among development phases by moving some activities from design time to deployment and run time hence asking for new and more efficient verification and validation techniques. Dependability is achieved with a comprehensive life cycle approach from requirements to operation, to maintenance by analyzing models, testing code, monitor, and repair execution. Many software models are involved, from requirements to specification, to code. In order to support dependability of adaptable applications new modeling notations are required. These should permit to express and deal with characteristics that are crucial for a Softure, i.e., QoS, resource-awareness, evolution, reconfiguration, variability, and uncertainty. At the same time they should allow for validation techniques affordable at run time. Their cost must be sustainable under the execution environment resource constraints, e.g. time and computational resources. In order to easily and consistently integrate the modeling layer with the analysis and implementation ones, model transformation and evolution techniques should be exploited.

The paper is structured as follows. In the following section we discuss the Softure characteristics in order to identify the two key challenges: *adaptability* and *dependability.* Section 3 discusses and compares different notions of adaptability with different degrees of dependability. This discussion will bring us to consider the Softure issues in a software process perspective. In Section 4, based on the previous discussion and comparison of different adaptability and dependability degrees, we discuss the requirements that the modeling notations to the design, development, and validation of Softure should satisfy. Section 5 proposes a new software process and discusses it in the scope of the PLASTIC project [13]. In Section 6 we conclude by summarizing the thesis originating from the discussion carried on through the paper.

2 Softure Challenges: Setting the Context

Softure is supposed to execute in an ubiquitous, heterogeneous infrastructure under mobility constraints. This means that the software must be able to carry on operations while changing different execution environments or *contexts*. Execution contexts offer a variability of resources that can affect the software operation. *Context awareness* refers to the ability of an application to *sense* the context in which it is executing and therefore it is the base to consider (self-)adaptive applications, i.e., software systems that have the ability to change their *behavior* in response to external changes.

It is worthwhile stressing that although a change of context is measured in terms of availability of resources, that is in quantitative terms, an application can only be adapted by changing its behavior, i.e., its functional/qualitative specification. In particular, (Physical) Mobility allows a user to move out of his proper context, traveling across different contexts. To our purposes the difference among contexts is determined in terms of available resources like connectivity, energy, software, etc. However other dimensions of contexts can exist relevant to the user, system and physical domains, which are the main context domains identified in the literature [15]. In the software development practice when building a system the context is determined and it is part of the (non-functional) requirements (operational, social, organizational constraints). If context changes, requirements change therefore the system needs to change. In standard software the pace at which context changes is slow and they are usually taken into account as evolutionary requirements. For SOFTURE context changes occur due to physical mobility while the system is in operation. This means that if the system needs to change this should happen dynamically. This notion leads to consider different ways to modify a system at run time that can happen in different forms namely *(self-)adaptiveness/dynamicity* and at different levels of granularity, from software architecture to line of code.

Softure needs also to be dependable. *Dependability* is an orthogonal issue that depends on QoS attributes, like performance and all other -bilities. Dependability impacts all the software life cycle.

In general dependability is an attribute for software systems that operate in specific application domains. For Softure we consider dependability in its original meaning as defined in [5], that is *the trustworthiness of a computing system which allows reliance to be justifiably placed on the service it delivers ... Dependability includes such attributes as reliability, availability, safety, security.* Softure encompasses any kind of software system that can operate in the future ubiquitous infrastructure. The dependability requirement is therefore extended also to applications that traditionally have not this requirement. Dependability in this case represents the user requirement that states that the application must operate in the unknown world (i.e., out of a confined execution environment) with the same level of reliance it has when operating at home. At home means in the controlled execution environment where there is complete knowledge of the system behavior and the context is fixed. In the unknown world, the knowledge of the system is undermined by the absence of knowledge on contexts, thus the dependability requirement arises also for conventional applications. Traditionally dependability is achieved with a comprehensive approach all along the software life cycle from requirements to operation to maintenance by analyzing models, testing code, monitor and repair execution.

Therefore the overall challenge is to provide dependable assurance for highly adaptable applications. Since dependability is achieved throughout the life cycle many software artifacts are involved, from requirements specification to code. In the rest of this paper we will consider as such artifacts only *models* that is idealized view of the system suitable for reasoning, developing, validating a real system. Models can be functional and non-functional and can represent different level of abstractions of the real system, from requirements to code. Our research bias is on Software Architecture, therefore we will often consider software architectural systems models. An architectural model allows the description of the static and dynamic components of the system and explains how they interact. Software architectures support early analysis, verification and validation of software systems. Software architectures are the earliest comprehensive system model along the software lifecycle built from requirements specification. They are increasingly part of standardized software development processes because they represent a system abstraction in which design choices relevant to the correctness of the final system are taken. This is particularly evident for dependability requirements like security and reliability and quantitative ones like performance.

3   Adaptabilty: 3 Examples

In this section we discuss the notion of adaptability. According to what presented so far, adaptability is the ability to change a system according to context variations, e.g., driven by QoS requirements. However, the change should maintain the essence of the system that from now on we will call invariant. From Section 3.2 to Section 3.4, we will focus on evolving systems that change through adaptation. In order to classify them we propose to use a 4 dimension metric: the four Ws.

3.1   The Four Ws

The systems we consider can change through adaptability either their *structure* and/or their *behavior*. The four Ws characterize the nature of the change along the following four dimensions:

- *Why* there is the need to change?
- *What* does (not) change?
- *When* does the change happen?
- *What/Who* manages the change?

Why: this dimension makes explicit the need for the change. In a Software Engineering perspective this change is always done to meet requirements. It can be because the requirements evolved or it can be that the system does not behave properly according to the stated requirements. It is also worthwhile mentioning that requirements can be functional and non functional requirements. The former class captures the qualitative behavior of a software system, its functional specification. The latter defines the systemss quantitative attributes like, performance, reliability, security, etc.

What: here we discuss the part of the system that is affected by the change. Referring to architectural models, changes can affect the structure and/or the behavior. For the structure, components can get in and out, new connectors can be added and removed. For the behavior components can change their functionality and connectors can change their interaction protocols.

When: this dimension captures the moment during the systems lifetime in which the change occurs. It does not mean that the change happens necessarily at run time. This dimension is related with the Static versus Dynamic issue.

What/Who: this is the description of the mechanisms to achieve the change. It can be a configuration manager or it can be the system itself. Involves monitoring the system to collect relevant data, evaluating this data, make a decision about the change alternatives and then perform the actual change.

In the following we will provide 3 examples of functional and non-functional adaptation. The first one has been developed in the Software Engineering research group at University of L'Aquila.

3.2 Synthesis: An Approach to Automatically Build Failure-Free Connectors for Component-Based Architectures

Synthesis is a technique equipped with a tool [2,16] that permits to assemble a component-based application in a deadlock-free way [7,8,18]. Starting from a set of components Off The Shelf (OTS), Synthesis assembles them together according to a so called connector-based architecture by synthesizing a connector that guarantees deadlock-free interactions among components. The code that implements the new component representing the connector is derived, in an automatic way, directly from the OTS (black-box) components interfaces. Synthesis assumes a partial knowledge of the components interaction behavior described as finite state automata plus the knowledge of a specification of the system to assemble given in terms of Message Sequence Charts (MSC) [9,19,20]. Furthermore, by exploiting that MSC specification, it is possible to go beyond deadlock. Actually, the MSC specification is an implicit failure specification. That is we assume to specify all the *desired* assembled system behaviors which are failure-free from the point of view of the system assembler, rather than to explicitly specify the failure. Under these hypotheses, Synthesis automatically derives the assembling code of the connector for a set of components. The connector is derived in such a way to obtain a failure-free system. It is shown that the connector-based system is equivalent according to a suitable equivalence relation to the initial one once depurated of all the failure behaviors. The initial connector is a *no-op* connector that serves to model all the possible component interactions (i.e., the failure-free and the failing ones). Acting on the initial connector is enough to automatically prevent both deadlocks and other kinds of failure hence obtaining the failure-free connector.

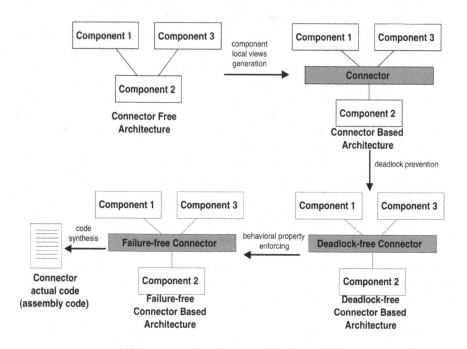

Fig. 1. The Synthesis Application Adaptation

As illustrated in Figure 1, the Synthesis framework realizes a form of system adaptation. The initial software system is changed by inserting a new component, the connector, in order to prevent interactions failures.

The framework makes use of the following models and formalisms. An architectural model, the connector-based architecture that constrains the way components can interact, by forcing interaction to go through the connector. A set of behavioral models for the components that describe each single components interaction behavior with the *ideal*[1] external context in the form of Label Transition Systems (LTSs). A behavioral equivalence on LTS to establish the equivalence among the original system and the adapted one. MSC are used to specify the behavioral integration failure to be avoided, and then LTSs and *LTS*

---

[1] The one expected by the component's developer.

synchronous product [1,10] plus a notion of *behavioral refinement* [11] to synthesize the failure-free connector specification, as it is described in detail in [18]. From the connector specification the actual code can then be automatically derived as either a centralized component [18] or a distributed one [3]. The latter is implemented as a set of *wrappers*, one for each component, that cooperatively realize the same behavior as the centralized connector.

SythesisRT. Recently, the Synthesis approach and its related tool has been extended to the context of real-time systems [17]. This extension, hereafter called SynthesisRT, has been developed by the Software Engineering research group at University of L'Aquila in cooperation with the POP ART project team at INRIA Rhône-Alpes. In [17], it is shown how to deal with the compatibility, communication, and QoS issues that can raise while building a real-time system from reusable black-box components within a lightweight component model where components follow a data-flow interaction model. Each component declares input and output ports which are the points of interaction with other components and/or the execution environment. Input (resp., output) ports of a component are connected to output (resp., input) ports of a different component through synchronous links. Analogously to the version of Synthesis without real-time constraints, a component interface includes a formal description of the *interaction protocol* of the component with its expected environment in terms of sequences of writing and reading actions to and from ports. The interface language is expressive enough to specify QoS constraints such as writing and reading *latency*, *duration*, and *controllability*, as well as the component's *clock* (i.e., its activation frequency). In order to deal with incompatible components (e.g., clock inconsistency, read/write latency/duration inconsistency, mismatching interaction protocols, etc.) we synthesize component *adaptors* interposed between two or more interacting components. An adaptor is a component that mediates the interaction between the components it supervises, in order to harmonize their communication. Each adaptor is automatically derived by taking into account the interface specification of the components it supervises. The adaptor synthesis allows the developer to automatically and *incrementally* build *correct-by-construction* systems from third-party components.

Figure 2 shows the main steps of the method performed by SynthesisRT by also highlighting the used formalisms/models.

We take as input the architectural specification of the network of components to be composed and the component interface specifications. The behavioral models of the components are generated in form of LTSs that make the elapsing of time explicit (step 1). Connected ports with different names are renamed such that complementary actions have the same label in the component LTSs (see actions a and d in Figure 2). Possible mismatches/deadlocks are checked by looking for possible sink states into the parallel composition of the LTSs. The adaptor synthesis process starts only if such deadlocks are detected.

The synthesis first proceeds by constructing a *Petri net* (PN) [12] representation of the environment expected from a component in order not to block it (step 2). It consists in complementing the actions in the component LTSs that

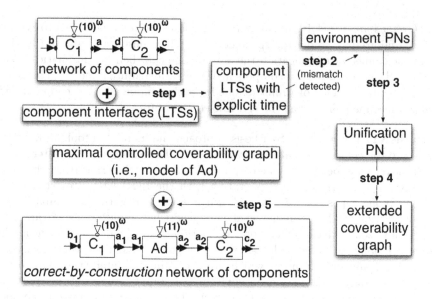

Fig. 2. Main steps of adaptor synthesis for real-time components

are performed on connected ports, considering the actions performed on unconnected ports as internal actions. Moreover, a buffer storing read and written
values is modeled as a place in the environment PN for each IO action. Each
such PN represents a partial view of the adaptor to be built. It is partial since it
reflects the expectation of a single component. In particular, a write (resp. read)
action gives rise to a place (buffer) without outgoing (resp. incoming) arcs.

The partial views of the adaptor are composed together by building causal
dependencies between the reading/writing actions and by unifying time-elapsing
transitions (step 3). Furthermore, the places representing the same buffer are
merged in one single place. This *Unification PN* models an adaptor that solves
deadlocks using buffers to desynchronize received events from their emission.

However, the unification PN may be not completely correct, in the sense
that it can represent an adaptor that may deadlock and/or that may require
unbounded buffers. In order to obtain the most permissive and correct adaptor,
we generate an extended version of the graph usually known in PNs theory [12]
as the coverability graph [4] (step 4).

Our method automatically restricts the behavior of the adaptor modeled by
the extended coverability graph in order to keep only the interactions that are
deadlock-free and that use finite buffers (i.e., bounded interactions). This is done
by automatically constructing, if possible, an "instrumented" version of our extended coverability graph, called the *Controlled Coverability Graph (CCG)*. The
CCG is obtained by pruning from the extended coverability graph both the *sinking*
paths and the *unbounded* paths, by using a *controller synthesis* step [14] (step 5).

This process also performs a *backwards error propagation* step in order to
correctly take into account the case of sinking and unbounded paths originating
from the firing of uncontrollable transitions.

If it exists, the maximal CCG generated is the LTS modeling the behavior of the correct (i.e., deadlock-free and bounded) adaptor. This adaptor models the correct-by-construction assembly code for the components in the specified network. If it does not exist, a correct adaptor assembling the components given as input to our method cannot be automatically derived, and hence our method does not provide any assembly code for those components.

Let us now analyze the Synthesis(RT) approach to adaptation by means of the four *Ws* metric:

Why there is the need to change? Here the purpose of the change is to *correct* functional behavior and to *make* the non-functional one fit. That is to avoid interaction deadlocks (due to possible clock inconsistency, inconsistent latency / duration for the component actions, mismatching interaction protocols) and / or enforce a certain interaction property P. This adaptation is not due to changes of context simply because, at assembly time, the context does not to change. The change here aims at both correcting a functional misbehavior and making different non-functional characteristics of the components fit.

What does (not) change? It changes the topological structure and the interaction behavior. A new component is inserted in the system and the overall interaction behavior is changed. The invariant part of the system is represented by all the correct behaviors. The proof that the adaptation preserves the invariant is by construction.

When does the change happen? It happens at assembly time, thus prior to deployment and execution. Thus it is actually part of the development process.

What/Who manages the change? An external entity: The developer through the Synthesis(RT) framework.

3.3 Topological Evolution: Graph Grammars to Describe Software Architecture Styles

In this section we summarize and discuss (w.r.t. the four Ws) the work by D. Le Métayer described in [24]. In this work the author proposes to describe software architectures formally in terms of graphs. The nodes of the graph represent the individual system entities (i.e., components, in a very general meaning). The edge corresponds to the communication links (i.e., connectors) between entities. Architectural styles are defined as context-free graph grammars since they can be seen as a set of architectures (and, hence, graphs) sharing a common shape. In other words, an architectural style is the "type" (i.e., form) that an architecture conform to the style must have at run time, that is the possible interconnections between its individual entities. A "coordinator" is used to pilot the overall application, and it is in charge of managing the architecture itself (creating and removing entities and links). As an illustration, the graph shown in Figure 3 represents an example of a client-server architecture.

The architecture represented by the graph shown in Figure 3 involves two clients $c1$ and $c2$, two servers $s1$ and $s2$, a manager $m0$ and $x0$. It is formally defined as the set D:

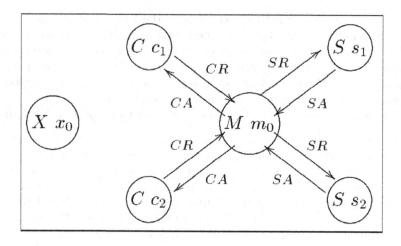

Fig. 3. A client-server architecture

$\{CR(c1, m0), CA(m0, c1), C(c1), CR(c2, m0), CA(m0, c2), C(c2), SR(m0, s1),$
$SA(s1, m0), S(s1), SR(m0, s2), SA(s2, m0), S(s2), X(x0), M(m0)\}$

where C, S, M, and X correspond, respectively, to the client, server, manager and external entity types. The external entity stands for the external world; it records requests for new clients wanting to be registered in the system. CR and CA correspond to client request links and client answer links (they are link types), respectively (SR and SA are the dual links for servers).

D is just one particular representative of a more general class of client-server architectures. Architectures belonging to this class must include values $X(x0)$ and $M(m0)$ and any number of servers and clients. Furthermore, they must follow the communication link pattern exhibited by D. Such a class is specified as a context-free graph grammar:

$$HCS = [\{CS, CS1\}, \{M, X, C, S, CR, CA, SR, SA\}, R, CS]$$

where $\{CS, CS1\}$ is the set of non-terminal symbols with CS the axiom (i.e., the origin of any derivation produced by applying the production rules in R), $\{M, X, C, S, CR, CA, SR, SA\}$ is the set of terminal symbols, and R the set of the following four production rules:

1. $CS \rightarrow CS1(m)$
2. $CS1(m) \rightarrow CR(c, m), CA(m, c), C(c), CS1(m)$
3. $CS1(m) \rightarrow SR(m, s), SA(s, m), S(s), CS1(m)$
4. $CS1(m) \rightarrow M(m), X(x)$

It is often the case that the architecture of an application should be able to evolve dynamically. For instance, a client-server organization must allow for the introduction of new clients or their departure. In the theoretical framework described in this section, the evolution of the architecture is defined by a coordinator. As an illustration, the following coordinator Coo_{CS} can be applied to a client-server architecture:

$$X(x), M(m) \rightarrow X(x), M(m), CR(c, m), CA(m, c), C(c)$$
$$CR(c, m), CA(m, c), C(c) \rightarrow \emptyset$$

The coordinator is defined as a set of production rules. The two rules above describe the introduction of a new client in the architecture and its departure, respectively.

The possibility of expressing architecture transformations is definitely a useful feature but it also raises a question: is it possible to ensure that a coordinator does not break the constraints of a given architectural style? For example, had we forgotten, say $CR(c, m)$ in the right-hand side of the first rule, then the coordinator would have been able to transform a client-server architecture into an architecture which would not belong any longer to the client-server class defined by HCS. To answer this question, in [24], the author defines a static style checking algorithm which would be the counterpart for coordinators of the type checking algorithms of classical languages. The algorithm has been applied to a real-scale case study, see [24] for further details.

Let us analyze the theoretical framework based on graph grammars, that is summarized in this section, with the four Ws metric:

Why there is the need to change? The change allows the *topological* evolution of the system (e.g., new components entering or quitting the system) according to the constraints imposed by the architectural style the system's software architecture conforms to.

What does (not) change? The topological structure of the system changes since its software architecture changes, but the imposed architectural style is preserved. Moreover, the interaction behavior does not change since the system's components are constrained to always exhibit the same "style" of interaction.

When does the change happen? At run time with the introduction of a new component acting as both a coordinator of the other components in the system and a manager of the links between the system components.

What/Who how is the change managed? By the coordinator and an external entity that allows the system to be open in the sense that its structure can evolve.

3.4 Topological and Behavioral Evolution: ArchJava

In this section we recall and discuss (w.r.t. the four Ws) the work by Aldrich et al. concerning the ArchJava[2] language [25,26]. ArchJava is an extension to Java which allows programmer to specify the architecture of the software within the program.

Software architecture is the organization of a software system as a collection of components, connections between the components, and constraints on how the components interact. Architecture description languages (ADLs) can be used

---

[2] http://www.cs.washington.edu/homes/jonal/archjava/

to specify and analyze the software architecture and, by equipping/integrating an ADL with a verification tool, Architecture specifications can be also automatically analyzed. Architecture specification is helpful in software development and maintenance since it represents the reference skeleton used to compose the system components and let them interact.

The motivation for ArchJava is the following: using an ADL for specifying the architecture causes problems since there could be inconsistencies between the implementation and the specification. This becomes a bigger problem as the software changes. ArchJava extends Java with constructs for specifying the architecture of the software. Using ArchJava software developers specify the architecture of the software within the program. Therefore, the architecture and the program are always consistent in the sense that a certain set of architectural constraints always hold in the implementation of the architecture.

Communication integrity is one of the architectural constraints that is worth checking when implementing an architectural specification into a program. Communication integrity means that the components only communicate directly with the components they are connected to in the architecture. By using ArchJava to implement an architectural specification into a program, the communication integrity, defined at the architectural-level, is guaranteed by the implemented program.

The new language constructs introduced by ArchJava are *Components*, *Ports*, and *Connections*. Components are the same as usual Java classes plus architectural constraints. They define architectural objects and must obey the declared architectural constraints. Ports are points of interaction of the components with the external environment, that is they define the communication interfaces of the components by declaring the set of methods that are *required* and *provided* to enable communication. Components communicate through ports and they can send and receive ordinary (i.e., non-component) objects between each other through the ports. As an illustration, the following is a part of the ArchJava code defining a component, Parser, with an input port declaring a required method, nextToken, and an output port declaring a provided method, parse. In order to implement parse the "private" method parseExpr is used.

```
public component class Parser {
  public port in {
    requires Token nextToken();
  }
  public port out {
    provides AST parse();
  }
  AST parse() {
    Token tok=in.nextToken();
    return parseExpr(tok);
  }
  AST parseExpr(Token tok) { ... }
  ...
}
```

Components can have sub-components, i.e., several components can be composed to form a composite component. Sub-components communicate through the connected ports. Connections are used to connect different ports and components can only communicate with their sub-components (through ports) and the components that they are connected to. As an illustration, the following is a part of the ArchJava code implementing the composite component `Compiler`:

```
public component class Compiler {
    private final Scanner scanner = new Scanner();
    private final Parser parser = new Parser();
    private final CodeGen codegen = new CodeGen();
    connect scanner.out, parser.in;
    connect parser.out, codegen.in;
    ...
```

`Compiler` is formed by three components, `Scanner`, `Parser`, and `Codegen`. The output port of `Scanner` (resp., `Parser`) is connected to input port of `Parser` (resp., `Codegen`). The `connect` primitive will bind each required method to a provided method with the same signature. The arguments to connect may be a components own ports or those of subcomponents in final fields. Connection consistency checks are performed to ensure that each required method is bound to unique provided method.

For the sake of clarity, in Figure 4, we show the software architecture of `Compiler`.

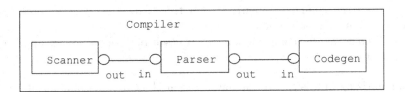

Fig. 4. Software architecture of a composite component

As mentioned above, ArchJava enforces communication integrity since no method calls are permitted from one component to another except either from a parent to its immediate sub-component or through connections in the architecture. This means that, on the one hand, ArchJava allows calls either between connected components, or from a parent to its immediate sub-component, or to shared objects. On the other hand, ArchJava forbids calls either that are external to sub-components, or between unconnected sub-components, or through shared objects.

In ArchJava, communication integrity can be statically checked (i.e., at compile time). This is due to way the ArchJava Type System has been designed. It enforces the following invariant: components can only get a typed reference to sub-components and connected components. Therefore, it is not possible to cast a component to an Object and avoid the restrictions on communication between components. This will cause an exception.

By using ArchJava, it is also possible to establish dynamic architectures. Instances of components can be dynamically created using new syntax as with ordinary objects. At creation time each component records the component instance that created it as its parent component. Communication integrity puts restrictions on how component instances can be used. Typed references to subcomponents should not escape the scope of their parent component. This requirement is enforced by putting restrictions on how component types can be used. Connections can be formed dynamically using a connect expression. A connect expression must match a connect pattern declared at the enclosing component. A connection pattern is used to describe a set of connections that can be instantiated at run time. A connect expression matches a connection pattern if the connected ports are identical and each connected component instance is an instance of the type specified in the pattern.

Let us analyze the features of the ArchJava language, that are recalled in this section, with the four *Ws* metric:

Why there is the need to change? The change allows both the topological and behavioral evolution of the system.

What does (not) change? The topological structure and the behavior of the system, e.g., new type of components can enter the system or old ones quitting it, and also new types of connections can be instantiated among components hence, possibly, introducing new interaction behavior. Whatever change is applied, communication integrity is kept, i.e., it is the invariant.

When does the change happen? At run time with the dynamic creation of component and connection instances.

What/Who how is the change managed? It is self-managed since the application itself steers it.

Summarizing in this section we have presented 5 examples of adaptation that differ with respect to several dimensions. One issue that is raised by the *when* dimension in the four Ws metric is whether *adaptability* is static or dynamic. The system adapts at run time, how and when the adaptation is computed or carried out does not change the problem, it is just a matter of *cost*. The cost we are referring to here is the cost of carrying out the adaptation maintaining the original integrity of the part of the application that does not change, i.e. the *invariant*. Thus if the application A that exhibits property P is changed into an application A' and the change is supposed to preserve the property P, then this means that also A' must satisfy P. For example the property P could be type integrity, thus we require that the change does not undermines type integrity in the changed application. Obviously, in this case, carrying out the change statically, i.e. before the system is running permits to prove type integrity of A' in a less expensive way than if done at run time.

4 Requirements on the Modelling Notations to Support Adaptation and Dependability

In this section we discuss the requirements that the modelling notations for Softure should satisfy in order to specify, and reason about, computational entities that will be adaptable to the environment they will be deployed and executed. We recall that adaptability is, here, intended as the ability to change a system according to requirement changes and context variations possibly driven by QoS requirements. However, the change should maintain the behavioural essence of the system that we call invariant. This premise allows us to set a number of requirements on the notations that should be used in the context of Softure. The first consideration is that a sole unifying notation will not suffice. This implies that a bunch of modelling notations should be used and consistently integrated. These notations will characterize the software at different levels of granularity, according to the adaptation variability. They will express different attributes of interest for validation purposes. It shall be possible to characterize the invariant behaviour of the software as well as its variability and it shall be possible to define accordingly a notion of cost for the validation of the invariant part upon adaptation. The adaptation logic itself needs to be described, either embedded in the software or external but dependent on the observation of the software to adapt. Besides notations for the adaptable software, notations for characterizing the context, both statically and at run time, must be defined. Each one of the above represents a research challenge itself and opens new research opportunities. All these new notations will be used to provide a common base for behavioural and dependability analysis, model checking, model transformation, correct-by-construction code synthesis and testing. A further challenge then is to let all the different notations coexist in a common evolutionary development framework based on model-transformations, which allows the definition of relationships between the different Softure notations. Summarizing, these notations should allow the developer to express context-aware adaptation in conjunction with the desired degree of dependability. In this direction, new modelling notations should be defined to support the effective development of Softure. These notations should be able to:

- Express the attributes of interest, operational profile (e.g., workload, probability of usage), user preferences, testability concepts (e.g., verdict, test case, test purpose), etc.
- Model relevant context characteristics to be monitored at run time to enable applications to adapt accordingly. Such notations should facilitate the management of context information (and their variations) being retrieved by different sources in a homogeneous way. They should also allow for advanced operations on contextual data, e.g., by comparing and reasoning on data for checking consistency and by combining different types of data.
- Define: (i) which behavioural properties have to be considered as invariants (i.e., no matter what adaptation will be performed, these properties must be always guaranteed), and (ii) which ones can be considered parametric

in the possible deployment environments. Depending on the system, on the properties and on the possible adaptations a static verification can be carried on. However, in general, their verification needs to be performed dynamically, under a certain notion of reasonable cost, in conjunction with the validation of the discovered deployment environment. Thus, how to model this notion of verification cost should also be another challenge to face.

– Express how to embed the adaptation logic in the system that we assume to be made of components. Two types of approaches are possible: (i) endogenous, that requires enriching the modelling language to provide this ability into the component logic; and (ii) exogenous, that refers to an external entity able to monitor the state exported from each component and adapt the component behaviour to dynamic changes in the environment. The first case amounts to provide in the component modelling notation higher-order capabilities. The latter amounts to make the component state available (and, hence, modelled) to be inspected and managed. Both of them require notations to effectively specify a kind of "make before break policies" for preparing the adaptation before the application consistency breaks. For instance, when switching from a given context to a different one the application might change its "internal" status according to the new environment it is entering into.

– Express variability in a declarative style in order to support property verification for evolving systems [34]. This requires capability in the notation to express degrees of generality in the component specification that can be instantiated, maintaining the correctness of the component, at run time depending on the execution context. The challenge, here, is providing the right balance between generality and verifiability.

All these new notations would be used to provide a common base for behavioural and dependability analysis, model checking, model transformation, correct-by-construction code synthesis, testing, and reconfiguration. Since a unique notation incorporating all such aspects is unreasonable (as discussed also in [35]), we envision that all the different notations should be let coexist in a common evolutionary development framework based on model-transformations, which allows the definition of relationships between different Softure notations.

5   Softure: The Process View

In this section we cast the above discussed challenges in a process view. The process view focuses on the set of activities that characterize the production and the operation of a software system. These activities are traditionally divided into activities related to the actual production of the software system and activities that are performed when the system can be executed and goes into operation. Specification, Design, Validation, and Evolution activities vary depending on the organization and the type of system being developed. Each Activity requires its Language, Methods and Tools and works on suitable artifacts of the system. For validation purposes each artifact can be coupled with a *model*. Models are an idealized view of the system suitable for reasoning, developing, validating a real system. To achieve dependability a large variety of models are used from behavioral to stochastic. These models represent the systems at very different levels of abstraction from requirements specification to code. The ever growing complexity of software has exacerbated the dichotomy development/static/compile time versus execution/dynamic/interpreter time concentrating as many analysis and validation activities as possible at development time.

Softure puts new requirements on this standard process. The evolutionary nature of Softure makes unfeasible a standard approach to validation since it would require before the system is in execution to predict the system behavior with respect to virtually any possible change. Therefore in the literature most approaches that try to deal with the validation of dynamic software system concentrate the changes to the structure by using graph and graph grammars formalisms or topological constraints [24,27,28,29,30,31]. As far as changes to behavior are concerned, only few approaches exist that make use either of behavioral equivalence checks or of the type system [25,26,32] or through code certification [23,33]. If dependability has to be preserved through adaptation, whatever the change mechanism is, at the time the change occurs a validation check must be performed. This means that all the models necessary to carry on the validation step must be available at run time and that the actual validation time becomes now part of the execution time.

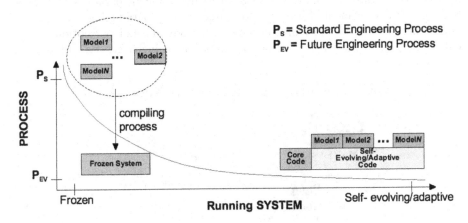

Fig. 5. The Future Engineering Process

The Future development process therefore has to explicitly account for complex validation steps at run time when all the necessary information are available. Figure 5 represents the process development plane delimited on one side by the standard process and on the other side by the future development one. The vertical dimension represents the static versus dynamic time with respect to the analysis and validation activities involved in the development process. The horizontal axis represents the amount of adaptability of the system, that is its ability to cope with evolution still maintaining dependability. The standard development process carries out most of the development and validation activities before the system is running that is during development. The result is a running system that, at run time, is frozen with respect to evolution. Considering development processes that allow increasingly degrees of adaptability allows to move along the horizontal axis thus ideally tending to a development process that is entirely managed at run time. In the middle we can place development processes that allow larger and larger portions of the system to change at run time and that make use for validation purposes of artifacts that can be produced statically. In the following section we introduce an instance of the Future Engineering Process that has been proposed in the scope of the PLASTIC project.

5.1   PLASTIC Services: An Instance of Softure

The PLASTIC project aims to offer a comprehensive provisioning platform for software services deployed over B3G networks (see Figure 6). A characteristic of this kind of infrastructure is its heterogeneity, that is it is not possible to assume that the variety of its components QoS is homogenized through a uniform layer. PLASTIC aims at offering B3G users a variety of application services exploiting the network's diversity and richness, without requiring systematic availability of an integrated network infrastructure. Therefore the PLASTIC platform needs to enable dynamic adaptation of services to the environment with respect to resource availability and delivered QoS, via a development paradigm based on Service Level Agreements (SLA) and resource-aware programming.

The provided services should meet the user demand and perception of the delivered QoS, which varies along several dimensions, including: type of service,

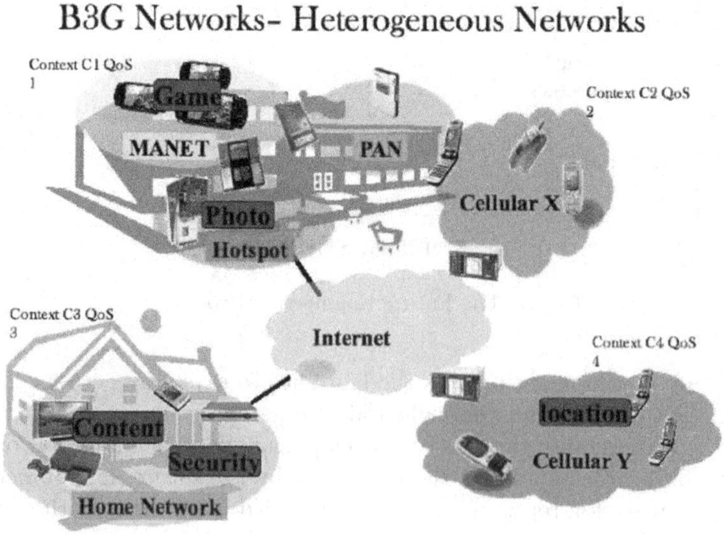

Fig. 6. B3G Networks

type of user, type of access device, and type of execution network environment. Referring to the challenges discussed in Section 2, this means that services must be *dependable* according to the users expected QoS.

This demands for a software engineering approach to the provisioning of services, which encompasses the full service life cycle, from development to validation, and from deployment to execution.

The PLASTIC answer to the above needs is to offer a comprehensive platform for the creation and provisioning of lightweight, adaptable services for the open wireless environment. Supporting the development of resource-aware and self-adapting components composing adaptable services requires focusing on the QoS properties offered by services besides the functional ones. The whole development environment is based on the PLASTIC Conceptual Model [36] whose main role is to provide an abstract characterization of B3G networks so as to ease the development of applications that effectively exploit them. To this end, the model proposes an elicitation of base abstractions that need to be accounted for developing applications for B3G networking infrastructures. Starting from the analysis of the characteristics of B3G networks, the relevant abstractions have been identified and refined according to the PLASTIC goals. The model considers the Service-Oriented Architecture (SOA), as it offers significant benefits for the development of applications in the open B3G networking environment. It relates and refines SOA concepts with concepts associated with B3G networking abstractions. The result is a reference model for service-oriented B3G applications, which formalizes the concepts needed to realize context-aware adaptable

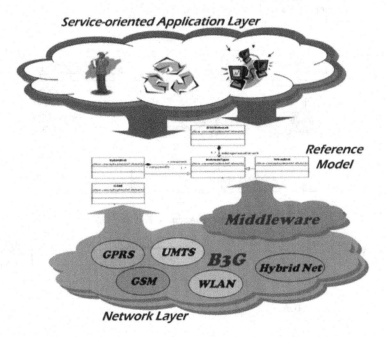

Fig. 7. A reference model for B3G networks

applications for B3G networks. The model is specified using UML diagrams, and is aimed at both application and middleware developers (see Figure 7). Indeed, a number of abstractions may be made available by the middleware layer, thus reusable by applications.

Recently, several approaches to conceptualize the world of services have been proposed. The PLASTIC model takes the move from the SeCSE conceptual model [37,38] that it has been suitably extended to reflect all the concepts related to B3G networks and service provision in B3G networks. In particular, it focusses on the following key concepts:

– *Service Level Agreement* that clearly set commitment assumed by consumers and providers and builds on services descriptions that are characterized functionally, via a service interface and non-functionally via a Service Level Specification (*SLS*).
– *Context awareness and adaptation* as the context is a key feature distinguishing services in the vast B3G networking environment. B3G networking leads to have diverse user populations, changing availability in system resources, and multiple physical environments of service consumption and provisioning. It is then crucial that services adapt as much as possible to the context for the sake of robustness and to make themselves usable for given contexts.

As illustrated in Figure 8 adaptability is achieved by transferring some of the validation activities at run time by making available models for different kind

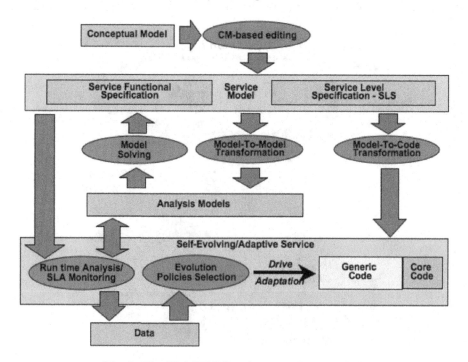

Fig. 8. The PLASTIC Development Process Model

of analysis. In particular stochastic models and behavioral ones will be made available at run time to allow the adaptation of the service to the execution context and service on line validation, respectively.

In PLASTIC all the development tools will be based on the conceptual model exploiting as much as possible model-to-model transformations. The definition of a service will consists of a functional description and of a SLS that defines the QoS characteristics of the service. The overall service description is obtained by means of an iterative analysis specification phase that makes use of behavioral and stochastic models. These models suitably refined with pieces of information coming from the implementation chain, will then be made available as artifacts associated to the service specification.

The main novelties of the PLASTIC process model is to consider SLS as part of a Service Model, as opposite to existing approaches where SLS consists, in best cases, in additional annotations reported on a (service) functional model. This peculiar characteristic of our process brings several advantages: (i) as the whole service model is driven by the conceptual model, few errors can be introduced in the functional and non-functional specification of a service; (ii) SLS embedded within a service model better supports the model-to-model transformations towards analysis models and, on the way back, better supports the feedback of the analysis; (iii) in the path to code generation, the SLS will drive the adaptation strategies.

With respect to the spectrum presented in Figure 5 the PLASTIC development process will present a limited form of adaptability as shown in Figures 9 and 13. The components implementing PLASTIC services will be programmed using the resource aware programming approach described in [21,22] by using Java.

In PLASTIC adaptation happens at the time the service request is matched with a service provision. To better understand how the matching process might operate, it is useful to refer to the reference style for SOA. Moreover it also useful to recall the roles played by the main logic entities (Service registry, Service

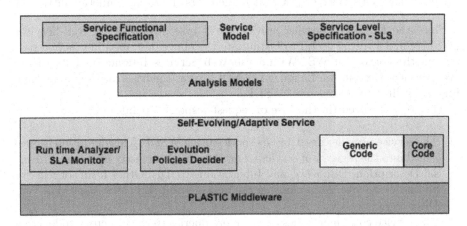

Fig. 9. The PLASTIC Artifacts to be registered at deployment time

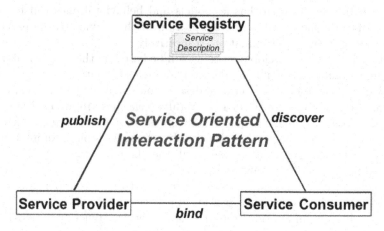

Fig. 10. Service Oriented Interaction Pattern

Provider and Service Consumer) involved in the Service Oriented Interaction Pattern for service publications, discovery and binding (see Figure 10).

The steps involved in the service provision and consumption are:

1. Service providers publish their service descriptions into a service registry (the directory of services) so that the service consumer can locate them.
2. According to the service request format, service consumers query the service registry to discover service providers for a particular service description.
3. If one or more providers are present in the service registry at the moment of the request the service consumer can select and bind to any of them. The service registry communicate (according to the service response format) to the service consumer how to communicate with that provider.
4. When a service requester binds to the service provider, the latter returns a reference to a service object that implements the service functionality.

Since the PLASTIC service provision will take advantage of Web Services (WS) technology, it is useful to instantiate the above described interaction pattern in the context of WS. Within the Web Services Interaction Pattern the Web Services Description Language (WSDL) forms the basis for the interaction. Figure 11 illustrates the use of WSDL.

The steps involved (in the case of request-response operation call) are:

1. The service provider describes its service using WSDL. This definition is published into the registry of services. For instance the registry could use Universal Description, Discovery, and Integration (UDDI). Other forms of registry and other discovery meccanisms can also be used (e.g., WS-Inspection WS-Discovery).
2. The service consumer issues one or more queries to the directory to locate a service and determine how to communicate with that service.

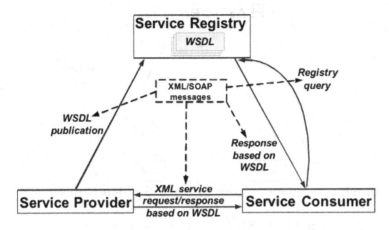

Fig. 11. Web Services Interaction Pattern

3. Part of the WSDL provided by the service provider is passed to the service consumer. This tells the service consumer what the requests and responses are for the service provider.
4. The service consumer uses the WSDL to send a request to the service provider.
5. The service provider provides the expected response to the service consumer.

In Figure 11 all the messages are sent using the envelope provided by SOAP and, usually, HTTP is used as communication protocol. In general other means of connection may be used since WSDL does not force a specific communication protocol.

Considering PLASTIC adaptation, the WS interaction pattern is slightly modified in order to reach the SLA at the end of the discovery phase. The steps involved in the PLASTIC service provision and consumption might be the ones as shown in Figure 12.

In particular, the discovery process has to take into account the user's QoS request (i.e., the requested SLS) and the service SLSs (i.e., the offered SLSs). The result of the match (between the user's QoS and the service SLSs) will produce the SLA that defines the QoS constraints of the service provision. During this matching process, in order to reach an SLA the service code might need to be adapted according to the previously mentioned resource aware programming approach hence resulting in a customized service code that satisfies the user's QoS request and results in a SLA.

Figure 13 shows an instance of the process model shown in Figure 8. It is a particular example of the PLASTIC development process.

With respect to the service model analysis, in Figure 13 we have focused on performance and reliability. SAP•one/XPRIT starts from annotated UML diagrams and generates a performance model that may be a Queueing Network (QN) that represents a Software Architecture, if no info about the executing

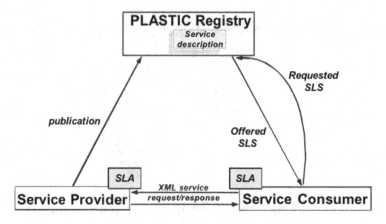

Fig. 12. PLASTIC Services Interaction Pattern

platform is available; or it may be an Execution Graph (representing the software workload) and a QN (representing the executing platform) if (some alternative for) the executing platform is available. The model solution provides performance indices that are parametric in the first case and numerical in the second one. A QN solver like SHARPE provides values of these performance indices. COBRA is a tool that, starting from annotated UML diagrams, generates a reliability model for component-based or service-based systems. The model takes into account the error propagation factor. The COBRA solver performs reliability analysis on the basis of the generated model. Model-to-Model transformations are performed by means of the ATLAS Transformation Language (ATL) [39] that has been developed in the context of the MODELWARE European project [40].

With respect to service validation/testing, two kinds of validation are performed: off-line and on-line validation. The former is performed before the service execution and it serves to generate test cases. The latter is performed whilst the service is running and exploits the previously generated test cases. The validation framework of the PLASTIC project is described in Chapter 5 of this tutorial volume. Thus we refer this chapter for further details.

5.2   The PLASTIC Development Environment

In this section we provide an overall description of the PLASTIC development environment that implements a part of the PLASTIC development process shown in Figure 13 (i.e., those process activities regarding the service model specification, model functional and non-functional analysis, resource-aware analysis and development, and code synthesis).

The PLASTIC development environment is one of the three main blocks forming the integrated PLASTIC platform (see Figure 14).

As it is shown in Figure 14, in order to enable the development of robust distributed lightweight services in the B3G networking environment, the PLASTIC platform can be organized into three main blocks: (i) a development environment, (ii) a middleware, and (iii) a validation framework.

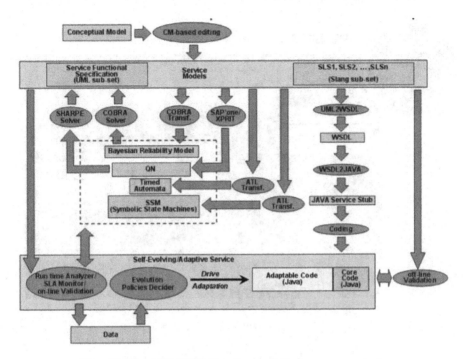

Fig. 13. The PLASTIC Development Process: an example

In the following, we discuss the main aspects of the PLASTIC development environment that concern our main contribution to the PLASTIC project. The middleware and the validation framework will not be further discussed. We refer to [36] and to Chapter 5, of this tutorial volume, for a detailed description of the middleware and the validation framework, respectively.

As it has been already mentioned above, all the architectural elements of the PLASTIC platform rely on a concrete implementation of concepts defined in the PLASTIC conceptual model. The PLASTIC conceptual model has to be considered more than documentation and a basis for common understanding. In fact, it defines all the guide principles and the main conceptual elements that should be considered in order to rigorously design an integrated framework for the modeling, analysis, development, validation, and deployment of robust lightweight services over B3G networked environments.

The PLASTIC development environment can be organized into five main blocks (see Figure 15): (i) modeling tools, (ii) non-functional analysis tools, (iii) code generation tools, (iv) resource- aware programming model, and (v) resource-aware adaptation tools. The PLASTIC development environment allows the developer to perform all the service design, analysis and development activities defined by the PLASTIC development process and to manage the process artifacts produced by these activities. The overall design depicted in Figure 15 should be interpreted as a layered architecture: an architectural block that is situated at an upper layer depends on some artifacts produced by using an architectural

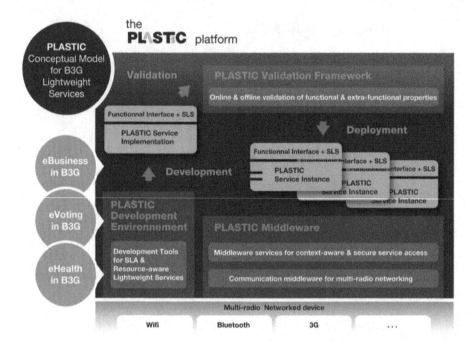

Fig. 14. The integrated PLASTIC platform

block that is situated at a lower layer. For instance, the service model built by using the modeling tools is exploited by both the non-functional analysis and code generation tools or, just to give another example, "Universal Queueing Network solver" exploits the output of "UML to Queueing Network transformation tool". The PLASTIC development environment relies on the Eclipse framework [41], i.e., all the tools of the PLASTIC development environment are implemented as Eclipse plug-ins. In this way, the development environment results in a fully-integrated environment relying on the Eclipse IDE. Although a single tool of the development environment is implemented as an Eclipse plug-in, it has been developed in a modular way hence providing also an API that would allow a developer to use the tool also outside Eclipse. This has been done to promote the use of PLASTIC solutions also outside the development scenario considered within the PLASTIC project.

The **modeling tools** block is constituted of two modeling tools: the service model editor, and the SLA editor. The former is an UML2 modeling editor customized in order to be PLASTIC oriented. That is, it embeds a customized UML2 profile which is suited to model dependable and adaptable services over B3G networked environments. It is called "PLASTIC UML2 profile" and it is a concrete implementation of the PLASTIC conceptual model. The service model editor allows the developer to specify the functional interface of the service plus its behavioral and non-functional characteristics (e.g., the orchestration of those (sub-)services that form the service under design, or the QoS characteristics of a service operation respectively). Furthermore, it allows the specification of

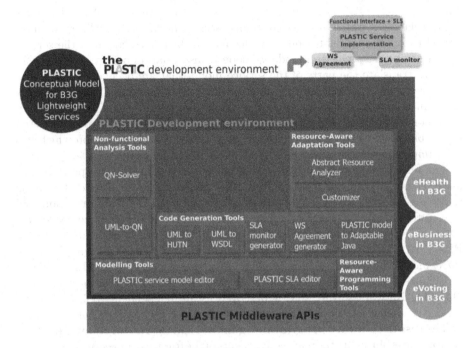

Fig. 15. The PLASTIC development environment

context-aware behavior with respect to two kinds of context: the *device context* and the *network context*. The device context is given in terms of the set of resources (and their characteristics) available on a possible execution environment (e.g., a device modeled as a set of a "display" resource with specific "resolution" and "refresh frequency" values, and a "CPU" resource with a specific "clock frequency" value). The network context is given in terms of "mobility patterns" [42], i.e., the set of the different network types the device over which the service runs can possibly move on. Once the context-aware behavior of the service is specified, by using the service model editor, the developer can also specify how the service has to adapt to the possible context changes by still maintaining a certain degree of dependability. The SLA editor is a GUI for "SLAng" which is a language for writing SLAs. It allows the developer to specify which are the parties involved in the agreement (e.g., "doctor" and "eHealth provider"), the contractual constraints defining the agreement (e.g., "service availability greater than 80%"), and the penalties that must be applied in the case of agreement violation (e.g., "the eHealth provider will provide one month of the service for free"). The syntax and semantics of SLAng are defined by means of EMOF (a language similar to UML class diagrams) and OCL, respectively. In particular, EMOF models specify the meta-model of SLAng, that is its abstract syntax in terms of the modeling constructs and their relationships (such as throughput constraints, availability, environment, schedules, etc.) that will be used for specifying SLAs. The models conforming to the SLAng meta-model are checked with respect to OCL constraints which specify the semantics of the language in a declarative way. The service model editor and the SLA editor are integrated through a model-to-code transformation. In particular, once the service model has been specified, a model-to-code transformation can be performed in order to translate the parts of the service model that are needed for specifying the agreement (e.g., parties, possible services, operations, etc.) into a HUTN (Human-Usable Textual Notation) file which is one of the file format that can be imported by the SLA editor. The "PLASTIC Model to HUTN" tool, depicted in the block "Code Generation Tools", performs this transformation which has been implemented using the JET transformation technology [41].

The **non-functional analysis tools** block is constituted of two performance analysis tools: "UML to Queueing Networks transformation tool" and "Universal Queueing Network solver". The former is a model-to-model transformation tool that automatically translates the parts of the service model that are needed for performance analysis (they are annotated UML2 diagrams which conform to the PLASTIC UML2 profile) into a performance model that is a Queueing Network (QN) model. This tool has been implemented by using the UML2 APIs available in Eclipse [43]. Then, the QN model solution is performed by using "Universal Queueing Network solver" that is deployed as an independent tool, i.e., a web service so that it can be used also outside the PLASTIC development scenario.

The **resource-aware programming model** and the **resource-aware adaptation tools** blocks are the main constituents of the framework described in [21,22]. Since a discussion on these two blocks is not crucial for the purposes of this paper, for the sake of brevity, we refer to [21,22] for them.

The **code generation tools** block is constituted of five model-to-code transformation tools. The functionality provided by the "PLASTIC Model to HUTN" transformation tool has been briefly described above in the discussion concerning the integration between the service model editor and the SLA editor. The "PLASTIC Model to WSDL" transformation tool starts from the PLASTIC service functional interface, modeled by using the service model editor, and automatically generates the WSDL of the provider-side code of the service. Once this WSDL is obtained, in order to automatically derive the skeleton of the provider-side code of the service, it is enough to use the facilities provided by a suitable application server or SOAP engine (e.g., Axis in the case of Web Services). The "SLA monitor generator" transformation tool starts from the HUTN file completed by using the SLA editor and automatically generates the code of Axis handlers used to the run-time monitoring of SLAs. Analogously, "WS-Agreement generator" takes into account the HUTN file and automatically generates WS-Agreements. SLAng is maintained for SLA specification purposes while WS-Agreement is used for validation purposes. The "WS-Agreement generator" enables the integration between the modeling layer of the PLASTIC platform and the validation one. The "PLASTIC Model to Adaptable JAVA" tool starts from a specific part of the service model called "implementation view". The implementation view models how the service is implemented in terms of software components (and their relationships) which, in turn, are implemented in terms of "adaptable" classes. By taking into account such an implementation view, the "PLASTIC Model to Adaptable JAVA" transformation tool automatically translates the implementation view into the corresponding adaptable JAVA code. This is only a skeleton code and its logic has to be coded by hand.

6 Conclusions

In this paper we have discussed our point of view on software in the future. Adaptability and Dependability will play a key role in influencing models, languages and methodologies to develop and execute future software applications. In a broader software engineering perspective it is therefore mandatory to reconcile the static/compile time development approach to the dynamic/interpreter oriented one thus making models and validation technique manageable lightweight tools for run time use. There are several challenges in this domain. Programming Language must account in a rigorous way of *quantitative* concerns, allowing programmers to deal with these concerns declaratively. Models must become simpler and lighter by exploiting compositionality and partial evaluation techniques. Innovative development processes should be defined to properly reflect these new concerns arising from software for ubiquitous computing. We presented the Plastic approach to service development and provision in B3G networks as a concrete instance of the problem raised by Softure. The solutions we are experimenting in Plastic are not entirely innovative *per se* rather they are used in a completely new and non trivial fashion. Summarizing our message is that in the Softure domain it is important to think and research *point to point* theories and techniques but it is mandatory to re-think the whole development process in order to cope with the complexity of Softure and its requirements.

References

1. Arnold, A.: Finite Transition Systems. International Series in Computer Science. Prentice Hall International, UK (1989)
2. Autili, M., Inverardi, P., Navarra, A., Tivoli, M.: Synthesis: A tool for automatically assembling correct and distributed component-based systems. In: 29th International Conference on Software Engineering (ICSE 2007), Minneapolis, MN, USA, pp. 784–787. IEEE Computer Society, Los Alamitos (2007),
   http://doi.ieeecomputersociety.org/10.1109/ICSE.2007.84
3. Autili, M., Mostarda, L., Navarra, A., Tivoli, M.: Synthesis of decentralized and concurrent adaptors for correctly assembling distributed component-based systems. Journal of Systems and Software (2008),
   http://dx.doi.org/10.1016/j.jss.2008.04.006
4. Finkel, A.: The minimal coverability graph for Petri nets. In: Proc. of the 12th APN. LNCS, vol. 674. Springer, Heidelberg (1993)
5. IFIP WG 10.4 on Dependable Computing and Fault Tolerance,
   http://www.dependability.org/wg10.4/
6. Inverardi, P.: Software of the future is the future of Software? In: Montanari, U., Sannella, D., Bruni, R. (eds.) TGC 2006. LNCS, vol. 4661, pp. 69–85. Springer, Heidelberg (2007)

7. Inverardi, P., Tivoli, M.: Deadlock-free software architectures for com/dcom applications. Elsevier Journal of Systems and Software - Special Issue on component-based software engineering 65(3), 173–183 (2003)
8. Inverardi, P., Tivoli, M.: Software Architecture for Correct Components Assembly. In: Bernardo, M., Inverardi, P. (eds.) SFM 2003. LNCS, vol. 2804, pp. 92–121. Springer, Heidelberg (2003)
9. ITU Telecommunication Standardisation sector, ITU-T reccomendation Z.120. Message Sequence Charts. (MSC 1996). Geneva
10. Keller, R.: Formal verification of parallel programs. Communications of the ACM 19(7), 371–384 (1976)
11. Milner, R.: Communication and Concurrency. Prentice Hall, New York (1989)
12. Murata, T.: Petri nets: Properties, analysis and applications. Proceedings of the IEEE 77(4) (1989)
13. PLASTIC IST Project, http://www.ist-plastic.org
14. Ramadge, P., Wonham, W.: The control of discrete event systems. Proceedings of the IEEE 1(77) (1989)
15. Schilit, B., Adams, N., Want, R.: Context-aware computing applications. In: IEEE Workshop on Mobile Computing Systems and Applications, Santa Cruz, CA, US (1994)
16. Tivoli, M., Autili, M.: SYNTHESIS, a Tool for Synthesizing Correct and Protocol-Enhanced Adaptors. RSTI L Objet journal 12(1), 77–103 (2006)
17. Tivoli, M., Fradet, P., Girault, A., Goessler, G.: Adaptor synthesis for real-time components. In: Grumberg, O., Huth, M. (eds.) TACAS 2007. LNCS, vol. 4424, pp. 185–200. Springer, Heidelberg (2007)
18. Tivoli, M., Inverardi, P.: Failure-free coordinators synthesis for component-based architectures. Science of Computer Programming 71(3), 181–212 (2008), http://dx.doi.org/10.1016/j.scico.2008.03.001
19. Uchitel, S., Kramer, J.: A workbench for synthesising behaviour models from scenarios. In: Proceeding of the 23rd IEEE International Conference on Software Engineering (ICSE 2001) (2001)
20. Uchitel, S., Kramer, J., Magee, J.: Detecting implied scenarios in message sequence chart specifications. In: ACM Proceedings of the joint 8th ESEC and 9th FSE. ACM press, New York (2001)
21. Inverardi, P., Mancinelli, F., Nesi, M.: A Declarative Framework for adaptable applications in heterogeneous environments. In: Proceedings of the 19th ACM Symposium on Applied Computing (2004)
22. Mancinelli, F., Inverardi, P.: Quantitative resource-oriented analysis of Java (adaptable) applications. In: ACM Proceedings Workshop on Software Performance (2007)
23. Necula, G.C.: Proof-Carrying Code. In: Jones, N.D. (ed.) Proceedings of the Symposium on Principles of Programming Languages, Paris, France, January 1997, pp. 106–119. ACM Press, New York (1997)
24. Le Métayer, D.: Describing Software Architecture Styles Using Graph Grammars. IEEE Transaction on software engineering 24(7) (1998)
25. Aldrich, J., Chambers, C., Notkin, D.: ArchJava: Connecting Software Architecture to Implementation. In: Proceedings of ICSE 2002 (May 2002)
26. Aldrich, J., Chambers, C., Notkin, D.: Architectural Reasoning in ArchJava. In: Magnusson, B. (ed.) ECOOP 2002. LNCS, vol. 2374. Springer, Heidelberg (2002)
27. Hirsch, D., Inverardi, P., Montanari, U.: Graph grammars and constraint solving for software architecture styles. In: Proc. of the 3rd Int. Software Architecture Workshop (ISAW-3), pp. 69–72. ACM Press, New York (1998)

28. Georgiadis, I., Magee, J., Kramer, J.: Self-organising software architectures for distributed systems. In: Proc. of the 1st Work. on Self-Healing Systems (WOSS 2002), pp. 33–38. ACM Press, New York (2002)
29. Magee, J., Kramer, J.: Dynamic structure in software architectures. In: Proc. of the 4th ACM SIGSOFT Symp. On Foundations of Software Engineering (FSE-4), pp. 3–14. ACM Press, New York (1996)
30. Taentzer, G., Goedicke, M., Meyer, T.: Dynamic change management by distributed graph transformation: Towards configurable distributed systems. In: Ehrig, H., Engels, G., Kreowski, H.-J., Rozenberg, G. (eds.) TAGT 1998. LNCS, vol. 1764, pp. 179–193. Springer, Heidelberg (2000)
31. Baresi, L., Heckel, R., Thöne, S., Varró, D.: Style-Based Refinement of Dynamic Software Architectures. In: WICSA 2004, pp. 155–166 (2004)
32. Allen, R., Garlan, D.: A Formal Basis for Architectural Connection. ACM Transactions on Software Engineering and Methodology 6(3), 213–249 (1997)
33. Barthe, G.: Mobius, securing the next generation of java-based global computers. ERCIM News (2005)
34. Inverardi, P., Mostarda, L.: DESERT: a decentralized monitoring tool generator. In: IEEE Proceeding of ASE 2007, tool demo (2007)
35. Cortellessa, V., Di Marco, A., Inverardi, P., Mancinelli, F., Pelliccione, P.: A framework for integration of functional and non-functional analysis of software architectures. ENCS 116, 31–44 (2005)
36. PLASTIC IST Project, http://www.ist-plastic.org
37. SeCSE Project, http://secse.eng.it
38. Colombo, M., Di Nitto, E., Di Penta, M., Distante, D., Zuccalà, M.: Speaking a common language: A conceptual model for describing service-oriented systems. In: Benatallah, B., Casati, F., Traverso, P. (eds.) ICSOC 2005. LNCS, vol. 3826, pp. 48–60. Springer, Heidelberg (2005)
39. Jouault, F., Kurtev, I.: Transforming Models with ATL. In: Bruel, J.-M. (ed.) MoDELS 2005. LNCS, vol. 3844, pp. 128–138. Springer, Heidelberg (2006)
40. ModelWare, IST European project 511731, http://www.modelware-ist.org
41. Budinsky, F., Steinberg, D., Merks, E., Ellersick, R., Grose, T.J.: Eclipse Modeling Framework. Addison-Wesley, Reading (2003)
42. Di Marco, A., Mascolo, C.: Performance Analysis and Prediction of Physically Mobile Systems. In: WOSP 2007 (2007)
43. Eclipse project. Model Development Tools UML2, http://www.eclipse.org/modeling/mdt/?project=uml2

Autonomic Computing
Now You See It, Now You Don't
Design and Evolution of
Autonomic Software Systems

Hausi A. Müller, Holger M. Kienle, and Ulrike Stege

Department of Computer Science
University of Victoria
{hausi,kienle,stege}@cs.uvic.ca
http://webhome.cs.uvic.ca/~{hausi,stege}

Abstract. With the rapid growth of web services and socio-technical ecosystems, the management complexity of these modern, decentralized, distributed computing systems presents significant challenges for businesses and often exceeds the capabilities of human operators. Autonomic computing is an effective set of technologies, models, architecture patterns, standards, and processes to cope with and reign in the management complexity of dynamic computing systems using feedback control, adaptation, and self-management. At the core of an autonomic system are control loops which sense their environment, model their behavior in that environment, and take action to change the environment or their own behavior. Computer science researchers often approach the design of such highly dynamical systems from a software architecture perspective whereas engineering researchers start with a feedback control perspective. In this article, we argue that both design perspectives are needed and necessary for autonomic system design.

Keywords: Continuous evolution, software ecosystems, software complexity management, autonomic computing, self-managing systems, self-adaptive systems, feedback loops, autonomic element, autonomic computing reference architecture, autonomic patterns.

1   Introduction

Two important trends are dominating the computing world in the new millennium. First, many companies are moving from a goods-centric way to a service-centric way of conducting business [34]. In this service-oriented world, we perform everyday tasks, such as communication, banking, or shopping, without human-to-human interaction from the comfort of our living rooms. This apparently seamless integration of services and computing power has put enormous demands on its underlying information technology (IT) infrastructure. Second, with the proliferation of computing devices and enterprise systems, software systems have evolved from software intensive systems to systems of systems [56], and now to ultra-large-scale systems and socio-technical ecosystems [51]. With the rapid growth of web

A. De Lucia and F. Ferrucci (Eds.): ISSSE 2006–2008, LNCS 5413, pp. 32–54, 2009.

services and socio-technical ecosystems, the management complexity of these modern, decentralized, distributed computing systems presents significant challenges for businesses and often exceeds the capabilities of human operators who manage these systems.

The continuous evolution from goods-centric to service-centric businesses and from software intensive systems to socio-technical ecosystems requires new and innovative approaches for building, running, and managing software systems. Understanding, managing, and controlling the run-time dynamics of these computing systems—given the onslaught of ever-changing IT infrastructure—is nowadays a crucial requirement for the survival and success of many businesses. Therefore, end-users increasingly demand from business that they provide software systems that are versatile, flexible, resilient, dependable, robust, service-oriented, mashable, inter-operable, continuously available, decentralized, energy-efficient, recoverable, customizable, self-healing, configurable, or self-optimizing.

One of the most promising approaches to achieving some of these properties is to equip software systems with feedback control to address the management of inherent system dynamics. The resulting self-managing and self-adapting computing systems, which embody multiple feedback control loops at their core, are better able to cope with and even accommodate changing contexts and environments, shifting requirements, and computing-on-demand needs.

Over the past decade, many industrial and academic research initiatives have emerged to attack these problems and challenges head-on and produced impressive and profitable solutions for many businesses. One of the best-documented and most successful research initiatives is IBM's Autonomic Computing initiative, launched in 2001 with Horn's grand challenge for the entire IT sector [26]. The rest of the computing industry followed quickly with major initiatives to take on this formidable challenge. For example, the goal of Sun's N1 management software is to enable application development across heterogeneous environments in a consistent and virtualized manner [58]. The Dynamic Systems Initiative (DSI) is Microsoft's technology strategy for products and solutions to help businesses meet the demands of a rapidly changing and adaptable environment [44]. Hewlett-Packard's approach to autonomic computing is reified in its Adaptive Enterprise Strategy [25]. Intel is deeply involved in the development of standards for autonomic computing [60].

The goal of this paper is to illustrate the broad applicability of autonomic computing techniques from IT complexity problems to continuous software evolution problems, to motivate the benefits of mining the rich history of control theory foundations for autonomic, self-managing and self-adaptive systems, and to present selected challenges for the future. Section 2 characterizes the problem of continuous software evolution using different perspectives. Section 3 discusses selected approaches, issues, and challenges when designing dynamic computing systems using feedback control. Section 4 introduces the field of autonomic computing and illustrates how autonomic computing technology can be used to reduce complexity and solve continuous evolution problems of software-intensive systems. Section 5 relates traditional feedback control, such as model reference adaptive control (MRAC) or model identification adaptive control (MIAC), to feedback control for dynamic computing systems. Sections 6 and 7 describe cornerstones of IBM's autonomic computing technology, including the autonomic computing reference architecture (ACRA) and two key architecture components, autonomic element and autonomic manager. Section 8 presents some lessons learned and outlines selected research challenges for this exciting field, and Section 9 draws some conclusions and points out selected entries in the references as good starting points for newcomers to the autonomic computing field.

2   Continuous Evolution of Software Systems

In a world where continuous evolution, socio-technical ecosystems, and service-centric businesses are prevalent, we are forced to re-examine some of our most fundamental assumptions about software and its construction. For the past 40 years, we have embraced a traditional engineering perspective to construct software in a centralized, top-down manner where functional or extra-functional requirements are either satisfied or not [51]. Today, many software-intensive systems of systems emerge through continuous evolution and by means of regulation rather than traditional engineering. For example, firms are engineered—but the structure of the economy is not; the protocols of the Internet were engineered—but not the web as a whole [51]. While software ecosystems, such as the web, exhibit high degrees of complexity and organization, it is not built through traditional engineering. However, individual components and subsystems of such ecosystems are still being built using traditional top-down engineering [51].

Three independent studies, conducted in 2006, seem to confirm that this notion of continuous evolution is taking hold [3,5,51]. In particular, the acclaimed report of Carnegie Mellon Software Engineering Institute (SEI) on ultra-large-scale (ULS) systems suggests that traditional top-down engineering approaches are insufficient to tackle the complexity and evolution problems inherent in decentralized, continually evolving software [51].

While there has been recent attention to the problem of continuous evolution, several researchers have already articulated this problem at the end of the nineties. In his dissertation, Wong envisioned the *Reverse Engineering Notebook* to cope with and manage continuous evolution issues of software systems [62]. At the same time, Truex et al. recognized that the traditional assumption where "software systems should support organizational stability and structure, should be low maintenance, and should strive for high degrees of user acceptance" might be flawed [61]. They suggested an alternate view where "software systems should be under constant development, can never be fully specified, and are subject to constant adjustment and adaptation".

Having investigated software systems and their engineering methods for many years, we have come to realize that their alternate, continuous evolution view is as important today—or even more important for certain application domains—than the traditional view. For narrow domains, well-defined applications, or safety-critical tasks, the traditional view and engineering approach still applies.

For highly dynamic and evolving systems, such as software ecosystems, the continuous evolution view clearly applies. This is good news for the software engineering research community at large since this shift guarantees research problems for many years to come. The not so good news is that most software engineering textbooks, which only treat and advocate the traditional view, will have to be rewritten or at least updated to incorporate the notion of continuous evolution [46].

In a 2004 Economist article, Kluth discussed how other industrial sectors previously dealt with complexity [36]. He and others have argued that for a technology to be truly successful, its complexity has to disappear. He illustrates this point by showing how industries such as clocks, automobiles, and power distribution overcame complexity challenges. For example only mechanics were able to operate early automobiles successfully and in the early days of the 20th century, companies had a prominent position of Vice President of Electricity to deal with power generation and consumption issues. In both cases, the respective industries managed to reduce the need of human expertise and simplify the usage of the underlying technology with traditional engineering methods. However, usage simplicity comes with an increased complexity of the overall system complexity (e.g., what is under the hood). Basically for every mouse click or key stroke we take out of the user experience, 20 things have to happen in the software behind the scenes [36]. Given this historical perspective with this predictable path of technology evolution, there may be hope for the information technology sector [45].

Today, there are several research communities (cf. Section 1) which deal with highly dynamic and evolving systems from a variety of perspectives. For example, Inverardi and Tivoli argue that the execution environment for future software systems will not be known a priori at design time and, hence, the application environment of such a system cannot be statically anticipated [32]. They advocate reconciling the static view with the dynamic view by breaking the traditional division among development phases by moving some activities from design time to deployment and run time. What the approaches of these different communities have in common is that the resulting systems push design decisions towards run-time and exhibit capabilities to reason about the systems' own state and their environment. However, different communities emphasize different business goals and technological approaches.

The goal of autonomic computing or self-managing systems is to reduce the total cost of ownership of complex IT systems by allowing systems to self-manage by combining a technological vision with on-demand business needs [16,17]. Autonomic communication is more oriented towards distributed systems and services and the management of network resources [13]. Research on self-adaptation spans a wide range of applications from user-interface customization and web-service composition, to mechatronics and robotics systems, to biological systems, and to system management. As a result, distinct research areas and publication venues have emerged, including adaptive, self-adaptive, self-managing, autonomic, autonomous, self-organizing, reactive, and ubiquitous systems.

Feedback control is at the heart of self-managing and self-adaptive systems. Building such systems cost-effectively and in a predictable manner is a major engineering challenge even though feedback control has a long history with huge successes in many different branches of engineering [59,63]. Mining the rich experiences in these fields, borrowing theories from control engineering [1,6,23,12,50], and then applying the findings to software-intensive self-adaptive and self-managing systems is a most worthwhile and promising avenue of research. In the next section we introduce a generic model of an autonomic control loop that exposes the feedback control of self-managing and self-adaptive systems, providing a first step towards reasoning about feedback control (e.g., properties of the control loop during design, and implications of control loops during maintenance).

3   Design and Maintenance Issues of Feedback-Based Systems

Self-adaptive and self-managing systems have several properties in common. First and foremost such systems are "reflective" in nature and are therefore able to reason about their state and environment. Secondly these systems address problems for which selected design decisions are necessarily moved towards runtime [55,9,2]. Müller et al. proposed a set of problem attributes which suggest considering self-adaptive and self-managing solutions [47]:

- Uncertainty in the environment, especially uncertainty that leads to substantial irregularity or other disruption or may arise from external perturbations, rapid irregular change, or imprecise knowledge of the external state.
- Nondeterminism in the environment, especially of a sort that requires significantly different responses at different times.
- Requirements, especially extra-functional requirements, which can best be satisfied through regulation of complex, decentralized systems (as opposed to traditional, top-down engineering) especially if substantial trade-offs arise among these requirements.
- Incomplete control of system components (e.g., the system incorporates embedded mechanical components, the task involves continuing action, or humans are in the operating loop).

The reasoning about a system's state and environment typically involves feedback processes with four canonical activities—*collect, analyze, decide,* and *act*— as depicted in Figure 1 [13]. Sensors, or probes, "collect" data from the executing process and its context about their current states. The accumulated data is then cleaned, filtered, and finally stored for future reference to portray an accurate model of past and current states. The diagnosis engine then "analyzes" the data to infer trends and identify symptoms. The planning engine then attempts to predict the future to "decide" on how to "act" on the executing process and its context through effectors.

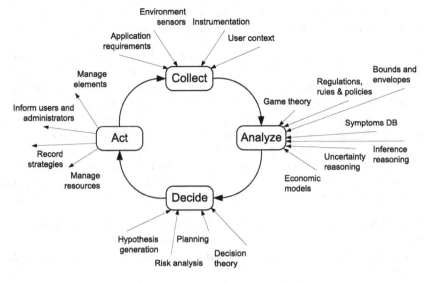

Fig. 1. Generic control loop [13]

This generic model provides a good overview of the main activities around the feedback loop, but ignores many properties of the control and data flow around the loop. In the following we give examples of control loop properties for each activity (cf. Figure 1) [9]:

Collect

What kinds of data and events are collected from which sources, sensors, or probes? Are there common event formats? What is the sampling rate and is it fixed or varying? Are the sampled sources fixed or do they change dynamically? What are appropriate filters for the data streams?

Analyze

How are the collected data represented and stored? What are appropriate algorithms or diagnosis methods to analyze the data? How is the current state of the system assessed? How much past state needs to be kept around? How are critical states archived? How are common symptoms recognized (e.g., with the help of a symptoms database)?

Decide

How is the future state of the system inferred and how is a decision reached (e.g., with off-line simulation, quality of service (QoS) objectives, or utility/goal functions)? What models and algorithms are used for trade-off analysis? What are the priorities for adaptation across multiple control loops and within a single control loop? Under what conditions should adaptation be performed (e.g., allow for head-room or avoid system thrashing while considering timing issues relating to the required adaptations)?

Act

What are the managed elements and how can they be manipulated (e.g., by parameter tuning or by injecting new algorithms)? Are changes of the system pre-computed (e.g., switching between known configurations) or opportunistically assembled, composed, or generated?

Only a system designed to be self-adaptive is able to self-manage by monitoring and responding to changes in its own state or its external operating environment. As a result, designers and maintainers of such systems must take uncertainty into account because the environment may change in unexpected ways and cause the system to adapt in such a way that was not foreseeable at design time. Introducing uncertainty requires trade-offs between flexibility and assurance. For a maintainer it is critical to know which parts of the environment are assumed to be fixed and which are expected to introduce uncertainty.

Two key maintenance questions arise in the context of self-adaptive and self-managing systems [64]:

– How different are the maintainability concerns for self-adaptive and self-managing systems compared to static systems?
– Is a system that is designed for dynamic variability or adaptation easier to maintain?

It is reasonable to expect that differences in maintenance exist between the two kinds of systems because self-managing systems, for instance, have to (1) introduce pervasive monitoring functionality, (2) reify part of the system's state in an executable meta-model (i.e. reflectivity), and (3) include functionality that performs reasoning and adaptations at run-time. This means that system properties of a self-managing system have to be verified during run-time whenever the system dynamically changes or evolves. In contrast, for a static system the properties can be often assured with off-line analyses before deployment.

Self-adaptation in software-intensive systems comes in many different guises, including static and dynamic forms. In static self-adaptation all possible adaptations are explicitly defined by the designers for the system to choose from during execution whereas, in dynamic self-adaptation possible adaptations are determined and selected by the system at run-time. One way to characterize self-adaptive software systems is by the implementation mechanism used to achieve self-adaptation [52,53]. Static and dynamic mechanisms include design-time (e.g., architectural alternatives or hard-wired decision trees), compile-time (e.g., C++ templates or aspects), load-time (e.g., Java beans or plug-ins), and run-time (e.g., feedback loops or interpreters of scripting languages). Self-adaptive and self-managing systems are typically implemented using feedback mechanisms to control their dynamic behavior—for example, to keep web services up and running, to load-balance storage and compute resources, to diagnose and predict system failures, and to negotiate an obstacle course in a warehouse.

McKinley et al. distinguish between *parameter adaptation* and *compositional adaptation* [43]. Parameter adaptation modifies program variables that determine behavior whereas compositional adaptation exchanges algorithmic or structural system components with others to adapt to its environment. With compositional adaptation, an application can adopt new algorithms for addressing concerns that were unforeseen during development.

In this article, we mostly concentrate on a particular approach for realizing self-adaptive and self-managing systems, namely autonomic computing. In the next section we briefly outline the origins of autonomic computing and the community that has emerged around it. We then discuss selected issues of autonomic computing, including feedback control (cf. Section 5), autonomic element design (cf. Section 6), and architectures for autonomic systems (cf. Section 7). Even though this paper concentrates on autonomic computing, we believe that most of the findings also apply to most solutions dealing with dynamic and evolving computing systems in general. As Huebscher and McCann in their recent survey article on autonomic computing, in this article we basically use the terms autonomic system, self-Managing system, and self-adaptive system interchangeably [27].

4   Autonomic Computing Systems

A software system is called *autonomic*[1] if it operates mostly without human or external intervention or involvement according to a set of rules or policies. Such a system can, for example, self-configure at run-time to meet changing operating environments, self-tune to optimize its performance, recognize symptoms, determine root causes, and self-heal when it encounters unexpected obstacles during its operation.

The autonomic computing community often refers to the human Autonomic Nervous System (ANS) with its many control loops as a prototypical example [35]. The ANS monitors and regulates vital signs such as body temperature, heart rate, blood pressure, pupil dilation, digestion blood sugar, breathing rate, immune response, and many more involuntary, reflexive responses in our bodies. Furthermore the ANS consists of two separate divisions called the parasympathetic nervous system, which regulates day-to-day internal processes and behaviors and sympathetic nervous system, which deals with stressful situations. Studying the ANS might be instructive for the design of autonomic software systems; for example, physically separating the control loops which deal with normal and out-of-kilter situations might be a useful design idea for designing autonomic computing systems. Over the past decade distinct architectural patterns have emerged for specific autonomic problem domains. For example, Brittenham et al. have distilled common patterns for IT service management based on the best practices in the IT Infrastructure Library [4,31].

Autonomicity may be addressed at different points along a system-application dimension. Specifically, it can be built into a design at the hardware level (e.g., self-diagnosing hardware), the operating system level (e.g., self-configuring upgrades or security management), middleware (e.g., self-healing infrastructure), or the application level (e.g., self-tuning storage management, or optimization of application performance and service levels). Autonomicity is not an all-or-nothing property. One can conceive of software applications that require none, little, or considerable user input in order to self-manage at run-time. Kephart and Chess

---

[1] The Greek origin for autonomic ($\alpha\nu\tau o\nu o\mu o\varsigma$), literally means "self-governed".

in their seminal paper state that the essence of autonomic computing is system self-management, freeing administrators from low-level task management while delivering more optimal system behavior [35]. In many cases however, users and operators usually remain in the loop by assisting and approving self-management processes.

The IBM autonomic computing initiative has generated an impressive research community spanning academia and industry. Researchers have founded journals such as *ACM Transactions on Autonomous and Adaptive Systems (TAAS)*, produced special issues for established journals on the subject [24,8], and founded several conferences, including *IEEE International Conference on Autonomic Computing (ICAC), ACM/IEEE Workshop on Software Engineering for Adaptive and Self-Managing Systems (SEAMS), ACM International Conference on Autonomic Computing and Communication Systems (Autonomics), IEEE International Conference on Self-Adaptive and Self-Organizing Systems (SASO), and IBM CASCON Workshop on Engineering Autonomic Systems*. The produced research results are significant and have influenced and penetrated many commercial products in different companies. The results have recently also been embraced by architectural strategists and standards communities [60], including web services, service-oriented architecture (SOA) [14], and ubiquitous computing [28].

IBM has defined the widely applicable autonomic computing reference architecture (ACRA) [28] and the highly practical autonomic toolkit [30] which together comprise a collection of components, tools, scenarios, and documentation designed for users wanting to learn, adapt, and develop autonomic behavior in their products and systems. Thus, after almost a decade of intense research and development in this realm, autonomic computing constitutes an effective set of technologies, models, architecture patterns, standards, and processes to cope with and reign in the management complexity of dynamic computing systems using feedback control, adaptation, and self-management.

5   Feedback Control for Autonomic Computing

While the term autonomic computing was coined at the beginning of this decade, many of the foundations of autonomic computing have a rich history in engineering [59], operations research [63], and artificial intelligence [54,11]. Feedback control is really the heart of a self-managing, autonomic or self-adaptive system. Feedback control, with its control theory history in many branches of engineering and mathematics, is about regulating the behavior of dynamical systems as depicted in Figure 2.

A feedback control system consists of a set of components that act together to maintain actual system attribute values close to desired specifications. The main idea is to sense output measurements to adjust control inputs to meet the specified goals. For example, a thermostat controls the temperature of a house by sensing the air temperature and by turning the heater or air conditioner on and off. Another canonical example frequently analyzed and implemented in control theory textbooks is the automotive cruise-control system [1,6,50]. Control

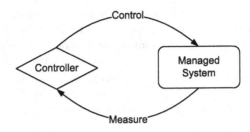

Fig. 2. Ubiquitous feedback loop

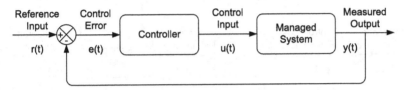

Fig. 3. Block diagram of a general feedback system [1,6,50]

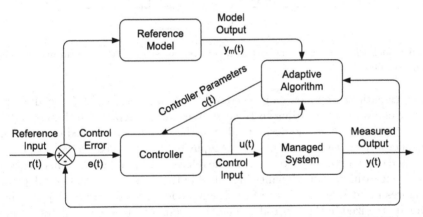

Fig. 4. Basic structure of model reference adaptive control (MRAC)

theory literature describes control systems using block diagrams and well-defined terminology as shown in Figure 3.

Control engineering textbooks contain many reference architectures for different application domains. One of the most common models is the model-reference adaptive control (MRAC) architecture depicted in Figure 4, which was originally proposed for the flight control problem [1,15]. MRAC is also known as model reference adaptive system (MRAS). MRAC implementations can be used to realize compositional adaptation.

Significant flexibility and leverage is achieved by defining the model and algorithm separately. Because of the separation of concerns, this solution is ideal for software engineering applications in general and self-adaptive or self-managed software-intensive systems in particular. While feedback control of this sort is common in the construction of engineered devices to bring about desired behavior despite undesired disturbances, it is not as frequently applied as one might hope for realizing dynamic computing systems—in part due to the inaccessibility of control theory for computing practitioners. With the publication of IBM's architectural blueprint for autonomic computing [28] and Hellerstein et al.'s book on *Feedback Control of Computing Systems* [23], computing practitioners are now in a much better position to address the dynamics of resource management and other related problems of autonomic computing.

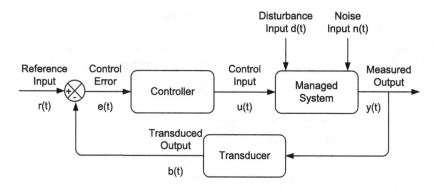

Fig. 5. Block diagram of a feedback control system with disturbance input for computing systems [23,12]

The essential components of a feedback control system suitable for dynamic computing systems according to Hellerstein et al. are depicted in Figure 5 [23]. The reference input is the desired value of the system's measured output. The controller adjusts the setting of control input to the managed system so that its measured output converges towards to the referenced input [23,12]. This feedback control encapsulates functionality identified in the generic control loops depicted in Figures 1 and 3, and in Figure 4 the MRAC reference model and adaptive algorithm are realized in the controller. The main components are as follows [23,12]:

- Control input is a parameter that affects the behavior of the managed system and can be adjusted dynamically.
- The controller determines the setting of the control input needed to achieve the reference input. The controller computes values for the control input based on the history (i.e., current and past values) of the control error (i.e., the difference between the reference input and the measured output).
- Disturbance input is any change that affects the way in which the control input influences the measured output. These are factors that affect the measured output but for which there is no direct governing control input (e.g., workload variations such as running back-ups, and downloading and updating virus definitions).
- Noise input is any effect that changes the measured output produced by the managed system. This is also called sensor noise or measurement noise.
- Measured output is a measurable characteristic of the managed system (e.g., response time).

- Reference input (also referred to as set point) is the desired value of the measured outputs.
- Managed system (also referred to as process or plant) is the computing system to be controlled.
- The transducer transforms the measured output so that it can be compared with the reference input (e.g., relating and converting output units to input units).

The application determines the control objective. Hellerstein et al. concentrate on regulatory control (e.g., to maintain reserve capacity), disturbance and noise rejection (e.g., to maximize throughput subject to guaranteed response times for different customers), and optimization (e.g., optimizing operations according to service level agreements and compliance requirements) [23]. The crux of the matter is the construction of a suitable model to quantify the control objective. Fields such as performance engineering and queuing theory have arrived at mature models. However, in many application domains are still at their infancy of modeling the relationships between controlled inputs and outputs.

The feedback loop is a central element of control theory, which provides well-established mathematical techniques to analyze system performance and correctness. It is not clear if general principles and properties established by this discipline (e.g., observability, controllability, stability, and hysteresis) are applicable for reasoning about autonomic systems. Generally, systems with a single control loop are easier to reason about than systems with multiple loops—but multi-loop systems are more common and have to be dealt with.

Good engineering practice calls for reducing multiple control loops to a single one—a common approach in control engineering, or making control loops independent of each other. If this is impossible, the design should make the interactions of control loops explicit and expose how these interactions are handled. Another typical scheme from control engineering is organizing multiple control loops in the form of a hierarchy where due to the employed different times unexpected interference between the levels can be excluded. This scheme seems to be of particular interest if we separate different forms of adaptation such as component management, change management, and goal management as proposed by Kramer and Magee [37,38].

In order to structure an autonomic system's control loops and to reason about them, the concept of autonomic element is helpful because it encapsulates a single control loop and provides an explicit abstraction for it.

6   The Autonomic Element

IBM researchers introduced the notion of an *autonomic element* as a fundamental building block for designing self-adaptive and self-managing systems [28,35]. An autonomic element consists of an autonomic manager (i.e., controller), a managed element (i.e., process), and two manageability interfaces.

The core of an autonomic manager constitutes a feedback loop, often referred to as monitor-analyze-plan-execute (MAPE) or monitor-analyze-plan-execute-knowledge (MAPE-K) loop, as depicted in Figure 6. The manager gathers measurements from the managed element as well as information from the current and past states from various knowledge sources via a service bus and then adjusts the managed element if necessary through a manageability interface (i.e., the sensors and effectors at the bottom of this figure) according to the control objective. Note that an autonomic element itself can be a managed element—the sensors and effectors at the top of the autonomic manager in Figure 6 are used to manage the element (i.e., provide measurements through its sensors and receive control input (e.g., rules or policies) through its effectors). If there are no such effectors, then the rules or policies are hard-wired into the MAPE loop. Even if there are no effectors at the top of the element, the state of the element is typically still exposed through its top sensors.

One of the greatest achievements and most compelling benefits of the autonomic computing community is the standardization of the manageability interfaces and manageability endpoints (i.e., a manageability endpoint exposes the state and the management operations for a resource or another autonomic element) across a variety of managed resources and the standardization of the information (e.g., events or policies) that is passed through these interfaces [60].

IN 2006 OASIS Web Services Distributed Management Technical Committee (WSDM TC) approved and published two sets of specifications on Web Services Distributed Management entitled Management Using Web Services (MUWS) and Management of Web Services (MOWS) [49]. The standardization of WSDM 1.0 is an important milestone for autonomic computing because it defines the web services endpoints. Web services endpoints are a necessary technology for autonomic managers to bring self-managing capabilities to hardware and software resources of the IT infrastructure.

The autonomic manager is a controller, which controls the managed element (i.e., a set of resources or other autonomic elements). Thus, the autonomic manager and the managed element of an autonomic element correspond to the controller and the managed system in the general feedback system (cf. Figure 3). This connection is depicted in Figure 7 below.

The autonomic element structure can also be characterized as MIAC or MRAC structure (cf. Section 5). The MIAC or MRAC reference model is stored in the knowledge base and the adaptive algorithm is decomposed into the four MAPE components.

The controller, with its MAPE loop, operates in four phases over a knowledge base to assess the current state of the managed elements, predict future states, and bring about desired behavior despite disturbances from the environment and changes in the process. The monitor senses the managed process and its context, filters the accumulated sensor data, and stores relevant events in the knowledge base for future reference. The analyzer compares event data against patterns in the knowledge base to diagnose symptoms and stores the symptoms [29]. The planner interprets the symptoms and devises a plan to execute the change in the managed process through the effectors.

While there is plenty of existing literature for designing and implementing each MAPE component (e.g., artificial intelligence planning algorithms), the

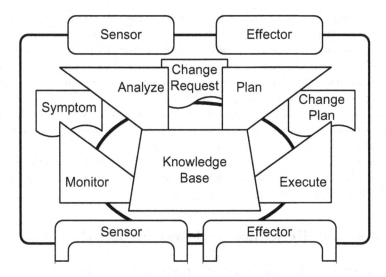

Fig. 6. Autonomic Manager [28,35]

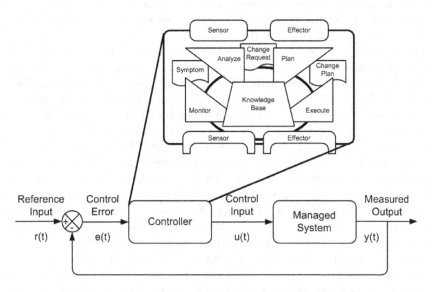

Fig. 7. Autonomic Manager as Controller in Feedback Loop

modeling of control objectives is hard. Therefore, human operators are often kept in the loop (i.e., performing some of the tasks of the MAPE loop manually). For example, for root cause analysis in enterprise systems, the monitor and analyze tasks are frequently fully automated whereas the plan and execute tasks are completed by experienced human operators. Even if all components of a MAPE loop can be executed without human assistance, the autonomic manager can typically be configured to perform only a subset of its automated functions.

The four components of a MAPE loop work together by exchanging knowledge to achieve the control objective. An autonomic manager maintains its own knowledge (e.g., information about its current state as well as past states) and has access to knowledge which is shared among collaborating autonomic managers (e.g., configuration database, symptoms database, business rules, provisioning policies, or problem determination expertise).

To realize an autonomic system, designers build an arrangement of collaborating autonomic elements working towards a common goal. In this case, the maintainability concerns increase significantly due to the interactions of the control loops of the different autonomic elements. To synthesize arrangements of autonomic elements, designers employ various techniques including goal models [39,40] and architectural patterns [64].

7 Autonomic Reference Architecture and Patterns

Autonomic system solutions consist of arrangements of interdependent, collaborative autonomic elements. A hierarchy of autonomic managers where higher level managers orchestrate lower level managers or resources is the most common and natural arrangement. For example, it reflects how organizations work or how IT professionals organize their tasks [4].

The autonomic computing reference architecture (ACRA) is a three-layer hierarchy of orchestrating managers, resource managers, and managed resources which all share management data across an enterprise service interface [28] as depicted in Figure 8. The ACRA also includes manual managers or operators, who have access to all levels through dashboards or consoles [42]. Hierarchical arrangements of autonomic managers also afford separation of concerns (e.g., managing performance, availability, or capacity relatively independently).

Brittenham et al. define a set of autonomic architecture and process patterns called delegation for progressing from manual management, to autonomic management [4]. Some of the intermediate stages include automated assistance, supervised delegation, conditional delegation, task delegation, and full loop delegation. For example, in conditional delegation the IT professional trusts an autonomic manager to perform some but not all requests whereas in task delegation the IT professional trusts an autonomic manager to perform a complete task.

Kramer and Magee proposed a three layer reference architecture for self managed systems consisting of goal management, change management, and component management [38]. They follow Gat's architecture for autonomous robotics systems [20] and address different time scales of management or control with the three levels. Immediate feedback actions are controlled at the component level and the longest actions requiring deliberation are at the goal level.

Litoiu et al. use three levels autonomic management for provisioning, application tuning, and component tuning [41]. Another typical scheme from control engineering is organizing multiple control loops in the form of a hierarchy where, due to the employed different time periods, unexpected interference between the levels can be excluded.

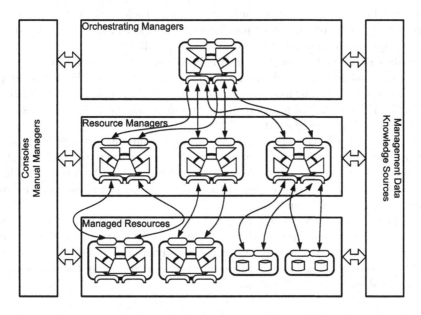

Fig. 8. Autonomic computing reference architecture (ACRA) [28]

Lapouchnian et al. proposed a novel design technique for autonomic systems based on goal-driven requirements engineering which results in more complicated autonomic element topologies [39,40]. Goal models capture a spectrum of alternative system behaviors and/or system configurations, which are all delivering the same functionality and are able to select at run-time the best behavior or configuration based on the current context. Goal models provide a unifying intentional view of the system by relating goals assigned to autonomic elements to high-level system objectives and quality concerns. This method produces an arrangement of autonomic elements that is structurally similar to the goal hierarchy of the corresponding goal model. One extreme solution is to realize the entire goal model using a single autonomic element. On the other side of the spectrum is a solution that allocates an autonomic element for each node in the goal model. A combination of these two extreme mappings appears to be most practical. Realizing a subtree (i.e., rather than a single node) of a goal model using an autonomic element seems more appropriate for many applications. Trade-offs among goal subtrees can be tuned and optimized using higher-level autonomic elements. Thus, a goal model affords a first architectural decomposition of a self-managing system into components. Of course, much design information has to be added to implement the four phases of each autonomic element.

Out of a need to include autonomic features into legacy applications, Chan and Chieu proposed an autonomic design that treats the monitoring of a software application as a separate and independent concern [7]. This approach utilizes aspect-oriented programming to intercept, analyze, and decompose the application states of a software application before linking appropriate non-invasive constructs into the software application code to provide application state information to an autonomic manager through sensors. Kaiser et al. proposed a similar approach to externalizing monitoring logic [33].

Garlan's Rainbow framework, which is based on reusable infrastructure, also uses external adaptation mechanisms to allow the explicit specification of adaptation strategies for multiple system concerns. [18,19]. The Rainbow project investigated the use of software architectural models at runtime as the basis for reflection and dynamic adaptation.

Zhu et al. [64] identify and categorize types of common forms of autonomic element patterns grounded in Hawthorne and Perry's architectural styles [21,22], and Neti and Müller's attribute based architectural styles (ABASs) [48]. They also reveal the inherent relationships among these patterns and assess their particular maintainability concerns.

The field of autonomic computing has produced control-centric as well as architecture-centric reference models and patterns. To this point little research has been devoted to compare and evaluate the advantages and disadvantages of these two strategies. The selected research challenges outlined in the next section present good steps in this direction.

8   Lessons Learned and Research Challenges

While much progress has been made over the past decade, many open research problems and challenges remain in this exciting field of autonomic computing.

Model construction
    The process of designing feedback-based computing systems requires the construction of models which quantify the effect of control inputs on measured outputs [23]. Fields such as performance engineering and queuing theory have developed advanced models for many different applications. However, performance, albeit important, constitutes just one dimension of the modeling problem. There are many other quality criteria that come into play in dynamic autonomic applications. For some of these criteria (e.g., trust) quantification is difficult [48]. In addition, models are needed to design trade-off analyses schemes for combinations of quality criteria. Thus, developing feedback models using quality criteria for various application domains is a major challenge and critical for the success of this field. Models and quality criteria related to governance, compliance, and service-level agreements are of particular importance for service-oriented autonomic business processes and applications.

Managing and leveraging uncertainty
    When we model potential disturbances from the environment of an autonomic system (e.g., unexpected saturation of the network) or satisfy requirements by regulation (i.e., trade-off analysis among several extra-functional requirements), we introduce some uncertainty. Therefore, designers and maintainers of such dynamical systems should manage uncertainty because the environment may change in unexpected ways and, as a result, the system may adapt

in such a way that was not foreseeable at design time. Introducing uncertainty requires trade-offs between flexibility and assurance [9]. For a maintainer it is critical to know which parts of the environment are assumed to be fixed and which are expected to introduce uncertainty [64]. Moreover, assurance and compliance criteria should be continuously validated at run-time (i.e., not just at system acceptance time). Hence, understanding, managing, and leveraging uncertainty is important for delivering autonomic systems with reliability and assurance guarantees.

Making control loops explicit

Software engineers are trained to develop abstractions that hide complexity. Hiding the complexity of a feedback loop seems obvious and natural. In contrast, Müller et al. advocate that feedback loops, which are the bread and butter of self-adaptive and autonomic systems, should be made first class design elements [47]. Designers of autonomic systems will realize significant benefits by raising the visibility of control loops and specifying the major components and characteristics of the control loops explicitly. Further benefits could be realized by identifying common forms of adaptation and then distilling design and V&V obligations for specific patterns. When arrangements of multiple control loops interact as in the ACRA (cf. Section 7), system design and analysis should cover their interactions. As control grows more complex, it is especially important for the control loops to be explicit in design and analysis. Hence, it is useful to investigate the trade-offs between hiding the complexity of feedback loops and treating feedback loops as first class objects with respect to the construction and operation of autonomic systems.

Characterizing architectural patterns and analysis frameworks

Another worthwhile avenue of research is to investigate patterns, quality criteria, and analysis frameworks for self-managing applications for different business and evolution contexts [48,64,10]. Quality attributes should not only include traditional quality criteria such as variability, modifiability, reliability, availability and security, but also autonomicity-specific criteria such as dynamic adaptation support, dynamic upgrade support, support for detecting anomalous system behavior, support for how to keep the user informed and in the loop, support for sampling rate adjustments in sensors, support for simulation of expected or predicted behavior, support for differencing between expected and actual behavior, or support for accountability (e.g., how users can gain trust by monitoring the underlying autonomic system).

9   Conclusions

On the one hand, dealing with software-intensive ecosystems seems rather daunting given that there are still many challenges in the top-down construction of traditional software systems and their subsequent maintenance. On the other hand, to be able to observe and control independent and competing processes in a dynamic and changing environment is a necessity in this new world of service-oriented, decentralized, distributed computing ecosystems.

After almost a decade of intense research and development, autonomic computing constitutes an effective set of technologies, models, architecture patterns, standards, and processes to cope with and reign in the management complexity of dynamic computing systems using feedback control, adaptation, and self-management. The feedback loops, which are at the core of an autonomic system, sense their environment, model their behavior in that environment, and take action to change the environment or their own behavior. In this article, we argued that we not only need architecture-centric views, but also control-centric views to construct, reason about, and operate highly dynamic autonomic systems. We illustrated that autonomic computing technology is not only useful for managing IT infrastructure complexity, but also to mitigate continuous software evolution problems. We also discussed how to leverage the rich history of control theory foundations for autonomic and self-adaptive systems. Finally, we presented some valuable lessons learned and outlined selected challenges for the future.

Previously, we advocated to teach the notion of a control loop, together with the concept of an autonomic element, early in computer science and software engineering curricula [46]. In contrast to traditional engineering disciplines, computing science programs seem to have neglected the control loop. If we assume that the two important trends dominating the computing world over the last decade and outlined at the beginning of this article—moving towards a service-centric way of conducting business and evolving towards socio-technical software ecosystems,—it might be time to give the control loop more prominence in undergraduate computing curricula so that the next generation of software engineers and IT professionals is intimately familiar with the foundations of self-adaptation and self-management. Over a decade ago, Shaw compared a software design method based on process control to an object-oriented design method [57]. Not surprisingly, the process control pattern described in that paper resembles an autonomic element. This method could be used to teach simple feedback loops in an introductory programming course.

The papers listed in the bibliography give a good indication of how quickly the field of autonomic computing has grown since 2001, but also show that there is a rich history for many of its foundations. The references contain a number of papers that can serve as good starting points for newcomers to the field (i.e., [4,9,12,13,16,23,28,35,38,51,60]).

Acknowledgments

This work grew out of collaboration with colleagues at IBM Toronto Center for Advanced Studies, CA Labs, and Carnegie Mellon Software Engineering Institute. We are also deeply indebted to many of friends and students, who contributed significantly to our appreciation and understanding of autonomic computing. In particular, we would like to thank John Mylopoulos, Marin Litoiu, Anatol Kark, Dennis Smith, Grace Lewis, Patricia Oberndorf, Mary Shaw, Linda Northrop, Ken Wong, Peggy Storey, Kostas Kontogiannis, Gabby Silbermann, Serge Mankovski, Joanna Ng, Kelly Lyons, Cheryl Morris, Scott Tilley, Andrea

De Lucia, Filomena Ferrucci, Qin Zhu, Piotr Kaminski, Sangeeta Neti, Sweta Gupta, and Dylan Dawson for their continued collaboration and support. This work was funded in part by the National Sciences and Engineering Research Council (NSERC) of Canada (CRDPJ 320529-04 and CRDPJ 356154-07) as well as IBM Corporation and CA Inc. via the CSER Consortium.

References

1. Astrom, K.J., Wittenmark, B.: Adaptive Control, 2nd edn. Addison-Wesley, Reading (1995)
2. Babaoğlu, Ö., Jelasity, M., Montresor, A., Fetzer, C., Leonardi, S., van Moorsel, A., van Steen, M. (eds.): SELF-STAR 2004. LNCS, vol. 3460, pp. 1–20. Springer, Heidelberg (2005)
3. Boehm, B.: A View of 20th and 21st Century Software Engineering. In: 28th ACM/IEEE International Conference on Software Engineering (ICSE 2006), pp. 12–29. ACM, New York (2006)
4. Brittenham, P., Cutlip, R.R., Draper, C., Miller, B.A., Choudhary, S., Perazolo, M.: IT Service Management Architecture and Autonomic Computing. IBM Systems Journal 46(3), 565–581 (2007)
5. Broy, M., Jarke, M., Nagl, M., Rombach, D.: Manifest: Strategische Bedeutung des Software Engineering in Deutschland. Informatik-Spektrum 29(3), 210–221 (2006)
6. Burns, R.S.: Advanced Control Engineering. Butterworth-Heinemann (2001)
7. Chan, H., Chieu, T.C.: An Approach to Monitor Application Status for Self-Managing (Autonomic) Systems. In: 18th ACM Annual SIGPLAN Conference on Object-Oriented Programming, Systems, Languages, and Applications (OOPSLA 2003), pp. 312–313. ACM, New York (2003)
8. Chao, L.: Special Issue on Autonomic Computing. Intel Technology Journal 10(4), 253–326 (2006)
9. Cheng, B.H.C., de Lemos, R., Giese, H., Inverardi, P., Magee, J., Andersson, J., Becker, B., Bencomo, N., Brun, Y., Cukic, B., Di Marzo Serugendo, J., Dustdar, S., Finkelstein, A., Gacek, C., Geihs, K., Grassi, V., Karsai, G., Kienle, H.M., Kramer, J., Malek, S., Mirandola, R., Müller, H.A., Park, S., Tichy, M., Tivoli, M., Weyns, D., Whittle, J.: A Research Roadmap: Software Engineering for Self-Adaptive Systems. Schloss Dagstuhl Seminar 08031 Report on Software Engineering for Self-Adaptive Systems, Wadern, Germany, 12 pages (2008); Presented at ACM/IEEE International ICSE Workshop on Software Engineering for Adaptive and Self-Managing Systems (SEAMS 2008). ACM, New York (2008), http://www.dagstuhl.de/08031/
10. Dawson, R., Desmarais, R., Kienle, H.M., Müller, H.A.: Monitoring in Adaptive Systems Using Reflection. In: 3rd ACM/IEEE International ICSE Workshop on Software Engineering for Adaptive and Self-Managing Systems (SEAMS 2008), pp. 81–88. ACM, New York (2008)
11. De Kleer, J., Mackworth, A.K., Reiter, R.: Characterizing Diagnosis and Systems. Artificial Intelligence 56(23), 197–222 (1992)
12. Diao, Y., Hellerstein, J.L., Parekh, S., Griffith, R., Kaiser, G.E., Phung, D.: A Control Theory Foundation for Self-Managing Computing Systems. IEEE Journal on Selected Areas in Communications 23(12), 2213–2222 (2005)

13. Dobson, S., Denazis, S., Fernández, A., Gaiti, D., Gelenbe, E., Massacci, F., Nixon, P., Saffre, F., Schmidt, N., Zambonelli, F.: A Survey of Autonomic Communications. ACM Transactions on Autonomous and Adaptive Systems (TAAS) 1(2), 223–259 (2006)
14. Draper, C.: Combine Autonomic Computing and SOA to Improve IT Management. IBM Developer Works (2006),
    http://www.ibm.com/developerworks/library/ac-mgmtsoa/index.html
15. Dumont, G.A., Huzmezan, M.: Concepts, Methods and Techniques in Adaptive Control. In: American Control Conference (ACC 2002), vol. 2, pp. 1137–1150. IEEE Computer Society, Washington (2002)
16. Ganek, A.G., Corbi, T.A.: The Dawning of the Autonomic Computing Era. IBM Systems Journal 42(1), 5–18 (2003)
17. Ganek, A.G.: Overview of Autonomic Computing: Origins, Evolution, Direction. In: Parashar, M., Hariri, S. (eds.) Autonomic Computing: Concepts, Infrastructure, and Applications. CRC Press, Boca Raton (2006)
18. Garlan, D., Cheng, S., Schmerl, B.: Increasing System Dependability through Architecture-based Self-repair. In: de Lemos, R., Gacek, C., Romanovsky, A. (eds.) Architecting Dependable Systems. LNCS, vol. 2677. Springer, Heidelberg (2003)
19. Garlan, D., Cheng, S., Huang, A.-C., Schmerl, B., Steenkiste, P.: Rainbow: Architecture-Based Self-Adaptation with Reusable Infrastructure. IEEE Computer 37(10), 46–54 (2004)
20. Gat, E.: On Three-layer Architectures. In: Kortenkamp, D., Bonasso, R., Murphy, R. (eds.) Artificial Intelligence and Mobile Robots: Case Studies of Successful Robot Systems. MIT/AAAI Press (1998)
21. Hawthorne, M.J., Perry, D.E.: Exploiting Architectural Prescriptions for Self-Managing, Self-Adaptive Systems: A Position Paper. In: 1st ACM SIGSOFT Workshop on Self-Managed Systems (WOSS 2004), pp. 75–79 (2004)
22. Hawthorne, M.J., Perry, D.E.: Architectural Styles for Adaptable Self-healing Dependable Systems. Technical Report, University of Texas at Austin, USA (2005), http://users.ece.utexas.edu/~perry/work/papers/MH-05-Styles.pdf
23. Hellerstein, J.L., Diao, Y., Parekh, S., Tilbury, D.M.: Feedback Control of Computing Systems. John Wiley & Sons, Chichester (2004)
24. Herger, L., Iwano, K., Pattnaik, P., Davis, A.G., Ritsko, J.J.: Special Issue on Autonomic Computing. IBM Systems Journal 42(1), 3–188 (2003), http://www.research.ibm.com/journal/sj42-1.html
25. Hewlett-Packard Development Company: HP Unveils Adaptive Enterprise Strategy to Help Businesses Manage Change and Get More from Their IT Investments (2003), http://www.hp.com/hpinfo/newsroom/press/2003/030506a.html
26. Horn, P.: Autonomic Computing. Online Whitepaper (2001), http://www.research.ibm.com/autonomic/manifesto/autonomic_computing.pdf
27. Huebscher, M.C., McCann, J.A.: A Survey of Autonomic Computing—Degrees, Models, and Applications. ACM Computing Surveys 40(3), 7, 1–28 (2008)
28. IBM Corporation: An Architectural Blueprint for Autonomic Computing, 4th edn. (2006),
    http://www-03.ibm.com/autonomic/pdfs/AC_Blueprint_White_Paper_4th.pdf
29. IBM Corporation: Symptoms Reference Specification V2.0 (2006),
    http://download.boulder.ibm.com/ibmdl/pub/software/dw/opensource/btm/SymptomSpec_v2.0.pdf
30. IBM Corporation: Autonomic Computing Toolkit User's Guide, 3rd edn. (2005),
    http://download.boulder.ibm.com/ibmdl/pub/software/dw/library/autonomic/books/fpu3mst.pdf

31. Information Technology Infrastructure Library (ITIL). Office of Government Commerce, UK (2007), http://www.itil.org.uk/
32. Inverardi, P., Tivoli, M.: The Future of Software: Adaptation and Dependability. In: De Lucia, A., Ferrucci, F. (eds.) ISSSE 2006–2008, University of Salerno, Italy. LNCS, vol. 5413, pp. 1–31. Springer, Heidelberg (2009)
33. Kaiser, G., Parekh, J., Gross, P., Valetto, G.: Kinesthetics eXtreme: An External Infrastructure for Monitoring Distributed Legacy Systems. In: 5th IEEE Annual International Active Middleware Workshop (AMS 2003), pp. 22–30. IEEE Computer Society, Washington (2003)
34. Kazman, R., Chen, H.-M.: The Metropolis Model: A New Logic for the Development of Crowdsourced Systems. Communications of the ACM, 18 pages (submitted, 2008)
35. Kephart, J.O., Chess, D.M.: The Vision of Autonomic Computing. IEEE Computer 36(1), 41–50 (2003)
36. Kluth, A.: Information Technology—Make It Simple. The Economist (2004), http://www.economist.com/surveys/displaystory.cfm?story_id=E1_PPDSPGP&CFID=17609242&CFTOKEN=84287974
37. Kramer, J., Magee, J.: Dynamic Structure in Software Architectures. ACM SIGSOFT Software Engineering Notes 21(6), 3–14 (1996)
38. Kramer, J., Magee, J.: Self-managed Systems: An Architectural Challenge. In: Future of Software Engineering (FoSE 2007), pp. 259–268. IEEE Computer Society, Washington (2007)
39. Lapouchnian, A., Liaskos, S., Mylopoulos, J., Yu, Y.: Towards Requirements-Driven Autonomic Systems Design. In: ICSE Workshop on Design and Evolution of Autonomic Application Software (DEAS 2005), pp. 45–51. ACM, New York (2005)
40. Lapouchnian, A., Yu, Y., Liaskos, S., Mylopoulos, J.: Requirements-Driven Design of Autonomic Application Software. In: ACM IBM Center for Advanced Studies Conference on Collaborative Research (CASCON 2006), pp. 80–93. ACM, New York (2006)
41. Litoiu, M., Woodside, M., Zheng, T.: Hierarchical Model-based Autonomic Control of Software Systems. In: ICSE Workshop on Design and Evolution of Autonomic Application Software (DEAS 2005), pp. 34–40. ACM, New York (2005)
42. Marcus, A.: Dashboards in Your Future. ACM Interactions 13(1), 48–49 (2006)
43. McKinley, P.K., Sadjadi, M., Kasten, E.P., Cheng, B.H.C.: Composing Adaptive Software. IEEE Computer 37(7), 56–64 (2004)
44. Microsoft Corporation: Dynamic Systems 2007: Get Started With Dynamic Systems Technology Today (2007), http://www.microsoft.com/business/dsi/dsiwp.mspx
45. Müller, H.A., O'Brien, L., Klein, M., Wood, B.: Autonomic Computing. Technical Report, Software Engineering Institute, Carnegie Mellon University, CMU/SEI-2006-TN-006, 61 pages (2006), http://www.sei.cmu.edu/pub/documents/06.reports/pdf/06tn006.pdf
46. Müller, H.A.: Bits of History, Challenges for the Future and Autonomic Computing Technology (Keynote). In: 13th IEEE Working Conference on Reverse Engineering (WCRE 2006), pp. 9–18. IEEE Computer Society, Washington (2006)
47. Müller, H.A., Pezzè, M., Shaw, M.: Visibility of Control in Adaptive Systems. In: 2nd ACM/IEEE International ICSE Workshop on Ultra-Large-Scale Software-Intensive Systems (ULSSIS 2008), pp. 23–26. ACM, New York (2008)
48. Neti, S., Müller, H.A.: Quality Criteria and an Analysis Framework for Self-Healing Systems. In: 2nd ACM/IEEE International ICSE Workshop on Software Engineering for Adaptive and Self-Managing Systems (SEAMS 2007), pp. 39–48. IEEE Computer Society, Washington (2007)

49. OASIS: Web Services Distributed Management: Management of Web Services (WSDM-MOWS) 1.1 OASIS Standard (2006),
    http://docs.oasis-open.org/wsdm/wsdm-mows-1.1-spec-os-01.htm
50. Ogata, K.: Discrete-Time Control Systems, 2nd edn. Prentice-Hall, Englewood Cliffs (1995)
51. Northrop, L., Feiler, P., Gabriel, R., Goodenough, J., R., L., Longstaff, T., Kazman, R., Klein, M., Schmidt, D., Sullivan, K., Wallnau, K.: Ultra-Large-Scale Systems—The Software Challenge of the Future. Technical Report, Software Engineering Institute, Carnegie Mellon University, 134 pages (2006),
    http://www.sei.cmu.edu/uls
52. Oreizy, P., Medvidovic, N., Taylor, R.N.: Architecture-Based Runtime Software Evolution (Most Influential Paper Award at ICSE 2008). In: ACM/IEEE International Conference on Software Engineering (ICSE 1998), pp. 177–186. IEEE Computer Society, Washington (1998)
53. Oreizy, P., Medvidovic, N., Taylor, R.N.: Runtime Software Adaptation: Framework, Approaches, and Styles. In: ACM/IEEE International Conference on Software Engineering (ICSE 2008), pp. 899–910. ACM, New York (2008)
54. Reiter, R.: A Theory of Diagnosis from First Principles. Artificial Intelligence 32(1), 57–95 (1987)
55. Schloss Dagstuhl Seminar 08031. Software Engineering for Self-Adaptive Systems, Wadern, Germany (2008), http://www.dagstuhl.de/08031/
56. SEI Software-Intensive Systems (ISIS). Integration of Software-Intensive Systems (ISIS) Initiative: Addressing System-of-Systems Interoperability (2007), http://www.sei.cmu.edu/isis/
57. Shaw, M.: Beyond Objects: A Software Design Paradigm Based on Process Control. ACM SIGSOFT Software Engineering Notes 20(1), 27–38 (1995)
58. Sun Microsystems: Sun N1 Service Provisioning System (2007),
    http://www.sun.com/software/products/service_provisioning/index.xml
59. Tanner, J.A.: Feedback Control in Living Prototypes: A New Vista in Control Engineering. Medical and Biological Engineering and Computing 1(3), 333–351 (1963), http://www.springerlink.com/content/rh7wx0675k5mx544/
60. Tewari, V., Milenkovic, M.: Standards for Autonomic Computing. Intel Technology Journal 10(4), 275–284 (2006)
61. Truex, D., Baskerville, R., Klein, H.: Growing Systems in Emergent Organizations. Communications of the ACM 42(8), 117–123 (1999)
62. Wong, K.: The Reverse Engineering Notebook. Ph.D. Thesis, Department of Computer Science, University of Victoria, Canada, 149 pages (1999) ISBN:0-612-47299-X
63. Tsypkin, Y.Z.: Adaptation and Learning in Automatic Systems. Mir Publishing, Moscow (1971)
64. Zhu, Q., Lin, L., Kienle, H.M., Müller, H.A.: Characterizing Maintainability Concerns in Autonomic Element Design. In: IEEE International Conference on Software Maintenance (ICSM 2008), 10 pages. IEEE Computer Society, Washington (2008)

Impact of Usability on Software Requirements and Design

Natalia Juristo

Facultad de Informática, Universidad Politécnica de Madrid
Campus de Montegancedo,
28660 Boadilla del Monte, Spain
natalia@fi.upm.es

Abstract. Like any other quality attribute, usability imposes specific constraints on software components. We have empirically corroborated that software design and usability are related. Therefore usability features impacting design need to be considered from a functional viewpoint at requirements stage. But discovering and documenting usability features is likely to be beyond the usability knowledge of most requirements engineers, developers and users. We propose an approach based on developing specific guidelines that capitalize upon key elements recurrently intervening in the usability features elicitation and specification. Developers can use these guidelines to ask the appropriate questions and capture usability requirements information. This practice should lead to build software with higher usability.

Keywords: SE-Usability gap, Usability requirements, Usability Impact.

1 Introduction

There are so many software systems with immature usability that you are sure to have had enough frustrating experiences to be able to recognise how little use is made of usability strategies, models and methods in software construction. Although usability is a topic that crops up over again in discussions with customers, it is evidently not properly addressed in most development projects [1] [2]. However, the importance of usability is growing. For instance, IBM is convinced that usability "makes business effective and efficient and it makes business sense" [3]. In the same line, the Boeing Co. changed the way it buys software making a product's usability a fundamental purchasing criterion [4].

A number of studies have pointed out a wide range of benefits stemming from usability [5] [6] [7]: it improves productivity and raises team morale, reduces training and documentation costs, improves user productivity, increases e-commerce potential, etc. Additionally the cost/benefit ratio of usability is highly worthwhile. Donahue stated that every dollar spent on usability offers a return of $30.25 [8]. There are also studies for e-commerce sites that show that a 5% improvement in usability could increase revenues by 10% to 35% [9].

Both the HCI and SE communities play a crucial role in the development of usable software systems. The HCI community has the knowledge about which features a

A. De Lucia and F. Ferrucci (Eds.): ISSSE 2006–2008, LNCS 5413, pp. 55–77, 2009.
© Springer-Verlag Berlin Heidelberg 2009

software system must provide to be usable. The SE community has the knowledge about software systems development.

The HCI community has developed over the last decades a variety of approaches to enhance usability in software systems, but they are not the everyday practice in SE. HCI approaches are usually regarded as being uncoupled from the mainstream software development lifecycles [1]. At the same time, software developers receive only rudimentary training in usability [10] so they do not have the knowledge to build usable software.

Two separated processes for building an interactive system –one from SE for the system development and another from HCI to enhance usability– are certainly not manageable. It is not possible to control and synchronize software development and usability design separately. Also, efficiency falls and costs increase because of the overlapping functions between the two processes. Milewski [11] argues that, despite improvements in SE-HCI interactions, problems of communication and efficiency still remain and deserve further investigation. One of the most significant difficulties that still stands in the way of HCI and SE cooperation is that there is little knowledge and communication about each others' practices. Both communities use different vocabulary and sometimes the same word to represent different artifacts. The word "design", for example, can be understood and used differently in both communities: to express the software modeling phase (in SE), and the final look and feel of the product (in HCI).

Some widespread expressions, such as "friendliness of the user interface", and "user interface" *per se*, are some of the underlying obstacles to more usable interactive systems [1]. Such terms give the impression that the user-centered approach and usability methods are only for "decorating a thin component sitting on top of the software or the "real" system". Some software engineers consider themselves the "real" designers of the software system, leaving the task of making the UI more "user friendly" to the usability people.

This paper aims to contribute in the direction of incorporating HCI knowledge in every day SE practice. To this end, we have analyzed what different types of impact usability heuristics and guidelines stated in the Human Computer Interaction (HCI) literature are likely to have on a software system. As we will see, some usability features appear to have some effect on software design. The next step then is to examine what sort of effect this is. With this aim in mind, we have conducted a study of several real systems into which we have incorporated the usability features in question. As a result of this analysis we have been able to demonstrate that usability really is not confined to the system interface and can affect the system's core functionality. The implications of the usability features for design materialize as the creation of special items (components, responsibilities, interactions, classes, methods, etc.) that affect both the presentation and application layer of the software system architecture.

We think usability should be brought forward in the development process and considered at requirements time. We propose an approach in which usability features with major implications for software functionality are incorporated as functional requirements. Addressing usability at the requirements stage has the same benefits as considering other quality attributes early on in the development process [12]: "The earlier key quality attribute requirements are identified and prioritized, the more likely it is that the essential quality attributes will be built into the system. It is more cost-effective to reason about quality attribute tradeoffs early in the lifecycle than later in the lifecycle when modifications are often difficult, impractical, or even impossible". Building usability into a software system has a cost and calls for negotiation with users and other stakeholders about which usability features should be included, the consequences of their inclusion, how to provide them, etc. As applies to other quality attributes, it is more cost-effective to reason about usability tradeoffs early on the lifecycle. This chapter focuses on particular usability features with high functional implications and discusses how to deal with them at the requirements stage.

2   Usability Is Not Confined to UI

Software usability is a quality attribute listed in a number of classifications [13][14][15]. Although it is not easy to find a standard definition of usability, Nielsen gave one of the most well-known descriptions concerning the learnability and memorability of a software system, its efficiency of use, its ability to avoid and manage user errors, and user satisfaction [16]. Similarly, ISO 9241-11 [17] defines usability as "the extent to which a product can be used by specified users to achieve specified goals with effectiveness, efficiency and satisfaction in a specific context of use". Usability is also generally referred to as "quality in use" [18]. Usability reflects the relationship between a software system and its users.

The most widespread view in the field of SE is that usability is chiefly related to the user interface UI. In other words, usability mainly affects the UI and not the core of the system. Therefore, the good design practice that separates the UI from the core functionality would be sufficient to support the development of a usable software system. This view means that dealing with usability could be put off until the later stages of software system development (commonly during system evaluation), as the changes required to improve this quality attribute should not involve a lot of rework.

To understand the depth and scope of the usability of a system, it is useful to make a distinction between the visible part of the user interface (buttons, pull-down menus, check-boxes, background color, etc.) and the interaction part of the system. By interaction we mean the coordination of information exchange between the user and the system. A system's usability deals not only with the user interface but mainly with the user-system interaction.

The interaction must be carefully designed and must be considered not just when designing the visible part of the user interface, but also when designing the rest of the system. For example, if our system has to provide continuous feedback to the user for usability reasons, we need to bear this in mind when designing the system. System operations have to be designed so as to allow information to be frequently sent to the user interface to keep the user informed about the current status of the operation. This information could be displayed to the user by different means (percentage-completed bar, a clock, etc.). These means are interface issues. It is not unusual to find development teams thinking that they can design the system and then make it usable afterwards just by designing a nice set of controls, having the right color combination and the right font. This approach is clearly wrong.

The improvements in system usability involve modifications beyond the interface, specifically, to the design of some software components and, therefore, to its core.

This relation between usability and software design makes the rework cost to achieve an acceptable level of usability much higher than expected according to the hypothesis of separation. Certain functionalities that improve usability are to be dealt with earlier in the development process in order to define and evaluate its impact on design as soon as possible.

Recommendations provided by HCI literature in order to obtain usable software systems can be put in three groups according to their effect on software development: Recommendations impacting on the UI, on the development process or on the design.

Usability recommendations with **impact on the UI** are HCI recommendations that affect system presentation through buttons, pull-down menus, check boxes, background color, fonts, etc. The impact of these features on software development can be illustrated by an example. Suppose we have a developed system and we want to change the color of one of the windows to highlight certain aspects of interest for the user or the text associated with certain buttons so that user can get a clearer idea of what option to select. These changes that help to improve the software usability would be confined to altering the value of some source code variable related to the window or buttons. Building these recommendations into a system involves slight modifications to the detailed UI design, and no other part of the system needs to be modified. If good design practices have been followed, this change would be confined to the interface component or subsystem, having no impact on the system core.

Usability recommendations with **impact on the development process** can only be taken into account by modifying the techniques, activities and/or products used during development. These recommendations include guidelines to encourage all user-system interaction to take place naturally and intuitively for the user. This is the goal of usability recommendations like natural mapping, develop a user conceptual model, know your uses, involve the user in software construction, reduce the user cognitive load, etc., which intend the user to be able to confidently predict the effect of his/her actions with the system. In order to incorporate such recommendations the software development process needs to be modified. This involves, for example, the use of more powerful elicitation techniques, probably coming from other disciplines like HCI. There are proposals aimed at modifying the software process for developing more usable software. Most of these proposals come from the HCI field [19] [20] with a perspective of software development removed from SE's view. Just a few [21] come from SE.

Usability recommendations with **impact on design** involve building certain functionalities into the software to improve user-system interaction. For example, features like cancel an ongoing task, undo a task, receive feedback on what is going on in the system or adapt the software functionalities to the user profile. Suppose that we want to build the cancel functionality for specific commands into an application. HCI experts mention "provide a way to instantly cancel a time-consuming operation, with no side effects" [22]. To satisfy such requirements the software system must at least: gather information (data modifications, resource usage, etc.) that allow the system to recover the status prior to a command execution; stop command execution; estimate the time to cancel and inform the user of progress in cancellation; restore the system to the status before the cancelled command; etc. Apart from the changes that have to be made to the UI to add the cancel button, specific components must be built into the software design to deal with these responsibilities. Therefore, building the cancel usability feature into a finished software system involves a substantial amount of design rework rather than minor changes to the UI. The same applies to other usability recommendations that represent specific functionalities to be incorporated into a software system,

We have termed this type of HCI recommendations functional usability features (FUF) [23], as most of these heuristics/rules/principles make recommendations on functionalities that the software should provide for the user. Table 1 shows the most representative FUFs that can be foreseen to have a crucial effect on system design. As we have seen with cancel, this effect is inferred from the detailed descriptions of the FUFs provided by HCI authors. In the remainder of this chapter we will focus on this category of usability features.

3 Making the Relationship between Usability and Software Design Visible

In order to confirm what the relationship between FUFs and software design is, we have worked on a number of real development projects carried out by UPM Master in Software Engineering students as part of their MSc dissertations from 2004 to 2005 [24]. Students originally developed the respective systems without any FUFs. These designs were then modified to include the FUFs listed in Table 1.

This section discusses an example illustrating the incorporation of one FUF on a system developed to manage on-line table bookings for a restaurant chain. The FUF addressed is one particular kind of feedback, system status feedback. This usability feature involves the system notifying the user of any change of state that is likely to be of interest. HCI experts recommend that the notification should be more or less striking for the user depending on how important the change is. The status changes that the client considered important referred to failures during the performance of certain system operations, owing either to runtime faults, insufficient resources or problems with devices or external resources (specifically Internet).

Table 1. Usability features with impact on software design

Functional Usability Features	Goal
Feedback	To inform users about what is happening in the system
Undo	To undo system actions at several levels
Cancel	To cancel the execution of a command or an application
Form/Field Validation	To improve data input for users and software correction as soon as possible
Wizard	To help do tasks that require different steps with user input
User Expertise	To adapt system functionality to users' expertise
Multilevel	To adapt system functionality to users' expertise
Help	To make users able to work with their own language, currency, ZIP code, etc.
Different Languages	To warn the user about an action with important consequences
Alert	

Figure 1 illustrates part of the UML class model for this system, including the classes involved in the restaurant table booking process only. The original classes designed without considering system status feedback are shown on a white background in the diagram and the classes derived from the later inclusion of this feature on a grey background. Let us first analyse this diagram without taking into account the system status feedback. The Interface class represents the part of the bookings terminal with which the user interacts to book a table at the restaurant over the Internet. The Restaurants-Manager and Reservations-Manager are two classes specialized in dealing with restaurants and bookings, respectively. They have been added to make the system more maintainable by separating the management processes so that they can be modified more efficiently in the future. The Reservations class accommodates the information related to each booking that is made at the restaurant, where the restaurant is represented by the Restaurant class and each of the tables at this restaurant that are not taken are identified by the Table class.

According to the previous definition of system status feedback, its inclusion into a software system involves the following specific responsibilities:

- R1: The software should be able to listen to commands under execution, because they can provide information about the system status. If this information is useful to the user, the system should be able to pass this information on as, when and where needed.
- R2: As the system may fail, the software should be able to ascertain the state of commands under execution, because users should be informed if the command is not working owing to outside circumstances. The system should be equipped with a mechanism by means of which it can check at any time whether a given command is being executed and, if the command fails, inform users that the command is not operational.
- R3: The software should be able to listen to or query external resources, like networks or databases, about their status, to inform the user if any resource is not working properly.
- R4: The software should be able to check the status of the internal system resources and alert users in advance to save their work, for instance, if the system is running short of a given resource and is likely to have to shut down.

The following changes (highlighted on a grey background) had to be made to the design illustrated in Figure 1 to deal with these responsibilities:

- Three new classes:
  - Internal-Resource-Checker, responsible for changes and for determining failures due to internal system resources like memory, etc.
  - External-Resource-Checker, responsible for changes and determining failures due to external system resources like networks, databases, etc.
  - Status-Feedbacker, responsible for providing the client with information stating the grounds for both changes and system failures in the best possible format and using the most appropriate heuristic in each case.

- Five new methods:
    - ExternalResourcesAvailable, to determine whether the external resources are available.
    - CheckSystemResources, to determine whether the system has the resources it needs to execute the booking operation for the restaurant.
    - AreYouAlive, to be able to ask whether the command under execution is still running correctly.
    - IAmAlive, for the Reservations-Manager to be able to tell the system that it is still running, that is, that it is alive.
    - Feedback, to tell the user of any changes or failures identified in the system while the table is being booked at the restaurant.
- Four new associations between:
    - Reservations-Manager&StatusFeedbacker, so that the ReservationsManager class can tell the StatusFeedbacker about changes or system failures that are relevant for the user and about which the user is to be informed.
    - Internal-Resource-Checker&Status-Feedbacker and External-Resource-Checker&Status-Feedbacker, to be able to tell the Status-Feedbacker class that a change or failure has occurred.
    - Reservations-Manager&Internal-Resources-Checker, so that the Internal-Resources-Checker can check that the reservation process is still active and working properly.

Table 2 summarizes the classes responsible for satisfying each of the identified responsibilities.

Table 2. Correspondence between responsibilities and static structure diagram classes

Class Name	Responsibility
Reservations-Manager	R1, R2
Internal-Resources-Checker	R1, R2, R4
External-Resources-Checker	R3
Status-Feedbacker	R1, R2, R3, R4

Figure 2 illustrates the sequence diagram for the case in which the user books a restaurant table over the Internet. Like Figure 1, this diagram shows the original classes designed without taking into account system status feedback on a white background, whereas as the classes derived from the inclusion of this usability feature are shaded grey. Let us analyze this diagram first without taking into account the information entered as a result of system status feedback. Looking at the sequence diagram, it is clear that the Client actor interacts with the Interface class to start to book a restaurant table. As of this point, the Reservations-Manager takes over to request the names of available restaurants from which the client is to select one and enter the date, time and table type (smoking or non-smoking).The system can use this information to check what tables have already been booked at the restaurant and determine which meet the conditions specified by the client. Once the system has gathered what information there is about tables, it displays a map of the restaurant showing the position of the vacant tables from which the user can select the one he or she likes best. After the user has selected the restaurant table, the system proceeds to materialize the booking providing the client with a booking code stating the table booked and giving him or her the option to print a ticket stating the booking information.

After including system status feedback, the following checks need to be run: i) the system has not stop while it was making the booking (see UML NOTE A); ii) the system has enough resources, memory, etc. (see UML NOTE B) for as long as it took to book the table, and iii) the Internet connection has worked properly (see UML NOTE C). As you can see, the above checks are done at different times throughout the booking process and, therefore, the interactions represented by UML NOTES A, B and C appear more than once.

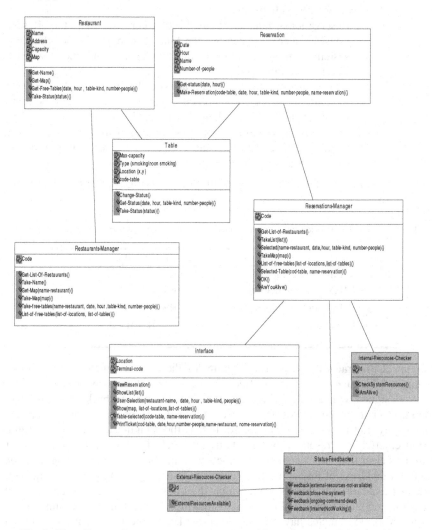

Fig. 1. Class diagram for restaurant management with system status feedback feature

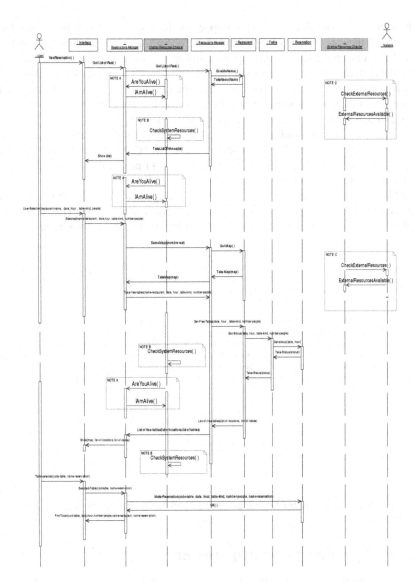

Fig. 2. Sequence diagram for reservations management with System Status Feedback feature

As shown in Figure 3, if an external resource, in this case the network, failed, the External-Resources-Checker would take charge of detecting this state of affairs (as no ExternalResourceAvailable message would be received) and it would alert the user through the Status-Feedbacker. If the shaded classes were omitted, the system would not be able to detect the network failure. Explicitly incorporating the components for this usability feature at design time provides some assurance that it will be included in the final system.

The above example illustrates what impact the inclusion of the system status feedback feature has on system design (and therefore on later system implementation). Other designers could have come up with different, albeit equally valid designs to satisfy the above-mentioned responsibilities. For example, a less reusable class model might not have included new classes for this type of feedback, adding any new methods needed to existing classes. In any case, the addition of this new feature to the system can be said to involve significant changes at design time.

Note that this example only shows the effect of this usability feature for a specific functionality (table booking). This effect is multiplied if this feature is added to the other system functionalities, and, as we will discuss in next section, even more so if we consider all the other FUFs.

In [24] we analyze what effect FUFs have on design in more detail We have quantified the impact of each feature to ascertain the different levels of FUFs complexity and, therefore, the level of impact on design. Table 3 shows this information.

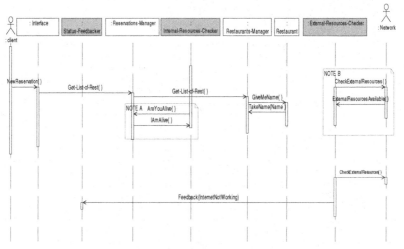

Fig. 3. Sequence diagram for bookings management with System Status Feedback feature and a network failure

4 Usability as Functional Requirement

Both Human HCI and SE disciplines deal with usability as a non-functional requirement. Typically usability requirements specify user effectiveness, efficiency or satisfaction levels that the system should achieve. These specifications can then be used as a yardstick at the evaluation stage: "A novice user should learn to use the system in less than 10 hours", or "End user satisfaction with the application should be higher than Z on a 1-to-5 scale". Dealing with usability in the shape of non-functional requirements does not provide developers with enough information about what kind of features to provide to satisfy such requirements.

The features described in Table 1 represent particular functionalities that can be built into a software system to increase usability. Since functional requirements describe the functions that the software is to execute [25], we consider that the usability features in

Table 1 should be treated as functional requirements (even though they are usability-related requirements). Such functional usability requirements need to be explicitly specified, just like any other functionality. If these usability functionalities are properly described in the requirements specification, they are more likely to be built into the system. They will improve the system's usability and contribute to the usability levels established in the non-functional requirements.

Usability functionalities could be specified by just stating the respective usability features. For example, "the system should provide users with the ability to cancel actions" or "the system should provide feedback to the user". This is actually the level of advice that most HCI heuristics provide. The HCI community assumes that this level of detail is sufficient for developers to properly build a usability feature into the system. For example, one of the most commonly recurring HCI guidelines is Nielsen's feedback heuristic: "The system should always keep users informed about what is going on through appropriate feedback within reasonable time" [16]. However, this description provides nowhere near enough information to satisfactorily specify the feedback functionality, let alone design and implement it correctly.

To illustrate what information is missing let us look at the complexity and diversity of the feedback feature. The HCI literature identifies four types of Feedback: Interaction Feedback to inform users that the system has heard their request; Progress Feedback for tasks that take some time to finish; System Status Display to inform users about any change in the system status, and Warnings to inform users about irreversible actions. Additionally, each feedback type has its own peculiarities. For example, many details have to be taken into account for a system to provide a satisfactory System Status Feedback: what states to report, what information to display for each state; how prominent the information should be in each case (e.g., should the application keep control of the system while reporting, or should the system let the user work on other tasks while status reporting), etc.

Therefore, a lot more information than just a description of the usability feature must be specified to properly build the whole feedback feature into a software system. Developers need to discuss this information with and elicit it from the different stakeholders.

Note that the problem of increasing functional requirements completeness is generally solved by adding more information to the requirements [26][27]. Even so, requirements completeness is never an easy problem to solve [28][29][30], and this is

Table 3. Functional Usability Features design impact

	FUF-Functionality	FUF-Classes	FUF-Methods Complexity	FUF-Interactions
Feedback	90%	27%	MEDIUM	66%
Undo	40%	10%	HIGH	66%
Cancel	95%	8%	HIGH	66%
User Errors Prevention	36%	11%	MEDIUM	6%
Wizard	7%	10%	LOW	70%
User Profile	8%	37%	MEDIUM	10%
Help	7%	6%	LOW	68%
Use of different languages	51%	10%	MEDIUM	70%
Alert	27%	7%	LOW	66%

even harder in the case of functional usability requirements. In most cases, neither users nor developers are good sources of the information needed to completely specify a usability feature. Users know that they want feedback; what they do not know is what kind of feedback can be provided, which is best for each situation, and less still what issues need to be detailed to properly describe each feedback type. Neither do software engineers have the necessary HCI knowledge to completely specify such functional usability requirements since they are not usually trained in HCI skills.

The HCI literature suggests that HCI experts should join software development teams to deal with this missing expertise [31][19]. However, this solution has several drawbacks. The first is that communication difficulties arise between the software developer team and HCI experts, as HCI and SE are separate disciplines. They use different vocabulary, notations, software development strategies, techniques, etc. Misunderstandings on these points can turn out to be a huge obstacle to software development. Another impediment is the cost. Large organizations can afford to pay for HCI experts, but many small-to-medium software companies cannot.

5   Guidelines for Gathering Information about Functional Usability Features

Our approach consists of packaging guidelines that empower developers to capture functional usability requirements without depending on a usability expert. These guidelines help developers to understand the implications of and know how to elicit and specify usability features for a software system.

The information provided by the HCI literature is not directly applicable for this purpose. We have analyzed this information from a software development point of view and have elaborated elicitation and specification guidelines. In the following we describe this work in detail. The usability features that we have worked on are listed in Table 4 along with their HCI sources of information.

First, we extracted and categorized the information about functional usability features provided by the different HCI authors. We found the most detailed information on usability features in [32][33][34][35][36] This information has served as a basis for identifying which issues should be discussed with stakeholders during the elicitation process. However, there is not enough HCI information to derive the essentials to be elicited and specified for all the functional usability features in Table 1. This is why features like Shortcuts and Reuse, for example, have been left out.

Each HCI author identifies different varieties of these usability features. We have denoted these subtypes as usability mechanisms, and have given them a name that is indicative of their functionality (see Table 2). Then we defined the elicitation and specification guides for the usability mechanisms.

We have packaged the elicitation guidelines we have generated in what we call a usability elicitation pattern. Our usability elicitation patterns capitalize upon elicitation know-how so that requirements engineers can reuse key usability issues intervening recurrently in different projects. Patterns help developers to extract the necessary information to specify a functional usability feature.

We have developed one usability elicitation pattern for each usability mechanism. They are available at http://is.ls.fi.upm.es/research/usability/usability-elicitation-patterns. Annex A shows an example of the System Status Feedback mechanism pattern. Let us briefly describe the fields making up this pattern:

- Identification of the usability mechanism addressed by the pattern (that is, its name, the family of usability features to which it belongs and possible aliases by which this usability mechanism may be known).
- Problem addressed by each pattern, that is, how to elicit and specify the information needed to incorporate in a software system the corresponding usability mechanism.
- Usability context in which this pattern will be useful.
- Solution to the problem addressed by the pattern. This is composed of two elements. The usability mechanism elicitation guide provides knowledge for eliciting information about the usability mechanism. It lists the issues to be discussed to properly define how the usability mechanism needs to be considered along with the corresponding HCI rationale. The usability mechanism specification guide provides an example of a specification skeleton.
- The related patterns refer to other usability elicitation patterns whose contexts are related to the one under study and could also be considered in the same application

We use an example of a software system for theatre ticket sales for use by box office operators to illustrate pattern use. This is a highly interactive system with a specific user type. These two factors condition the usability requirements to be considered quite a lot.

The use of elicitation patterns involves instantiating them for each particular system. They should be applied after a preliminary version of the software requirements has been created. There needs to be an initial common vision of system functionality before developers and users can discuss whether and how specific usability mechanisms affect the software.

After this initial understanding of the software to be built, the developer can use the identification part of the pattern to appreciate the generics of the usability mechanisms to be addressed. The discussion with the stakeholders starts by examining the pattern context section that describes the situations for which this mechanism is useful. If the mechanism is not relevant for the application, its use will be rejected. Otherwise, the respective usability functionality will be elicited and specified using the solution part of the pattern.

In the case of our theatre system, our client considered that the Object Specific Undo, Command Aggregation and User Profile-related mechanisms were of no interest. These application users do not get to be expert users because staff turnover is high. On this ground and because of the cost of incorporating the first two mechanisms, stakeholders decided that they were not to be built into the system. Again because of the high turnover, very few, if any, users are on the system long enough for the User Profile functionality to be warranted or even feasible.

The next step is to deal with the solution part of the pattern. Regarding the usability mechanism elicitation guide, it is important that developers read and understand the HCI rationales in the guide, that is, the HCI recommendations used to derive the respective issues to be discussed with stakeholders. This will help developers to understand why they need to deal with those issues. Not all questions in the patterns require the same level of involvement of all kinds of stakeholders. In fact, we can identify three groups of questions:

Table 4. Usability mechanisms for which usability elicitation and specification guides have been developed

Usability Feature	Usability Mechanism	Goal
Feedback	System Status	To inform users about the internal status of the system
	Interaction	To inform users that the system has registered a user interaction
	Warning	To inform users of any action with important consequences
	Long Action Feedback	To inform users that processing an action will take some time
Undo / Cancel	Global Undo	To undo system actions at several levels
	Object-Specific Undo	To undo several actions on an object
	Abort Operation	To cancel the execution of an action or the whole application
	Go Back	To go back to a particular state in a command execution sequence
User Error Prevention	Structured Text Entry	To help prevent the user from making data input errors
Wizard	Step-by-Step Execution	To help users to do tasks that require different steps
User Profile	Preferences	To record each user's options for using system functions
	Personal Object Space	To record each user's options for using the system interface
	Favourites	To record certain places of interest for the user
Help	Multilevel Help	To provide different help levels for different users
Command Aggregation	Command Aggregation	To express actions to be taken through commands built from smaller parts

1) Questions that the user/client can answer on his or her own (Which statuses are relevant in a particular application?);

2) Questions that the user/client can answer following the recommendations of a GUI expert (Which is the best place to locate the feedback information for each situation?- the GUI expert is able to provide guidance for displaying this kind of information, whereas the user will choose one of the options);

3) Questions that the developer must answer but on which the user should give his opinion (Does the user want the system to provide notification if there are not enough resources to execute the ongoing commands? If so,

which resources? – the developer must provide information about the internal resources needed to perform the different tasks, and the user will decide about which ones he or she wants to be informed.

4) Why it is applicable to this system and the specific functionalities that it affects.

The requirements related to the affected functionalities and/or possible new requirements that emerge from the usability issues discussed. In the case of the ticket system, no new requirements had to be added for the system status usability mechanism. The elicited usability information can be specified following the pattern specification guide. This guide is a prompt for the developer to modify each requirement affected by the incorporation of each mechanism. Figure 4 shows a fragment of a requirement modified to include all the usability mechanisms that affect it. The parts added as a result of using the respective usability elicitation patterns are highlighted in bold face and italics.

Modifying a requirement to include certain usability mechanisms involves adding the details describing how to apply these mechanisms to this functionality. As of this point, the remaining development phases are undertaken as always, and the new usability functionality is integrated into the development process. This prevents the rework that the alternative of incorporating usability features at later development stages would entail.

6 Evaluation

We have analyzed the potential benefits of the usability elicitation patterns at different levels. We have been working with SE Master students who have developed software systems to which they added the functional usability features. We worked with five groups of three students. Each group was randomly allocated a different software requirement specification (SRS) document in IEEE-830 format corresponding to a real application.

Each of the three students in the group was asked to add the functionality derived from the functional usability features to the original SRS independently and to build the respective software system. The procedure was as follows.

We gave one of the students the usability elicitation patterns discussed in this chapter. This student used the pattern content to elicit the usability functionality as explained in the last section.

Another student was given reduced patterns. This short pattern is just a compilation of information from the HCI literature about the usability mechanisms. We have not elaborated this information from a development perspective; i.e. the reduced patterns do not include the "Issues to be discussed with stakeholders" column in Table 5. The idea behind using the reduced patterns was to confirm whether our processing of the HCI information resulting in the formulation of specific questions was useful for eliciting the functionality related to the mechanisms or whether developers are able to extract such details just from the HCI literature.

Finally, the third student was given just the definitions of the usability features according to the usability heuristics found in the HCI literature and was encouraged to take information from other sources to expand this description.

Requirement 3.1.9. Ticket Booking

A booking can be created, but not modified. If you want to modify a booking, it will have to be cancelled (as specified in requirement 3.1.10) and another one created. Cancel implies deleting the booking.

The system will display a succession of windows for creating a booking. These windows contain the information described below and *three options: back, next and cancel booking* (Abort Operation, Go Back):

- First, a screen will be displayed listing *what theatres there are for the user to choose from* (Structured Text Entry).
- Then the system *will display the show times at that theatre for the user to choose from* (Structured Text Entry).
- Next the system displays a seating plan showing the seats booked and/or sold for the session in question. While this image is being loaded, *a non-obtrusive window (which the user can minimize) and an indicator will be displayed to inform the user that an image is being loaded and how many seconds it will take to finish* (Long Action Feedback). *Additionally, the user will be given the chance to cancel the operation, and the system will again display the selected theatre show times* (Abort Operation).
- *The user will mark the seats he or she would like to book on this image* (Structured Text Entry).
- *Once the user has selected the seats he or she would like to book, another window will be displayed containing all the information about the selected seats and asking the user to confirm or cancel the operation. This window will warn the user that once he or she has confirmed the booking, it cannot be modified* (Warning).
- If the user confirms the operation the system will mark the seats as reserved and they will be allocated a unique booking code. *If the user cancels, the system will go back to the first window listing what theatres there are* (Abort Operation).
- *At the end of the booking process, the system will display a window reporting whether or not the operation was a success or failure. This information will be displayed obtrusively in a dialogue box* (System Status Feedback). *The possible causes of the operation failing are: the seats had already been booked or there was a problem with the database connection.*

Fig. 4. Fragment of a requirement modified with usability functionality

Students of each group were randomly allocated the usability information they were to use (completed patterns, reduced patterns, and no patterns) to prevent student characteristics from possibly biasing the final result.

Final system usability was analyzed differently to determine how useful the elicitation patterns were for building more usable software. We ran what the HCI literature defines as usability evaluations carried out by users and heuristic evaluations done by usability experts.

The usability evaluations conducted by users are based on usability tests in which the users state their opinion about the system. Before doing the tests, users need to carry out a number of standard tasks, called a scenario, to get acquainted with the software.

We worked with three representative users for each system with whom our clients put us into touch. Each user evaluated the three versions of each application (one developed with full patterns, one with reduced patterns and one with no patterns). This way the users could appreciate any differences between versions, although they did not know which usability information had been used to develop which version. The users evaluated these versions in a different order to prevent scenario learning from possibly having a negative effect on the same version of the application.

All three representative users for each application were assembled in the same room. Each user executed the respective scenario for the first version of the application and completed the usability test. Users then enacted the same process for the second version of the application to be evaluated, and, finally, did the same thing for the third version.

The results of the evaluation are deeply discussed in [23]. Summarizing, the usability value for the systems developed using the full patterns was statistically greater than the score achieved using the reduced patterns, and both were greater than the usability value attained without any pattern. Therefore, we were able to confirm that the users perceived the usability of the systems developed with the full usability elicitation patterns to be higher.

With the aim of identifying the reasons that led users to assess the usability of the different types of applications differently, we had an expert in HCI run a heuristic evaluation.

A paid independent HCI expert ran the usability evaluation of the applications developed by our MSc students. The expert analyzed the applications focusing on how these systems provided the usability features listed in Table 1.

Again in [23] can be found the details of this evaluation. In the case of feedback, for example, the developers that used the respective elicitation patterns included, on average, 94% of the functionalities associated with this mechanism. Developers that used the reduced patterns incorporated 47% of the respective functionalities. Finally, developers that used no pattern included only 25%. The expert obtained these data working to a blind evaluation protocol, that is, the expert was not aware of the usability information used as input for each version of the applications.

We got similar results for each usability feature. All the usability features were built into the systems developed using the full patterns better than they were into systems developed using the reduced patterns, and both provided more usability details than systems developed without patterns (with feature definitions only). This explains why users perceived differences in the usability of the systems.

These findings give us some confidence in the soundness of the usability elicitation patterns as a knowledge repository that is useful in the process of asking the right questions and capturing precise usability requirements for developing software without an HCI expert on the development team.

7   Conclusions

It is critically important to elicit requirements early enough in the development process, especially such requirements as have a big impact on software functionality. Our work takes a step in this direction, suggesting that usability features with particular functional implications should be dealt with at the requirements stage. This is not a straightforward task as usability features are more difficult to specify than they may appear: a lot of details need to be explicitly discussed among stakeholders, and often neither software practitioners nor users have the HCI expertise to do this.

We propose an alternative solution when HCI experts are not available or the likely communication problems between development and HCI teams are not cost justified. We have developed specific guidelines that lead software practitioners through the elicitation and specification process. This approach supports face-to-face communication among the different stakeholders during requirements elicitation to cut down ambiguous and implicit usability details as early as possible. As we have shown, these guidelines help developers to determine whether and how a usability feature applies to a particular system, leading to benefits for the usability of the final system. The use of these patterns leads to an extra workload during development because more time and effort is required to answer questions, modify requirements, etc. On the other hand, they save effort by directing developers to proven usability solutions, reducing thinking time and rework.

Evidently, the use of usability patterns and any other artifact for improving software system usability calls for a lot of user involvement throughout the development process. This is a premise in the usability literature that is also necessary in this case. If this condition cannot be satisfied, the final system is unlikely to be usable. In our opinion, therefore, a trade-off has to be made at the beginning of the development between user availability, time and cost restrictions, on the one hand, and usability results, on the other.

Finally, note that the functional usability features addressed here are not sufficient to make software usable. As we point out in the paper, the usability literature contains a host of recommendations on how to do this, and we have focused on the ones with the biggest impact on functionality.

References

1. Seffah, A., Metzker, E.: The Obstacles and Myths of Usability and Software Engineering. Communications of the ACM 47(12), 71–76 (2004)
2. Bias, R.G., Mayhew, D.J.: Cost-Justifying Usability. An Update for the Internet Age. Elsevier, Amsterdam (2005)
3. IBM. Cost Justifying Ease of Use (2005), http://www-3.ibm.com/ibm/easy/eou_ext.nsf/Publish/23
4. Thibodeau, P.: Users Begin to Demand Software Usability Tests. ComputerWorld (2002), http://www.computerworld.com/softwaretopics/software/story/0,10801,76154,00.html
5. Trenner, L., Bawa, J.: The Politics of Usability. Springer, London (1998)

6. Battey, J.: IBM's redesign results in a kinder, simpler web site (1999),
   `http://www.infoworld.com/cgi-bin/displayStat.pl?/pageone/`
   `opinions/hotsites/hotextr990419.htm`
7. Griffith, J.: Online transactions rise after bank redesigns for usability. The Business Journal (2002), `http://www.bizjournals.com/twincities/stories/2002/12/09/focus3.html`
8. Donahue, G.M.: Usability and the Bottom Line. IEEE Software 16(1), 31–37 (2001)
9. Black, J.: Usability is next to profitability. BusinessWeek (2002),
   `http://www.businessweek.com/technology/content/dec2002/tc2002124_2181.htm`
10. Holzinger, A.: Usability Engineering Methods for Software Developers. Communications of the ACM 48(1), 71–74 (2005)
11. Milewski, A.E.: Software Engineers and HCI Practitioners Learning to Work Together: A Preliminary Look at Expectations. In: 17th Conference on Software Engineering Education and Training, pp. 45–49. IEEE Computer Society, Washington (2004)
12. Barbacci, M., Ellison, R., Lattanze, A., Stafford, J.A., Weinstock, C.B.: Quality Attribute Workshop, 3rd edn. CMU/SEI-2003-TR-016, Software Engineering Institute, CMU (2003)
13. IEEE Std 1061: Standard for Software Quality Metrics Methodology (1998)
14. ISO/IEC 9126: Information Technology - Software quality characteristics and metrics (1991)
15. Boehm, B., et al.: Characteristics of Software Quality. North Holland, New York (1978)
16. Nielsen, J.: Usability Engineering. AP Professional, Boston (1993)
17. ISO 9241-11, 98: Ergonomic Requirements for Office work with Visual Display Terminals. Part 11: Guidance on Usability (1998)
18. ISO/IEC ISO14598-1, 99: Software Product Evaluation: General Overview (1999)
19. Mayhew, D.J.: The Usability Engineering Lifecycle. Morgan Kaufmann, San Francisco (1999)
20. ISO 18529, 00: Human-Centered Lifecyle Process Descriptions (2000)
21. Ferre, X., Juristo, N., Moreno, A.: Integration of HCI Practices into Software Engineering Development Processes: Pending Issues. In: Ghaoui, C. (ed.) Encyclopedia of Human-Computer Interaction, pp. 422–428. Idea Group Inc. (2006)
22. Tidwell, J.: Designing Interfaces. Patterns for Effective Interaction Design. O'Reilliy, USA (2005)
23. Juristo, N., Moreno, A., Sánchez, M.: Guidelines for Eliciting Usability Functionalities. IEEE Transactions on SE (2007)
24. Juristo, N., Moreno, A., Sánchez, M.: Analysing the impact of usability on software design. Journal of System and Software 80(9) (September 2007)
25. Guide to the Software Engineering Body of Knowledge (2004),
   `http://www.swebok.org`
26. Kovitz, B.: Ambiguity and What to Do about It. In: IEEE Joint International Conference on Requirements Engineering (2002)
27. Benson, C., Elman, A., Nickell, S., Robertson, C.: GNOME Human Interface Guidelines,
   `http://developer.gnome.org/projects/gup/hig/1.0/index.html`
28. Chirstel, M.G., Kang, K.C.: Issues in Requirements Elicitation. Technical Report CMU/SEI-92-TR-012, Software Engineering Institute, CMU (1992)
29. Ebert, C., Man, J.D.: Requirements Uncertainty: Influencing Factors and Concrete Improvements. In: International Conference on Software Engineering, pp. 553–560 (2005)
30. Lauesen, S.: Communication Gaps in a Tender Process. Requirements Engineering 10(4), 247–261 (2005)

31. ISO Std 13407: Human-Centred Design Processes for Interactive Systems (1999)
32. Brighton. Usability Pattern Collection (2003),
    http://www.cmis.brighton.ac.uk/research/patterns/
33. Welie, M.: The Amsterdam Collection of Patterns in User Interface Design,
    http://www.welie.com
34. Tidwell, T.: The Case for HCI Design Patterns,
    http://www.mit.edu/jdidwell/common_ground_onefile.htm
35. Coram, T., Lee, L.: Experiences: A Pattern Language for User Interface Design (1996),
    http://www.maplefish.com/todd/papers/experiences/
    Experiences.html
36. Laasko, S.A.: User Interface Designing Patterns (2003), http://www.cs.helsinki.
    fi/u/salaakso/patterns/index_tree.html

Appendix A. System Status Feedback Usability Elicitation Pattern

IDENTIFICATION	
Name: System Status Feedback	
Family: Feedback	
Alias: Status Display	
Modelling Feedback Area	
PROBLEM	
Which information needs to be elicited and specified for the application to provide users with status information.	
CONTEXT	
When changes that are important to the user occur or when failures that are important to the user occur, for example: during application execution; because there are not enough system resources; because external resources are not working properly.	
Examples of status feedback can be found on status bars in windows applications; train, bus or airline schedule systems; VCR displays; etc.	
SOLUTION	
Usability Mechanism Elicitation Guide:	
HCI Rationale	**Issue to discuss with stakeholders**
1. HCI experts argue that the user wants to be notified when a change of status occurs.	*Changes in the system status can be triggered by user-requested or other actions or when there is a problem with an external resource or another system resource.*
	1.1 Does the user need the system to provide notification of system statuses? If so, which ones?
	1.2 Does the user need the system to provide notification of system failures (they represent any operation that the system is unable to complete, but they are not failures caused by incorrect entries by the user)? If so, which ones?
	1.3 Does the user want the system to provide notification if there are not enough resources to execute the ongoing commands? If so, which resources?
	1.4 Does the user want the system to provide notification if there is a problem with an external resource or device with which the system interacts? If so, which ones?

Appendix A. (*Continued*)

SOLUTION (Cont.)	
Usability Mechanism Elicitation Guide (Cont.):	
HCI Rationale (Cont.)	**Issue to discuss with stakeholders (Cont.)**
2. Well-designed displays of information to be shown should be chosen. They need to be unobtrusive if the information is not critically important, but obtrusive if something critical happens. Displays should be arranged to emphasize the important things, de-emphasize the trivial, not hide or obscure anything, and prevent one piece of information from being confused with another. They should never be re-arranged, unless users do so themselves. Attention should be drawn to important information with bright colours, blinking or motion, sound or all three – but a technique appropriate to the actual importance of the situation to the user should be used.	*2.1. Which information will be shown to the user?* *2.2. Which of this information will have to be displayed obtrusively because it is related to a critical situation? Represented by an indicator in the main display area that prevents the user from continuing until the obtrusive information is closed.* *2.3. Which of this information will have to be highlighted because it is related to an important but non-critical situation? Using different colours and sound or motion, sizes, etc.* *2.4. Which of this information will be simply displayed in the status area? For example, providing some indicator.* Notice that for each piece of status information to be displayed according to its importance, the range will be from obtrusive indicators (e.g., a window in the main display area which prevents the user from continuing until it has been closed), through highlighting (with different colors, sounds, motion or sizes) to the least striking indicators (like a status-identifying icon placed in the system status area). Note that during the requirements elicitation process, the discussion of the exact response can be left until interface design time, but the importance of the different situations about which status information is to be provided and therefore which type of indicator is to be provided does need to be discussed at this stage.
3. As regards the location of the feedback indicator, HCI literature mentions that users want one place where they know they can easily find this status information. On the other hand, aside from the spot on the screen where users work, users are most likely to see feedback in the centre or at the top of the screen, and are least likely to notice it at the bottom edge. The standard practice of putting information about changes in state on a status line at the bottom of a window is particularly unfortunate, especially if the style guide	*3.1. Do people from different cultures use the system? If so, the system needs to present the system status information in the proper way (according to the user's culture). So, ask about the user's reading culture and customs.* *3.2. Which is the best place to locate the feedback information for each situation?*

Appendix A. (*Continued*)

calls for lightweight type on a grey background.
Usability Mechanism Specification Guide:
The following information will need to be instantiated in the requirements document.
- The system statuses that shall be reported are X, XI, XII. The information to be shown in the status area is.... The highlighted information is … The obtrusive information is....
- The software system will need to provide feedback about failures I, II, III occurring in tasks A, B, C, respectively. The information related to failures I, II, etc.... must be shown in status area.... The information related to failures III, IV, etc., must be shown in highlighted format. The information related to failures V, VI, etc , must be shown in obtrusive format.
- The software system provides feedback about resources D, E, F when failures IV, I and VI, respectively, occur. The information to be presented about those resources is O, P, Q. The information related to failures I, II, etc....must be shown in the status area.... The information related to failures III, IV, etc., must be shown in highlighted format. The information related to failures V, VI, etc., must be shown in obtrusive format.
- The software system will need to provide feedback about the external resources G, J, K, when failures VII, VIII and IX, respectively, occur. The information to be presented about those resources is R, S, T. The information related to failures I, II, etc....must be shown in the status area.... The information related to failures III, IV, etc., must be shown in highlighted format. The information related to failures V, VI, etc., must be shown in obtrusive format.
RELATED PATTERNS: Does not apply

Service-Oriented Architectures Testing: A Survey

Gerardo Canfora and Massimiliano Di Penta

RCOST - Research Centre on Software Technology
University of Sannio
Palazzo ex Poste, Via Traiano 82100 Benevento, Italy
{canfora,dipenta}@unisannio.it

Abstract. Testing of Service Oriented Architectures (SOA) plays a critical role in ensuring a successful deployment in any enterprise. SOA testing must span several levels, from individual services to inter-enterprise federations of systems, and must cover functional and non-functional aspects.

SOA unique combination of features, such as run-time discovery of services, ultra-late binding, QoS aware composition, and SLA automated negotiation, challenge many existing testing techniques. As an example, run-time discovery and ultra-late binding entail that the actual configuration of a system is known only during the execution, and this makes many existing integration testing techniques inadequate. Similarly, QoS aware composition and SLA automated negotiation means that a service may deliver with different performances in different contexts, thus making most existing performance testing techniques to fail.

Whilst SOA testing is a recent area of investigation, the literature presents a number of approaches and techniques that either extend traditional testing or develop novel ideas with the aim of addressing the specific problems of testing service-centric systems. This chapter reports a survey of recent research achievements related to SOA testing. Challenges are analyzed from the viewpoints of different stakeholders and solutions are presented for different levels of testing, including unit, integration, and regression testing. The chapter covers both functional and non-functional testing, and explores ways to improve the testability of SOA.

1 Introduction

Service Oriented Architectures (SOA) are rapidly changing the landscape of today and tomorrow software engineering. SOA allows for flexible and highly dynamic systems through service discovery and composition [1,2,3], ultra-late binding, Service Level Agreement (SLA) management and automated negotiation [4], and autonomic system reconfiguration [5,6,7]. More important, SOA is radically changing the development perspective, promoting the separation of the ownership of software (*software as a product*) from its use (*software as a service*) [8].

The increasing adoption of SOA for mission critical systems calls for effective approaches to ensure high reliability. Different strategies can be pursued to increase confidence in SOA: one possibility is to realize fault tolerant SOA by redundancy. For example, Walkerdine *et al.* [9] suggest that each service invoked by a system could be replaced by a container that invokes multiple, equivalent, services, and acts as a voter.

A. De Lucia and F. Ferrucci (Eds.): ISSSE 2006–2008, LNCS 5413, pp. 78–105, 2009.

Another possibility is to continuously monitor a service-centric system during its execution [5] and apply corrective actions when needed: whenever an exceptional event is detected (e.g., a failure of a post condition or a violation of a Quality of Service—QoS—constraint), a recovery action is triggered. For example, if a temperature service, part of a whether forecasting system, is not available, an alternative one is located and invoked.

Whilst monitoring is an effective tool to build self-healing and self-repairing service-centric systems [10], it requires that adequate recovery actions be implemented for all possible exceptional events. Thus, testing remains a key process to reduce at a minimum the number of such exceptional events.

Several consolidated testing approaches, applied for years to traditional systems, apply to service-centric systems as well. Primarily, the idea that a combination of unit, integration, system, and regression testing is needed to gain confidence that a system will deliver the expected functionality. Nevertheless, the dynamic and adaptive nature of SOA makes most of the existing testing techniques not directly applicable to test services and service-centric systems. As an example, most traditional testing approaches assume that one is always able to precisely identify the actual piece of code that is invoked at a given call-site. Or, as in the case of object-centric programming languages, that all the possible (finite) bindings of a polymorphic component be known. These assumptions may not be true anymore for SOA, which exhibits run-time discovery in an open marketplace of services and ultra-late binding.

Examples of SOA unique features that add complexity to the testing burden include:

- systems based on services are intrinsically distributed, and this requires that QoS be ensured for different deployment configurations;
- services in a system change independently from each other, and this has impacts on regression testing;
- systems implement adaptive behaviors, either by replacing individual services or adding new ones, and thus integration testing has to deal with changing configurations;
- the limited trust service integrators and users have about the information service providers use to advertise and describe the service makes it complex the task of designing test cases;
- ownership over the system parts is shared among different stakeholders, and thus system testing requires the coordination of these stakeholders.

The adoption of SOA, in addition to changing the architecture of a system, brings changes in the process of building the system and using it, and this has effects on testing too. Services are used, not owned: they are not physically integrated into the systems that use them and run in a provider's infrastructure. This has several implications for testing: code is not available to system integrators; the evolution strategy of a service (that is, of the software that sits behind the service) is not under the control of the system owner; and, system managers cannot use capacity planning to prevent SLA failures.

This chapter overviews SOA testing, discussing issues and possible solutions for different testing levels and perspectives, introducing ways to improve service testability, and outlining open issues as an agenda for future research.

The chapter is organized as follows. Section 2 identifies key challenges of SOA testing, while Section 3 discusses testing needs, problems, and advantages from the perspectives of different stakeholders. Section 4 focuses on testing levels, namely unit, integration, regression, and non-functional testing, identifying problems and reviewing solutions in the literature. Section 5 discusses ways to increase testability in SOA. Finally, Section 6 concludes the chapter, highlighting open issues and future research directions.

2   Testing Challenges

When a new technology emerges and new software engineering approaches/processes have to be developed for such technology, a typical question is whether it is possible to reuse/adapt existing approaches, previously developed for other kinds of systems. In the context of this chapter, the question is whether testing approaches and techniques developed for traditional monolithic systems, distributed systems, component-based systems, and Web applications, can be reused or adapted to test service-centric systems. Answering this question requires an analysis of the peculiarities that make service-centric systems different from other systems as far as the testing process is concerned.

Key issues that limit the testability of service-centric systems include [11]:

- *lack of observability of the service code and structure:* for users and system integrators services are just interfaces, and this prevents white-box testing approaches that require knowledge of the structure of code and flow of data. When further knowledge is needed for testing purpose—e.g., a description of the dependencies between service operations, or a complete behavioral model of the service—either the service provider should provide such information, or the tester has to infer it by observing the service from the outside.
- *dynamicity and adaptiveness:* for traditional systems one is always able to determine the component invoked in a given call-site, or, at least, the set of possible targets, as it happens in (OO) systems in presence of polymorphism [12]. This is not true for SOA, where a system can be described by means of a workflow of abstract services that are automatically bound to concrete services retrieved from one or more registries during the execution of a workflow instance.
- *lack of control:* while components/libraries are physically integrated in a software system, this is not the case for services, which run on an independent infrastructure and evolve under the sole control of the provider. The combination of these two characteristics implies that system integrators cannot decide the strategy to migrate to a new version of a service and, consequently, to regression testing the system [13,14]. In other words, a service may evolve, however this is not notified to integrators/users accessing it. As a consequence, systems making use of the service can unexpectedly change their behavior or, although the functional behavior is preserved, might not meet SLAs anymore.
- *lack of trust:* a service might provide descriptions of its characteristics, for instance a behavioral model, information about the QoS levels ensured, etc. Such information can, in theory, be used by integrators to discover the service, to comprehend its characteristics, and to select it. However, it is not possible to guarantee that

any piece of information a service provides corresponds to the truth. In general, a service provider may lie, providing incorrect/inaccurate description of a service's functional and non-functional behavior, thus influencing decisions integrators may take on the use of the service.

– *cost of testing:* invoking actual services on the provider's machine has effects on the cost of testing, too, if services are charged on a *per-use* basis. Also, service providers could experience denial-of-service phenomena in case of massive testing, and repeated invocation of a service for testing may not be applicable whenever the service produces side effects, other than a response, as in the case of a hotel booking service [11].

Any level of SOA testing needs to develop new strategies, or to adapt existing ones, to deal with these issues. For example, SOA testing has similarities to commercial off-the-shelf (COTS) testing. The provider can test a component only independently of the applications in which it will be used, and the system integrator is not able to access the source code to analyze and retest it. However, COTS are integrated into the user's system deployment infrastructure, while services live in a foreign infrastructure. Thus, the QoS of services can vary over time more sensibly and unpredictably than COTS. This QoS issue calls for specific testing to guarantee the SLAs stipulated with consumers.

3   Testing Perspectives

SOA introduces different needs and challenges for different stakeholders involved in testing activities, i.e. developers, providers, integrators, certifiers, and end-users. Table 1 provides a summary of *pros* and *cons* stakeholders experience in different testing levels.

Service Developer. Aiming to release a highly reliable service, the service developer tests the service to detect the maximum possible number of failures. The developer owns the service implementation, thus s/he is able to perform white-box testing. Among the other things, the developer also tries to assess the service's non-functional properties and its ability to properly handle exceptions. Although testing costs are limited in this case (the developer does not have to pay when testing his own service), non-functional testing is not realistic because it does not account for the provider and consumer infrastructure, and the network configuration or load. In general, test cases devised by the developer may not reflect a real usage scenario.

Service Provider. The service provider tests the service to ensure it guarantees the requirements stipulated in the SLA with the consumer. Testing costs are limited. However, the provider might not use white-box techniques, since s/he may be an organization/person different from who developed the service. Finally, non-functional testing does not reflect the consumer infrastructure and network configuration or load and, once again, test cases do not reflect the service real usage scenario.

Service Integrator. The service integrator tests to gain confidence that any service to be bound to her own composition fits the functional and non-functional assumptions made at design time. Runtime discovery and ultra-late binding can make this more challenging because the bound service is one of many possible, or even unknown, services.

Table 1. Testing stakeholders: Needs and opportunities [11]. Roles/responsibilities are reported in italic, advantages with a (+), issues with a(-).

Testing levels	Testing Perspectives				
	Developer	Provider	Integrator	Third–party	End–User
Functional testing	+White-box testing possible	+Limited cost	+Tests the service in the context where it is used	+Small resource use for provider (one certifier tests the service instead of many integrators)	*Service-centric application self-testing to check that it ensures functionality at runtime*
	+Limited cost	-Needs service specification to generate test cases	+White-box testing for the service composition	+(Possible) impartial assessment	-Services have no interface to allow user testing
	+Service specification available to generate test cases	-Black-box testing only	-Black-box testing for services	-Assesses only selected services and functionality on behalf of someone else	
	-Non-representative inputs	-Non-representative inputs	-High cost	-Non-representative inputs -High cost	
Integration testing	*Can be service integrator on his/her own*	NA	*Must regression test a composition after reconfiguration or rebinding* -Test service call coupling challenging because of dynamic binding	NA	NA
Regression testing	*Performs regression testing after maintaining/evolving a service*	+Limited cost (service can be tested off-line)	-Might be unaware that the service s/he is using changed	+Lower-bandwidth usage than having many integrators	*Service-centric application self-testing to check that it works properly after evolution*
	+Limited cost (service can be tested off-line)	-Can be aware that the service has changed but unaware of how it changed	-High cost	-Re-tests the service during its lifetime only on behalf of integrators, not of other stakeholders -Nonrealistic regression test suite	
	-Unaware of who uses the service				
Non-functional testing	*Needed to provide accurate non-functional specifications to provider and consumers*	*Necessary to check the ability to meet SLAs negotiated with service consumers*	-SLA testing must consider all possible bindings	*Assesses performance on behalf of someone else*	*Service-centric application self-testing to check that it ensures performance at runtime*
	+Limited cost	+Limited cost	-High cost	+Reduced resource usage for provider (one certifier tests the service instead of many integrators)	
	-Nonrealistic testing environment	-The testing environment might not be realistic	-Results might depend on network configuration	-Nonrealistic testing environment	

Furthermore, the integrator has no control over the service in use, which is subject to changes during its lifetime. Testing from this perspective requires service invocations and results in costs for the integrator and wasted resources for the provider.

Third-Party Certifier. The service integrator can use a third-party certifier to assess a service's fault-proneness. From a provider perspective, this reduces the number of

stakeholders—and thus resources—involved in testing activities. To ensure fault tolerance, the certifier can test the service on behalf of someone else, from the same perspective of a service integrator. However, the certifier does not test a service within
any specific composition (as the integrator does), neither s/he performs testing from the
same network configuration as the service integrator.

End-User. The user has no clue about service testing. His only concern is that the
application s/he is using works while s/he is using it. For the user, SOA dynamicity
represents both a potential advantage—for example, better performance, additional features, or reduced costs—and a potential threat. Making a service-centric system capa-
ble of self-retesting certainly helps reducing such a threat. Once again, however, testing
from this perspective entails costs and wastes resources. Imagine if a service-centric
application installed on a smart-phone and connected to the network through a wireless network suddenly starts a self-test by invoking several services, while the network
usage is charged based on the bandwidth usage.

4   Testing Levels

This section details problems and existing solutions for different levels of testing, namely
(i) unit testing of atomic services and service compositions, (ii) integration/interoperabi-
lity testing, (iii) regression testing, and (iv) testing of non-functional properties.

4.1   Unit Testing

Testing a single atomic services might, in principle, be considered equivalent to component testing. As a matter of fact, there are similarities, but also differences:

- *observability:* unless when the service is tested by its developer, source code is
  not available. This prevents the possibility of using white-box testing techniques
  (e.g., code coverage based approaches). For stateful services, it would be useful to
  have models—e.g., state machines—describing how the state evolves. Such models
  could support, in addition to testing, service discovery [1,2], and composition [3].
  Unfortunately, these models are rarely made available by service developers and
  providers, due to the lack of proper skills to produce them, or simply to the lack
  of time and resources. Nevertheless, approaches for a black-box reverse engineering of service specifications—for example inspired by likely invariant detection
  approaches [15]—are being developed [16,17].
- *test data generation:* with respect to test data generation techniques developed so
  far—see for instance search-based test data generation [18]—the lack of source
  code observability makes test data generation harder. With the source code available, the generation heuristic is guided by paths covered when executing test cases
  and by distances from meeting control-flow conditions [19]; in a black-box testing
  scenario, test data generation can only be based on input types-ranges and output
  values.
- *complex input/output types:* with respect to existing test data generation techniques,
  most of which only handle simple input data generations, many real-world services have complex inputs defined by means of XML schema. Test data generation

should therefore be able to generate test data according to these XML schema. Thus, operators of test data generation algorithms for service operations should be able to produce forests of trees, corresponding to XML representations or operation parameter. To this aim genetic programming can be used, as it was done by Di Penta *et al.* [20].

- *input/output types not fully specified:* to apply functional testing techniques, e.g., category partition, it is necessary to know boundaries or admissible values of each input datum. In principle, XML schema defining service operation input parameters can provide such an information (e.g., defining ranges by means of *xs:minInclusive* and *xs:maxInclusive* XML Schema Definition—XSD—tags, or defining occurrences by means of the *xs:maxoccurs*) tag. However, in the practice, this is almost never done, thus the tester has to specify ranges/admissible values manually.
- *testing cost and side effects:* as explained in Section 2, this is a crosscutting problem for all testing activities concerning services. Unit testing should either be designed to limit the number of service invocations—making test suite minimization issues fundamental—or services should provide a "testing mode" interface to allow testers to invoke a service without being charged a fee, without occupying resources allocated for the service production version, and above all without producing side effects in the real world.

Bertolino *et al.* [21] propose an approach and a tool, named *TAXI* (Testing by Automatically generated XML Instances) [22], for the generation of test cases from XML schema. Although not specifically designed for web services, this tool is well-suited for performing service black-box testing. The tool partitions domains into sub-domains and generates test cases using category-partition [23].

Bai *et al.* [24] proposes a framework to deal with the generation of test data for operations of both simple and composite services, and with the test of operation sequences. The framework analyzes services WSDLs (Web Service Description Language) interfaces to produce test data. As known, service operation parameters can be simple XSD types, aggregate types (e.g., arrays) or user defined types. For simple types the framework foresees a database where, for each type and for each testing strategy a tester might want to adopt, a facet defines default values, minimum and maximum length (e.g., for strings), minimum and maximum values (e.g. numeric types), lists of admissible values (strings) etc. This information is used to generate test data for simple parameter types, while for complex and user defined types the structure is recursively analyzed until leaves defined in terms of simple types are encountered.

Other than generating test data, the approach of Bai *et al.* [24] also generates operation sequences to be tested, based on dependencies existing between operations. Bai *et al.* infer operation dependencies from the WSDL, based on the following assumptions:

1. two operations are input dependent if they have common input parameters;
2. two operations are output dependent if they have common output parameters;
3. two operations are input/output dependent if there exist at least one output produced by an operation that is input for the other.

Conroy *et al.* [25] exploit user interfaces of legacy applications—hereby referred as Reference APplications (RAP)—to generate test data for web services—hereby referred as Target APplications (TAP). Their approach is based on the following key ideas:

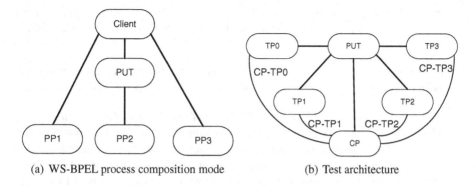

(a) WS-BPEL process composition mode   (b) Test architecture

Fig. 1. Li et al. [26] WS-BPEL Unit testing

1. GUI element may be (i) input data acceptors (e.g., input fields), (ii) action producers (e.g., buttons), (iii) output data retrievers (e.g., combo-boxes, tables), or (iv) state checkpoints (i.e., any GUI element that appear in a particular state in order to make the application to work correctly).
2. Data can be captured from the GUI using technologies conceived for accessibility purposes, e.g., to support screen reading for visually impaired.
3. Once data has been captured, the tester can map such data to inputs of the target application/service, and then enact the replay.

Unit Testing of Service Compositions. Other than atomic services, WS-BPEL processes also need unit testing. In this section, we analyze WS-BPEL testing issues from the perspective of a developer, who has access to the WS-BPEL process itself, and thus can test it using white-box testing strategies. We recall that black-box testing of a WS-BPEL process is equivalent to service testing, discussed in the previous section, since a WS-BPEL process is viewed, from an external point of view, as a service exposing a WSDL interface. It is very unlikely that WS-BPEL processes are tested in isolation, since it would require to produce stubs for all the process partners. On the other hand, the possibility of testing a WS-BPEL process without requiring the availability of partners would allows for testing it even before partners have been developed, or in general without involving partners in the testing phase.

Li *et al.* [26] define a framework for WS-BPEL Unit Testing. Such a framework is, to some extent, similar to other unit testing frameworks, such as JUnit. The framework comprises four components:

1. *the WS-BPEL process composition model* (Fig. 1-a), which includes the WS-BPEL Process Under Testing (PUT) and its Partner Processes (PPs).
2. *the test architecture* (Fig. 1-b), where PP are replaced by stubs, named test processes (TPs), coordinated by a Control Process (CP). Thus, TPs simulate PP, plus they contain testing control structure and behavior (e.g., error-detecting logic).
3. *lifecycle management*, that starts-up or stops CPs and TPs by means of a User Interface (UI). To this aim, the CP provides a *beginTest* and *endTest* interface, and the TPs have *startTest* and *stopTest* interface. When the tester starts the testing activity

by invoking *beginTest* through the CP interface, the CP on its own is responsible to start the TP it is coordinating. When all TPs complete their activity, the CP terminates as well.

A constraint-solver based approach for test case generation for WS-BPEL processes has been proposed by Yuan *et al.* [27]. Test case generation is performed in four steps:

1. WS-BPEL processes are represented as BPEL-Flow-Graphs (BFG), a variation of Control Flow Graphs (CFG) with fork, merge (the outgoing edge is activated by any incoming edge) and join (the outgoing edge is activated after all the incoming edges have been activated) nodes. Exception edges are made explicit, loop unfolded, and different control flow structures (e.g., switch and pick) are brought back to a single structure.
2. the BFG is traversed to identify test paths, defined as a partially-ordered list of WS-BPEL activities;
3. Infeasible paths are filtered out by means of constraint solving. Constraint solving is used to solve inequalities for path conditions: if no solution is found then the path is considered unfeasible. Test data produced by constraint solver can be complemented by means of randomly generated test data and manually-produced test cases.
4. Test cases are generated by combining paths and test data. To this aim, only input (e.g., message *receive*) and output (e.g., message *reply*) activities are considered, ignoring data handling activities such as assignments. Test case generation also requires to manually produce expected outputs, i.e., test oracles.

Tsai *et al.* [28] proposes a shift of perspective in service testing, moving from Individual Verification & Validation to Collaborative Verification & Validation. They propose a technique, inspired from blood testing, that overcomes the need for manually defining oracles. Testing is performed by invoking multiple, equivalent services and then using a voter to detect whether a service exhibited a failure; in other words, if voting is performed upon three equivalent services, and one out of the three provides a different output, then it is assumed to contain a fault.

4.2 Integration Testing

SOA shifts the development perspective from monolithical applications to applications composed of services, distributed over the network, developed and hosted by different organizations, and cooperating together according to a centralized orchestration (e.g., described using WS-BPEL) or in a totally-distributed way (as it happens in a peer-to-peer architectures). Moreover, service compositions can dynamically change to fulfill varying conditions, e.g., a service unavailability, or the publication of a new service with better QoS. In such a scenario, it becomes crucial to test services for interoperability, i.e., to perform service integration testing. This need is also coped by industrial initiative such as WS-Interoperability[1], aimed at suggesting best practices to ensure high service interoperability.

---

[1] http://www.ws-i.org/

The problem of integration testing for service compositions is discussed by Bucchiarone *et al.* [29]. With respect to traditional integration testing, the following issues have to be handled:

– *The lack of information about the integrated components*, which makes the production of stubs very difficult.
– *The impossibility of executing the integrated components in testing mode*: this requires to limit the involvement of services in testing activities, since it may cause costs, resource consumption, and even undesired side effects, as discussed earlier in this chapter.

As highlighted in our previous work [11], dynamic binding between service composition and partners make integration testing of service composition even more difficult. An invocation (hereby referred as *"abstract service"*) in a service composition (e.g., in a WS-BPEL process) can be dynamically bound to different end points.

Dynamic binding can be based on QoS constraints and objectives [30,31] or else on constraints defined upon service functional and non-functional properties (e.g., one might want to avoid services from a specific provider). This requires to perform integration testing with all possible bindings, as it happens when performing integration testing of OO systems [32]. For example, in Fig. 2-a the invocation from method *mc()* of class *A* to method *m()* of class B can be bound to *B::m()*, *C::m()* or *D::m()*. Regarding data-flow, for OO systems there is a *call coupling* between a method *mA* and a method *mB* when *mA* invokes *mB*, and a *parameter coupling* when *mB* has an input parameter that *mA* defines or an output parameter that *mA* uses. For such couplings, it can be possible to define:

– *call coupling paths*, beginning from the call site where (*mA* invokes *mB*) and finishing with a return site.
– *parameter coupling paths:* (see Fig. 2-b) for input parameters, it starts from the last definition of the parameter before the call, continues through the call site, and ends with the first use of the parameter in the callee. Similarly, for output parameters, it starts from the last definition of output parameter in the callee before the return, and ands with the first use after call in the caller.

Given the above paths, coverage criteria for OO systems include:

1. *all call sites:* test cases must cover all call-sites in the caller;
2. *all coupling definitions:* test cases must cover, for each coupling definition, at least one coupling path to at least one reachable coupling use;
3. *all coupling uses:* test cases must cover, for each coupling definition, at least one coupling path to each reachable coupling use;
4. *all coupling paths:* test cases must cover all coupling paths from the coupling definition to all coupling uses.

Ideally, such criteria could apply to test service compositions in the presence of dynamic binding. However:

– parameter coupling criteria cannot be applied as they are above defined, since the partners are invoked on providers' servers and thus viewed as black box entities. In

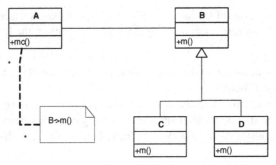

(a) Dynamic binding in OO

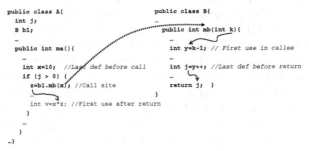

```
public class A{                         public class B{
   int j;                                  ...
   B b1;                                   public int mb(int k){
   ...                                        ...
   public int ma(){                           int y=k-1;  // First use in callee
      ...                                      ...
      int x=10;  //Last def before call        int j=y++;  //Last def before return
      if (j > 0) {                              ...
         z=b1.mb(x);  //Call site             return j;  }
         ...                                 }
         int v=x*z; //First use after return
      }
      ...
   }
   ...}
```

(b) Call coupling in OO

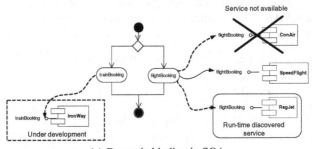

(c) Dynamic binding in SOA

```
<assign><copy>
   <from variable="a"/>          Last def before call
   <to variable="request"/>
</copy></assign>
...
<invoke name="invokeAssessor" partner="assessor"   Call site
        portType="asns:riskAssessmentPT"
        operation="check"
        inputVariable="request"
        outputVariable="riskAssessment">
   <target linkName="receive-to-assess"/>
   <source linkName="assess-to-setMessage"
           transitionCondition=
           "bpws:getVariableData('riskAssessment',
           'risk')!='low'"/>
   <source linkName="assess-to-approval"
           transitionCondition="
           bpws:getVariableData('riskAssessment',
           'risk')!='low'"/>
</invoke>
...
<assign><copy>
   <from variable="riskAssessment"/>          First use after return
   <to variable="bar"/>
</copy></assign>
```

(d) Call coupling in SOA

Fig. 2. Dynamic binding and call-coupling in OO and SOA

other words, for parameters defined in the caller, the only visible use is the partner invocation, while definitions in the callee are only visible from return points (see Fig. 2-d).

- the set of all possible concrete services for a given abstract service might not be known *a-priori*. In fact, some services available at design time might not be available at run-time, or else, if dynamic discovery in an open marketplace is used, new services can be made available at runtime (see Fig. 2-c).

- achieving the above coverage criteria for all possible bindings can be overly expensive and, in general, not possible when, as highlighted by Bucchiarone *et al.* [29], services cannot be invoked in testing mode.

Tsai *et al.* defines a framework for service integration testing, named Coyote [33], supporting both test execution and test scenario management. The Coyote tool consists of two parts: a test master and a test engine. The test master produces testing scenarios from the WSDL specifications, while the test engine interacts with the web service being tested and provides tracing information to the test master.

Bertolino and Polini [34] propose an approach to ensure the interoperability between a service being registered in a Universal Description, Discovery and Integration (UDDI) registry and any other service, already registered, that can potentially cooperate with the service under registration. As Bertolino and Polini suggest, an UDDI registry should change its role from a passive service directory towards the role of an active "audition" authority.

SOA calls for integration testing aimed at SLA, too. Since each abstract service in a workflow can be bound to a set of possible concrete services (equivalent from functional point-of-view, but with different QoS), there might be particular combinations of bindings that can cause SLA violations. This point is further discussed in Section 4.4.

An important issue, dicussed by Mei *et al.* [35], concerns the use WS-BPEL makes of XPath to integrate workflow steps. Services take as input, and produces as output, XML documents. Thus problems can arise when information is extracted from an XML document using an XPath expression and then used as input for a service. The authors indicate the case where a service looks for the availability of DSL lines in a given city. If the city is provided using a XML document like such as:

```
<address>
  <state>
    <name>Beijing</name>
    <city>Beijing</city>
  </state>
</address>
```

or

```
<address>
  <state />
  <city>Beijing</city>
</address>
```

Different XPaths can return different values in the two cases. For example, both `/city/` and `/state/city/` return Beijing for the first document, while for the second `/state/city/` returns an empty document. To perform BPEL data-flow testing, Mei *et al.* rewrite XPaths using graphs, named XPath Rewriting Graphs (XRG), that make explicit different paths through a XML schema. For example, the XPath expression `//city/` can be considered as `*//city/*` or just `*//city/`. An XRG is composed of *rewriting nodes*, containing the original expression (`//city/` in our case), having edges directed to *rewritten nodes*, representing the different forms of an XPath (`*//city/*` and `*//city/` in our case). Then, Mei *et al.* build models named X-WSBPEL, that combine CFG extracted from WS-BPEL with the XRG. To perform data-flow testing on the X-WSBPEL models, Mei *et al.* define a set of data-flow testing def-use criteria, based on variable definition and usages over XPaths.

An approach for data-flow testing of service compositions is proposed by Bartolini *et al.* [36], who essentially adapts data-flow criteria conceived for traditional CFGs to WS-BPEL processes to build, from a WS-BPEL process, an annotated CFG, and then generate test cases achieving different data-flow coverage criteria.

4.3 Regression Testing

An issue that makes service-centric systems very different from traditional applications is the lack of control a system integrator has over the services s/he is using. System integrators select services to be integrated in their systems and assume that such services will maintain their functional and non-functional characteristics while being used. However, this is not the case: a system exposed as a service undergoes—as any other system—maintenance and evolution activities. Maintenance and evolution strategies are out of the system integrators control, and any changes to a service may impact all the systems using it. This makes service-centric systems different from component-based systems: when a component evolves, this does not affect systems that use previous versions of the component itself. Component-based systems physically integrate a copy of the component and, despite the improvements or bug fixing performed in the new component release, systems can continue to use an old version. In such a context, several evolution scenarios may arise:

- Changes that do not require modifying the service interface and/or specification, e.g., because the provider believes this is a *minor* update, As a consequence, the changes remain hidden from whoever is using the service.
- Changes that do not affect the service functional behavior, but affect its QoS. Once again, these are not always documented by the service provider and, as a consequence, the QoS of the system/composition using such a service can be affected.
- A service can be, on its own, a composition of other services. As a matter of fact, changes are propagated between different system integrators, and it happens that the distance between the change and the actor affected by the change makes unlikely that, even if the change is advertised, the integrator will be able to get it and react accordingly.

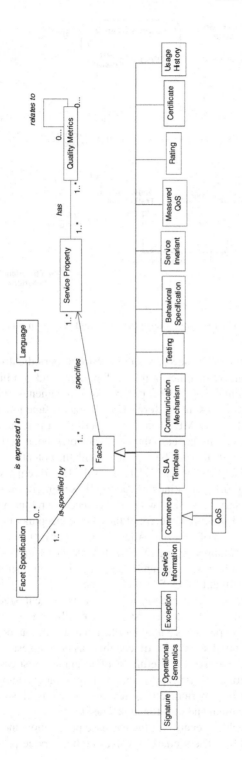

Fig. 3. Faceted specification of a service

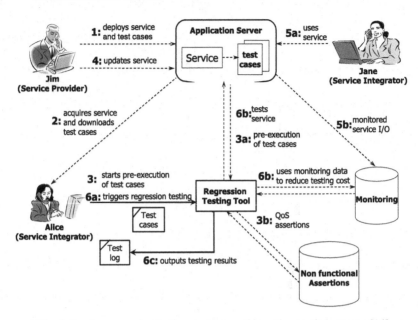

Fig. 4. Service regression testing: test generation and execution process [14]

The above scenarios raises the need for an integrator to periodically re-test the service she/he is using, to ensure that they still meet functional and non functional expectations. To this aim, Di Penta *et al.* [13,14] propose to complement service descriptions with a *facet* providing test cases, in the form of XML-based functional and non functional assertions. A facet is a (XML) document describing a particular property of a service, such as its interface (in this case the facet can correspond to the WSDL interface), its QoS, a SLA template that can be negotiated with the potential service users [4]. A faceted approach to describe services [37], extends the UDDI registry with an XML-based registry containing different kinds of facets. However, additional facets could simply be linked to the service WSDL without the need for requiring a customized, proprietary registry. Fig. 3 shows an excerpt of the SOA conceptual model [38] related to facets describing *properties* of a service. A facet is *specified* by means of a facet specification expressed using a language, e.g., WSDL for interfaces, or WS-Agreement for SLA. As shown in the figure, a service can be described by a number of facets related to signature, operational semantics, QoS, test cases, etc.

When a service integrator discovers a service and wants to use it, s/he downloads the testing facet and uses it to check whether the service exhibits the functional and non-functional properties s/he expects. As a matter of fact, a test suite can be used to support developers' comprehension of software artifacts: this has been investigated by Ricca *et al.* [39], who empirically assessed the usefulness of acceptance test cases expressed as Fit (Framework for Integrated Testing) [40] tables in requirement comprehension tasks. Then, the test suite is used to periodically re-test the service to check whether it still meets the integrator functional and non-functional needs.

Fig. 4 describes a possible scenario for the test case publication and regression testing process taken from [14]. The scenario involves both a service provider (*Jim*) and two system integrators (*Alice* and *Jane*), and explains the capabilities of the proposed regression testing approach.

1. At time t_0 *Jim* deploys a service, e.g., a *RestaurantService* that allows an user to search for restaurants, gets restaurants info and check for availability. The service is deployed together with its test suite (facet).
2. At time t_1 *Alice* discovers the service, negotiates the SLA and downloads the test suite; she can complement the test suite with her own test cases, performs a pre-execution of the test suite, and measures the service non-functional behavior. A SLA is agreed with the provider, and Alice stores both the test suite and the QoS assertions generated during the pre-execution.
3. Then, *Alice* regularly uses the service, until,
4. after a while, Jim updates the service. In the new version the *ID* return value for *getRestaurantID* is composed of five digits instead of four. Also, because of some changes in its configuration, the modified service is not able to answer in less than two seconds.
5. *Jane* regularly uses the new service with no problems. In fact, she uses a field that is large enough for visualizing a restaurant ID composed of five digits. Meanwhile, *Jane*'s interactions are monitored.
6. Since the service has changed, *Alice* decides to test it: data monitored from *Jane*'s executions can be used to reduce the number of service invocations during testing. A test log containing successes and failures for both functional test cases and QoS assertions is reported.

According to Di Penta *et al.* [14], facets to support service regression testing can either be produced manually by the service provider or by the tester, or can be generated from unit test cases of the system exposed as a service, as described in Section 5.

The idea of using test cases as a form of contract between service providers and service consumers [13,14] also inspired the work of Dai *et al.* [41]. They foresee a contract-based testing of web services. Service contracts are produced, in a Design by Contract [42] scenario, using OWL-S models. Then, Petri nets are used for test data generation. As for Di Penta *et al.*, test cases are then used to check whether during the time a service preserves the behavior specified in the contract.

Regression test suite reduction is particularly relevant in SOA, given the high cost of repeated invocations to services. Ruth and Tu [43,44] defines a safe regression test suite selection technique largely based on the algorithm defined by Rothermel and Harrold [45] for monolithic application. The proposed technique requires the availability of CFGs (rather than source code) for service involved in the regression testing activity. The idea is that CFGs should be able to highlight the changes that can trigger regression testing, while shielding the source code. Unfortunately, such assumption is, in most cases, pretty stronger in that service providers are unlikely to expose service CFGs.

4.4 Non-functional Testing

Testing non-functional properties is crucial in SOA, for a number of reasons:

- service providers and consumers stipulate a SLA, in which the provider guarantees to consumers certain pieces of functionality with a given level of QoS. However, under certain execution conditions, caused by unexpected consumer inputs or unanticipated service load, such QoS level could not be met;

- the lack of service robustness, or the lack of proper recovery actions for unexpected behaviors can cause undesired side effects even on the service side or on the integrator side;
- services are often exposed over the Internet, thus they can be subject to security attacks, for instance by means of SQL injection.

Robustness Testing. Different approaches have been proposed in the literature to deal with different aspects of service non-functional testing. Martin *et al.* [46,47] presents a tool for automatic service robustness testing. First, the tool automatically generates a service client from the WSDL. Then, any test generation tool for OO programs could be used to perform service robustness testing. In particular, the authors use JCrasher[2] [48], a tool that generates JUnit tests. The authors applied their tool on services such as Google search and Amazon; although no major failures were detected, the authors indicated that, sometimes, services hanged up, suggesting a possible presence of bugs.

Ensuring robustness also means ensuring that exceptional behavior is properly handled and that the service reacts properly to such behavior. However, very often the error recovery code is not properly tested. Fu *et al.* [49] proposes an approach for exception code data-flow testing, suited to web services developed in Java, but that can be applied to any Java program. In particular, they define the concept of *exception-catch* (e-c) link, i.e., the link between a fault-sensitive operation and a *catch* block in the program to be tested, and define coverage criteria for such links.

SLA Testing. SLA testing deals with the need for identifying conditions for which a service cannot be able to provide its functionality with a desired level of SLA. Before offering a SLA to a service consumer, the service provider would limit the possibility that it can be violated during service usage. Di Penta *et al.* [20] proposes an approach for SLA testing of atomic and composite services using Genetic Algorithms (GA). For a service-centric system such violations can be due to the combination of different factors, i.e., (i) inputs, (ii) bindings between abstract and concrete services, and (iii) network configuration and server load. In the proposed approach, GAs generate combinations of inputs and bindings for the service-centric system causing SLA violations. For atomic services, the approach generates test data as inputs for the service, and monitors the QoS exhibited by the service during test invocations. At minimum, the approach is able to monitor properties such as response time, throughput, and reliability. However, also domain specific QoS attributes [50] can be monitored. Monitored QoS properties are used as fitness function to drive the test data generation (the fitness is used to select the individuals, i.e., test cases, that should "reproduce" by means of GA crossover and mutation operators). In other words, the closer a test case is to produce a QoS constraint violation, the better it is. To allow for test data generation using GA, test inputs are represented as a forest, where each tree represents a service input parameter according to its XML schema definition. Proper crossover and mutation operators are defined to generate new test data from existing one, i.e., evolving the population of GA solutions.

---

[2] www.cc.gatech.edu/jcrasher/

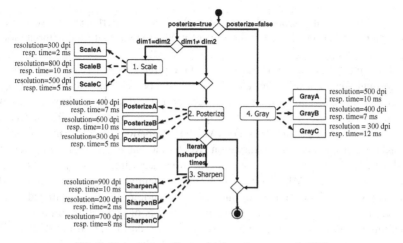

Fig. 5. SLA testing of composite service: example [50]

For service compositions, in particular where dynamic binding between *abstract services* in the workflow and *concrete services* is possible, GA aims at generating combinations of bindings and inputs that cause SLA violations. In fact, for the same inputs, different bindings might result in a different QoS. Fig. 5 shows an image processing workflow. Let us make the following assumptions:

- the service provider guarantees to consumers a response time less than 30 ms and a resolution greater or equal to 300 dots per inches (dpi);
- a user provides as inputs an image having a size smaller than 20 Mb (which constitutes a precondition for our SLA), $posterize = true$, $dim1 = dim2$, and $nsharpen = 2$;
- the abstract services are bound to *ScaleC*, *PosterizeC*, *SharpenB*, and *GrayA*, respectively.

In this case, while the response time will be lower-bounded by 24 ms, and therefore the constraint would be met, the resolution of the image produced by the composite service would be of 200 dpi, corresponding to the minimum resolution guaranteed by the invoked services. In other cases, the scenario can be much more complex, in particular when combinations of inputs for each service invoked in the workflow can, on its own, contribute to the overall SLA violation.

Testing for Dependability. The approach above described has a specific purpose, i.e., generating service inputs (and bindings) that violate the SLA. More generally, for services used in a business-critical scenario, it would be useful to generate service inputs that cause:

- security problems, e.g., allowing unauthorized access to sensible data;
- service hang up;
- unexpected, unhandled exceptions;
- a behavior not observable in the service response.

Many of the existing approaches rely on SOAP message perturbation. According to Voas [51], perturbation allows for altering an application internal state without modifying its source code.

To this aim, Offutt and Xu [52] foresee an approach to generate web service test cases through Data Perturbation (DP). Basically, the process consists in modifying the request messages, resending them to the web service and analyzing how the response message changed with respect to the original message. Specifically, the mechanism foresees two types of perturbation: Data Value Perturbation (DVP), Remote Procedure Call (RPC) Communication Perturbation (RCP), and Data Communication Perturbation (DCP). DVP produces data input modifications according to the types described in the service parameter XML schema, and is largely inspired to the concepts of boundary value testing [53]. For example, for numeric values minimum, maximum and zero are considered, while for strings the perturbation consists of generating minimum length or maximum length strings, and upper-casing or lower-casing the string. RCP modifies message in RPC and data communication, in particular considering data used within programs and data used as inputs to database queries. For data used within programs, mutation mechanisms are defined for different data types; for example a numeric datum n can be changed to to $1/n$ (*Divide*), $n \times n$ (*Multiply*), $-n$ (*Negative*), $|n|$ (*Absolute*). Another perturbation exchanges the order of arguments. When data is used to query a database, perturbation aims at SQL injection, which occurs when an user input, incorrectly filtered for string literal, escapes characters embedded in SQL statements, causing the execution of unauthorized queries.

Offutt and Xu provide the following example: if a service expects 2 input parameters, *username* and *password*, and then checks for the presence of username and password in a database table using the query:

```
SELECT username FROM adminuser
        WHERE username='turing' AND password='enigma'
```

then, the *Unhautorized* perturbation mechanism appends to both username and password the string ' OR '1'='1. As a result, the query becomes:

```
SELECT username FROM adminuser
WHERE username='turing'
        OR '1'='1' AND password ='enigma' OR '1'='1'
```

always providing authentication/access. They also provide an example of data perturbation: given a SOAP message containing a data structure describing, for instance, a book:

```
<book>
  <ISBN>0-781-44371-2</ISBN>
  <price>69.99</price>
  <year>2003</year>
</book>
```

Data perturbation entails sending (i) empty instances of the data structure, (ii) an allowable number of instances, (iii) duplicating instances from the message and (iv) removing an instance from the message. For example, the above message can be mutated by means of a duplication, as follows:

```
<book>
  <ISBN>0-781-44371-2</ISBN>
  <price>69.99</price>
  <year>2003</year>
</book>
<book>
  <ISBN>0-781-44371-2</ISBN>
  <price>69.99</price>
  <year>2003</year>
</book>
```

Such a perturbation test would be useful, for instance, to check whether the different behavior the service exhibits in presence of such a duplicate record is observable from the response message. A response like "true" or "false"—just indicating whether the insertion was successful or not—is not sufficient to see how many records have been inserted.

Looker *et al.* [54] propose to assess service dependability by means of fault injection techniques. They propose an approach and a tool named WS-FIT (Web Service Fault Injection Technology) inspired from network fault injection. Basically, they decode network messages based on SOAP and inject errors in these messages. They define a fault model for web services, considering different kinds of faults, namely (i) physical faults, (ii) software faults (programming or design errors), (iii) resource management faults (e.g., memory leakage), and (iv) communication faults. In particular, Looker *et al.* provide a detailed fault model for communication, considering message duplication, message omission, the presence of extra (attack) messages, change of message ordering, or the presence of delays in messages.

When injecting a fault, the service may react in different ways: (i) the service may crash, (ii) the web server may crash, (iii) the service may hang, (iv) the service may produce corrupted data, or (v) the response can be characterized message omission, duplication, or delay. Thus, the aim of the fault injection is to determine to what extent the service is able to properly react to faults seed in input messages, with proper exception handling and recovery actions, without exhibiting any of the above failures.

4.5 Summary Table

Table 2 briefly summarizes the approaches described in this section, providing, for each work, the reference, the testing level, and a short description.

5 Improving Testability

The intrinsic characteristics of SOA are a strong limit for service testability. According to Tsai *et al.* [55], service testability should account for several factors, such as:

- the service accessibility, i.e., source code accessibility, binary accessibility, model accessibility, signature accessibility;
- the "pedigree" of data describing a service. The origin of such information can constitute a crucial aspect since integrators might not trust it;
- the level of dynamicity of the SOA.

Below, we describe some approaches, summarized in Table 3, that deal with service testability.

Tsai *et al.* [56] propose that information to enhance service testability should be provided by extending WSDL. Specifically, the following information is proposed:

1. *Input-Output-Dependency:* they introduce a new complex type in the WSDL schema, named *WSInputOutputDependenceType*, to account for dependencies between service operation inputs and outputs;
2. *Invocation Sequences:* this represents a crucial issue when testing services, since a service might delegate to another service the execution of a particular task. The tester might want to be aware of such dependencies. A WSDL schema type *WSInvocation-DependenceType* is defined to represent caller-callee relationships between services;

Table 2. Summary of service testing approaches

Level	Reference	Description
Functional	Bertolino *et al.* [21,22]	Test data generation from XML schema using the category partition strategy
	Bai *et al.* [24]	WSDL test data generation from XSD types
	Conroy *et al.* [25]	Exploit user interfaces of legacy systems to perform capture-replay over web services
	Li *et al.* [26]	Define a framework for BPEL unit testing
	Yuan *et al.* [27]	Constraint-solver based approach for WS-BPEL test case generation
	Tsai *et al.* [28]	Builds automatic oracles by invoking multiple equivalent services and comparing results through a voter
Integration	Tsai *et al.* [33]	Coyote: a framework for service test integration testing
	Bertolino and Polini [34]	The UDDI registry plays the role of audition authority to ensure service interoperability
	Bucchiarone *et al.* [29]	Discusses problems related to service integration testing
	Mei *et al.* [35]	Data-flow testing of WS-BPEL process with focus on XPath expressions
	Bartolini *et al.* [36]	Data-flow testing of service composition
Regression	Di Penta *et al.* [13,14]	Generation of service testing facet from system JUnit test suite. Regression testing of service from the integrator side
	Dai *et al.* [41]	Services accompanied with a contract; Petri nets for generating test cases
	Ruth and Tu [43,44]	Applies the safe regression technique of Rothermel and Harrold [45] to web services where source code is unavailable.
Non-functional	Martin *et al.* [46,47]	Service robustness testing based on Axis and JCrasher
	Fu *et al.* [49]	Framework and criteria to perform exception code coverage
	Di Penta *et al.* [20]	Search-based SLA testing of service compositions
	Offutt and Xu [52]	Perturbation of SOAP messages
	Looker *et al.* [54]	WS-FIT: Service fault injection approach and tool

Table 3. Approaches for improving service testability

Reference	Description
Tsai et al. [56]	Complement WSDL with I/O dependencies, external dependencies, admissible invocation sequences, functional descriptions
Tsai et al. [57]	Extension of UDDI registry with testing features to test service I/O behavior
Heckel and Mariani [58]	Extension of UDDI registry with testing information; use of graph transformation systems to test single web services
Heckel and Lohmann [59]	Complement services with contracts at different (model, XML, and implementation) levels
Di Penta et al. [13,14]	Generate service test cases ("facet") to be used as contracts for regression testing purposed from system test cases
Bai et al. [60]	Framework for testing highly dynamic service-centric environments
Bertolino et al. [61]	Puppet: QoS test-bed generator for evaluating the QoS properties of a service under development
Bertolino et al [62]	Test-bed generator from extra-functional contracts (SLA) and functional contracts (modeled as state machines)

3. *Functional Description:* a service functional description can also be included as a form of hierarchy, to enhance black-box testing. To this aim Tsai et al. define two sub elements, *WSFParents* and *WSFChildren*, that permit the definition of functional structures. However, other than defining a hierarchical form for functional descriptions, the authors did not indicate which information such description must contain;

4. *Sequence Specification:* licit operation calling sequences are described using regular expressions, e.g., $OpenFile \cdot (ReadLine|WriteLine)* \cdot Close$ indicates that a file opening must be followed by zero or more read or write, then followed by a file closing.

Tsai et al. [57] also propose to extend the UDDI registry with testing features: the UDDI server stores test scripts in addition to WSDL specifications.

Heckel and Mariani [58] use graph transformation systems to test individual web services. Like Tsai et al., their method assumes that the registry stores additional information about the service. Service providers describe their services with an interface descriptor (i.e., WSDL) and some graph transformation rules that specify the behavior.

Heckel and Lohmann [59] propose to enable web service testing by using Design by Contract [42]. In a scenario where a service provider offers a piece of functionality through a service and a service consumer requests it, provider-consumer contracts describe the offered and required functionality. Heckel and Lohmann foresee service contract at different levels: (i) at model level, understandable by humans, (ii) at XML level, to be integrated into existing service standards like WSDL, and (iii) at implementation level, realized for example using JContract, and used by tools such as Parasoft Jtest[3] to generate test cases. Clearly, a mapping among different levels is required.

---

[3] http://www.parasoft.com

As described in Section 4.3, it would be useful to complement a service with facets containing test cases that can be used as a "contract" to ensure that the service, during the time, preserves its functional and non-functional behavior. To this aim, Di Penta *et al.* [13,14] propose to generate service test cases from test suites developed for the software system implementing the features exposed by the service. This is useful since, in most cases, developers are reluctant to put effort in producing a service test suite. On the other hand, legacy system unit test suites, such as Junit, are very often in use. Many software development methodologies, e.g., test-driven development, strongly encourage developers to produce unit test suites even before implementing the system itself. However, although these test suites are available, they cannot be directly used by a service integrator to test the service. This because assertions contained in the JUnit test cases can involve expressions composed of variables containing references to local objects and, in general, access to resources that are only visible outside the service interface. Instead, a test suite to be executed by a system integrator can only interact with the service operations. This requires that any expression part of a JUnit assertion, except invocations to service operations and Java static methods (e.g., methods of the Math class), needs to be evaluated and translated into a literal, by executing an instrumented version of the JUnit test class from the server-side. Such a translation is supported by the tester, that selectively specifies the operation invocation within the JUnit test suite that should be left in the testing facet and those that should be evaluated and translated in literals, since it regards operations not accessible from the service interface or operations not involved in the testing activity.

Testing activities in highly-dynamic environments, such as SOA with run-time discovery binding, require the presence of a test broker able to decouple test case definition from their implementation, and the testing environment from the system under test [60]. This allows for a run-time binding and reconfiguration of test agents in case the service under test change (i) interface operations, (ii) its bindings, or (iii) steps of its underlying process.

An important issue when testing service-centric systems is the need for test-beds that can be used to evaluate QoS properties of a service under development, but also, for instance, to evaluate/test the QoS of a service composition—as described in Section 4.4—without having component services available and, even if they are available, avoiding to invoke them to limit side-effects and reduce the testing costs. Bertolino *et al.* [61] proposed *Puppet* (Pick UP Performance Evaluation Test-bed), a test bed generator used to evaluate QoS properties of services uder development. Also, they propose an approach and a tool [62] to generate stubs from extra functional contracts expressed as SLA and functional contracts expressed as state machines. Further details can be found in Chapter 5 of this book.

6   Summary

Software testing has long been recognized as one of the most costly and risky activities in the life-cycle of any software system. With SOA, the difficulty of thoroughly testing a system increases because of the profound changes that this architectural style induces on both the system and the software business/organization models. Testing challenges derive primarily from the intrinsic dynamic nature of SOA and the clear separation of roles between the users, the providers, the owners, and the developers of a service and the piece of software behind it. Thus, automated service discovery and ultra-late binding mean that the complete configuration of a system is known only at execution time, and this hinder integration testing, while per-use-charge of a service affects unit testing and QoS testing of services and their compositions. Whilst SOA testing is a recent area of investigation, numerous contributions have been presented in the literature, primarily in the areas of unit testing of services and orchestrations, integration testing, regression testing, and testing of non-functional properties. The literature also reports several investigations into means to improve the testability of services and service-centric systems. Nevertheless, several problems remain open, calling for additional research work:

- *Combining testing and run-time verification.* The dynamic nature of SOA entails that testing-based validation needs to be complemented with runtime verification. On the one hand, testing is unable to cope with certain aspects of a service-centric system validation, primarily because of the impossibility to test all—often unforeseen—system configurations. On the other hand, run-time monitoring, while able to deal with the intrinsic dynamism and adaptiveness of SOA, is unable to provide confidence that a system will behave correctly before it is actually deployed. Thus, additional research is needed to fully comprehend the role of testing and monitoring in the validation of a service-centric system and to devise systematic ways to combine them with the aim of increasing the confidence and reducing the cost of validation [63].
- *Improving testability.* For system integrators and, more in general, users a service is just an interface, and this hinders the use of traditional white-box coverage approaches. Service usage may be charged based on the number of invocations; even worst, many services have permanent effects in the real world—e.g. booking a restaurant table—and this makes stress testing approaches infeasible. Lack of observability and cost of repeated invocations could be addressed by publishing a (state-full) model of a service and providing testing interface to query and change the state of a service without affecting the real world. Additional research work is needed to devise the right formalisms to express the models and to help standardizing the interfaces. As developing the models is costly and error prone, means to reverse engineering them from the observation of a service behavior are to be devised [16,17].
- *Validating fully decentralized systems.* Currently, the most widespread approach to service composition is orchestration, which entails the use of an engine that executes a process description and coordinates the invocations of services. With this approach, systems are intrinsically distributed —services run in independent administrative domains— but control remains centralized. Nowadays, different forms of compositions are emerging, such as peer-to-peer choreography, which makes control, in addition to services, completely decentralized. Fully decentralized compositions opens new scenarios, for example, propagation of a query in a network of active services that may subscribe it based on an introspective knowledge of their capabilities [64], which poses new challenges to testing and monitoring.

SOA has great potentials for reducing costs and risks of enterprise systems, improving efficiency and agility of organizations, and mitigating the effects of changing technology. However, many of the benefits of SOA become challenges to testing services and service-centric systems. Addressing these challenges requires a coherent combination of testing, run-time monitoring, and exception management.

Acknowledgements

This work is partially founded by the European Commission VI Framework IP Project SeCSE (Service Centric System Engineering) (*http://secse.eng.it*), Contract No. 511680, and by the Italian Department of University and Research (MIUR) FIRB Project ART-DECO.

References

1. Paolucci, M., Kawamura, T., Payne, T.R., Sycara, K.: Semantic matching of web services capabilities. In: Horrocks, I., Hendler, J. (eds.) ISWC 2002. LNCS, vol. 2342, pp. 333–347. Springer, Heidelberg (2002)
2. Bromberg, Y.D., Issarny, V.: INDISS: Interoperable discovery system for networked services. In: Alonso, G. (ed.) Middleware 2005. LNCS, vol. 3790, pp. 164–183. Springer, Heidelberg (2005)
3. Pistore, M., Traverso, P.: Assumption-based composition and monitoring of web services. In: Test and Analysis of web Services, pp. 307–335. Springer, Heidelberg (2007)
4. Di Nitto, E., Di Penta, M., Gambi, A., Ripa, G., Villani, M.L.: Negotiation of service level agreements: An architecture and a search-based approach. In: Krämer, B.J., Lin, K.-J., Narasimhan, P. (eds.) ICSOC 2007. LNCS, vol. 4749, pp. 295–306. Springer, Heidelberg (2007)
5. Baresi, L., Guinea, S.: Towards dynamic monitoring of WS-BPEL processes. In: Benatallah, B., Casati, F., Traverso, P. (eds.) ICSOC 2005. LNCS, vol. 3826, pp. 269–282. Springer, Heidelberg (2005)
6. Kephart, J., Chess, D.: The vision of autonomic computing. IEEE Computer (2003)
7. Hinchey, M.G., Sterritt, R.: Self-managing software. Computer 39, 107–109 (2006)
8. Turner, M., Budgen, D., Brereton, P.: Turning software into a service. IEEE Computer 36, 38–44 (2003)
9. Walkerdine, J., Melville, L., Sommerville, I.: Dependability properties of P2P architectures. In: 2nd International Conference on Peer-to-Peer Computing (P2P 2002), Linköping, Sweden, 5-7 September 2002, pp. 173–174 (2002)
10. Baresi, L., Ghezzi, C., Guinea, S.: Smart Monitors for Composed Services. In: Proc. 2nd International Conference on Service Oriented Computing (ICSOC 2004), pp. 193–202. ACM, New York (2004)
11. Canfora, G., Di Penta, M.: Testing services and service-centric systems: Challenges and opportunities. IT Professional 8, 10–17 (2006)
12. Milanova, A., Rountev, A., Ryder, B.G.: Parameterized object sensitivity for points-to analysis for Java. ACM Trans. Softw. Eng. Methodol. 14, 1–41 (2005)
13. Bruno, M., Canfora, G., Di Penta, M., Esposito, G., Mazza, V.: Using test cases as contract to ensure service compliance across releases. In: Benatallah, B., Casati, F., Traverso, P. (eds.) ICSOC 2005. LNCS, vol. 3826, pp. 87–100. Springer, Heidelberg (2005)
14. Di Penta, M., Bruno, M., Esposito, G., Mazza, V., Canfora, G.: Web services regression testing. In: Baresi, L., Nitto, E.D. (eds.) Test and Analysis of web Services, pp. 205–234. Springer, Heidelberg (2007)

15. Ernst, M.D., Cockrell, J., Griswold, W.G., Notkin, D.: Dynamically discovering likely program invariants to support program evolution. IEEE Trans. Software Eng. 27, 99–123 (2001)
16. Lorenzoli, D., Mariani, L., Pezzè, M.: Automatic generation of software behavioral models. In: 30th International Conference on Software Engineering (ICSE 2008), Leipzig, Germany, May 10-18, 2008, pp. 501–510 (2008)
17. Ghezzi, C., Mocci, A., Monga, M.: Efficient recovery of algebraic specifications for stateful components. In: IWPSE 2007: Ninth international workshop on Principles of software evolution, pp. 98–105. ACM, New York (2007)
18. McMinn, P.: Search-based software test data generation: a survey. Softw. Test. Verif. Reliab. 14, 105–156 (2004)
19. Wegener, J., Baresel, A., Sthamer, H.: Evolutionary test environment for automatic structural testing. Information & Software Technology 43, 841–854 (2001)
20. Di Penta, M., Canfora, G., Esposito, G., Mazza, V., Bruno, M.: Search-based testing of service level agreements. In: Proceedings of Genetic and Evolutionary Computation Conference, GECCO 2007, London, England, UK, July 7-11, 2007, pp. 1090–1097 (2007)
21. Bertolino, A., Gao, J., Marchetti, E., Polini, A.: Systematic generation of XML instances to test complex software applications. In: Guelfi, N., Buchs, D. (eds.) RISE 2006. LNCS, vol. 4401, pp. 114–129. Springer, Heidelberg (2007)
22. Bertolino, A., Gao, J., Marchetti, E., Polini, A.: TAXI - a tool for XML-based testing. In: 29th International Conference on Software Engineering (ICSE 2007), Minneapolis, MN, USA, May 20-26, 2007, pp. 53–54 (2007)
23. Ostrand, T., Balcer, M.: The category-partition method for specifying and generating functional tests. Communications of the Association for Computing Machinery 31 (1988)
24. Bai, X., Dong, W., Tsai, W.T., Chen, Y.: Wsdl-based automatic test case generation for web services testing. In: IEEE International Workshop on Service-Oriented System Engineering (SOSE), pp. 215–220. IEEE Computer Society, Los Alamitos (2005)
25. Conroy, K., Grechanik, M., Hellige, M., Liongosari, E., Xie, Q.: Automatic test generation from GUI applications for testing Web services. In: IEEE International Conference on Software Maintenance, ICSM 2007, pp. 345–354 (2007)
26. Li, Z., Sun, W., Jiang, Z.B., Zhang, X.: BPEL4WS unit testing: Framework and implementation. In: 2005 IEEE International Conference on web Services (ICWS 2005), Orlando, FL, USA, 11-15 July 2005, pp. 103–110 (2005)
27. Yuan, Y., Li, Z., Sun, W.: A graph-search based approach to BPEL4WS test generation. In: Proceedings of the International Conference on Software Engineering Advances (ICSEA 2006), Papeete, Tahiti, French Polynesia, October 28 - November 2, 2006, p. 14 (2006)
28. Tsai, W.T., Chen, Y., Paul, R.A., Liao, N., Huang, H.: Cooperative and group testing in verification of dynamic composite web services. In: 28th International Computer Software and Applications Conference (COMPSAC 2004), Design and Assessment of Trustworthy Software-Based Systems, Hong Kong, China, Proceedings, 27-30 September 2004, pp. 170–173 (2004)
29. Bucchiarone, A., Melgratti, H., Severoni, F.: Testing service composition. In: Proceedings of the 8th Argentine Symposium on Software Engineering (ASSE 2007) (2007)
30. Canfora, G., Di Penta, M., Esposito, R., Villani, M.L.: A framework for QoS-aware binding and re-binding of composite Web services. Journal of Systems and Software (in press, 2008)
31. Canfora, G., Di Penta, M., Esposito, R., Villani, M.L.: An approach for QoS-aware service composition based on genetic algorithms. In: Genetic and Evolutionary Computation Conference, GECCO 2005, Proceedings, Washington DC, USA, June 25-29, 2005, pp. 1069–1075. ACM Press, New York (2005)
32. Binder, R.V.: Testing Object-Oriented Systems: Models, Patterns, and Tools. Addison-Wesley Publishing Company, Reading (2000)

33. Tsai, W.T., Paul, R.J., Song, W., Cao, Z.: Coyote: An XML-based framework for Web services testing. In: 7th IEEE International Symposium on High-Assurance Systems Engineering (HASE 2002), Tokyo, Japan, 23-25 October 2002, pp. 173–176 (2002)
34. Bertolino, A., Polini, A.: The audition framework for testing Web services interoperability. In: 31st EUROMICRO Conference on Software Engineering and Advanced Applications (EUROMICRO-SEAA 2005), Porto, Portugal, 30 August - 3 September 2005, pp. 134–142. IEEE Computer Society, Los Alamitos (2005)
35. Mei, L., Chan, W.K., Tse, T.H.: Data flow testing of service-oriented workflow applications. In: 30th International Conference on Software Engineering (ICSE 2008), Leipzig, Germany, May 10-18, 2008, pp. 371–380 (2008)
36. Bartolini, C., Bertolino, A., Marchetti, E., Parissis, I.: Data flow-based validation of web services compositions: Perspectives and examples. In: de Lemos, V.R., Di Giandomenico, F., Muccini, H., Gacek, C., Vieira, M. (eds.) Architecting Dependable Systems. Springer, Heidelberg (2008)
37. Walkerdine, J., Hutchinson, J., Sawyer, P., Dobson, G., Onditi, V.: A faceted approach to service specification. In: International Conference on Internet and web Applications and Services (ICIW 2007), Le Morne, Mauritius, May 13-19, 2007, p. 20 (2007)
38. Colombo, M., Di Nitto, E., Di Penta, M., Distante, D., Zuccalà, M.: Speaking a common language: A conceptual model for describing service-oriented systems. In: Benatallah, B., Casati, F., Traverso, P. (eds.) ICSOC 2005. LNCS, vol. 3826, pp. 48–60. Springer, Heidelberg (2005)
39. Ricca, F., Torchiano, M., Di Penta, M., Mariano Ceccato, P.T.: Using acceptance tests as a support for clarifying requirements: A series of experiments. Information and Software Technology (in press, 2008)
40. Mugridge, R., Cunningham, W.: Fit for Developing Software: Framework for Integrated Tests. Prentice-Hall, Englewood Cliffs (2005)
41. Dai, G., Bai, X., Wang, Y., Dai, F.: Contract-based testing for web services. In: 31st Annual International Computer Software and Applications Conference (COMPSAC 2007), Beijing, China, 24-27 July 2007, pp. 517–526 (2007)
42. Meyer, B.: Object-Oriented Software Construction, 2nd edn. Prentice-Hall, Englewood Cliffs (1997)
43. Ruth, M., Tu, S.: Towards automating regression test selection for Web services. In: Proceedings of the 16th International Conference on World Wide Web, WWW 2007, Banff, Alberta, Canada, May 8-12, 2007, pp. 1265–1266 (2007)
44. Ruth, M., Oh, S., Loup, A., Horton, B., Gallet, O., Mata, M., Tu, S.: Towards automatic regression test selection for Web services. In: 31st Annual International Computer Software and Applications Conference (COMPSAC 2007), Beijing, China, 24-27 July 2007, pp. 729–736 (2007)
45. Rothermel, G., Harrold, M.J.: A safe, efficient regression test selection technique. ACM Trans. Softw. Eng. Methodol. 6, 173–210 (1997)
46. Martin, E., Basu, S., Xie, T.: WebSob: A tool for robustness testing of web services. In: 29th International Conference on Software Engineering (ICSE 2007), Minneapolis, MN, USA, May 20-26, 2007, pp. 65–66 (2007)
47. Martin, E., Basu, S., Xie, T.: Automated testing and response analysis ofweb services. In: 2007 IEEE International Conference on web Services (ICWS 2007), Salt Lake City, Utah, USA, July 9-13, 2007, pp. 647–654 (2007)
48. Csallner, C., Smaragdakis, Y.: JCrasher: an automatic robustness tester for Java. Softw. Pract. Exper. 34, 1025–1050 (2004)
49. Fu, C., Ryder, B.G., Milanova, A., Wonnacott, D.: Testing of Java Web services for robustness. In: Proceedings of the ACM/SIGSOFT International Symposium on Software Testing and Analysis, ISSTA 2004, Boston, Massachusetts, USA, July 11-14, 2004, pp. 23–34 (2004)

50. Canfora, G., Di Penta, M., Esposito, R., Perfetto, F., Villani, M.L.: Service composition (re)Binding driven by application–specific qoS. In: Dan, A., Lamersdorf, W. (eds.) ICSOC 2006. LNCS, vol. 4294, pp. 141–152. Springer, Heidelberg (2006)

51. Voas, J.M.: Fault injection for the masses. IEEE Computer 30, 129–130 (1997)

52. Offutt, J., Xu, W.: Generating test cases for Web services using data perturbation. In: SIG-SOFT Softw. Eng. Notes - SECTION: Workshop on testing, analysis and verification of Web services (TAV-WEB), vol. 29, pp. 1–10 (2004)

53. Beizer, B.: Software Testing Techniques, 2nd edn. International Thomson Computer Press (1990)

54. Looker, N., Munro, M., Xu, J.: Ws-fit: A tool for dependability analysis of Web services. In: Proceedings of 28th International Computer Software and Applications Conference (COMP-SAC 2004), Design and Assessment of Trustworthy Software-Based Systems, Hong Kong, China, 27-30 September 2004, pp. 120–123 (2004)

55. Tsai, W.T., Gao, J., Wei, X., Chen, Y.: Testability of software in service-oriented architecture. In: 30th Annual International Computer Software and Applications Conference (COMPSAC 2006), Chicago, Illinois, USA, 17-21 September 2006, pp. 163–170 (2006)

56. Tsai, W.T., Paul, R.J., Wang, Y., Fan, C., Wang, D.: Extending WSDL to facilitate Web services testing. In: 7th IEEE International Symposium on High-Assurance Systems Engineering (HASE 2002), Tokyo, Japan, 23-25 October 2002, pp. 171–172 (2002)

57. Tsai, W.T., Paul, R.J., Cao, Z., Yu, L., Saimi, A.: Verification of Web services using an enhanced UDDI server. In: Proceedings of the Eighth International Workshop on Object-Oriented Real-Time Dependable Systems, pp. 131–138 (2003)

58. Heckel, R., Mariani, L.: Automatic conformance testing of web services. In: Cerioli, M. (ed.) FASE 2005. LNCS, vol. 3442, pp. 34–48. Springer, Heidelberg (2005)

59. Heckel, R., Lohmann, M.: Towards contract-based testing of web services. Electr. Notes Theor. Comput. Sci. 116, 145–156 (2005)

60. Bai, X., Xu, D., Dai, G.: Dynamic reconfigurable testing of service-oriented architecture. In: 31st Annual International Computer Software and Applications Conference (COMPSAC 2007), Beijing, China, 24-27 July 2007, pp. 368–378 (2007)

61. Bertolino, A., De Angelis, G., Polini, A.: A QoS test-bed generator for web services. In: Baresi, L., Fraternali, P., Houben, G.-J. (eds.) ICWE 2007. LNCS, vol. 4607, pp. 17–31. Springer, Heidelberg (2007)

62. Bertolino, A., De Angelis, G., Frantzen, L., Polini, A.: Model-Based Generation of Test-beds for Web Services. In: Suzuki, K., Higashino, T., Ulrich, A., Hasegawa, T. (eds.) Test-Com/FATES 2008. LNCS, vol. 5047, pp. 266–282. Springer, Heidelberg (2008)

63. Canfora, G., Di Penta, M.: SOA: Testing and self-checking. In: Keynote speech at the International Workshop on Web Services - Modeling and Testing (WS-MATE 2006) (2006)

64. Forestiero, A., Mastroianni, C., Papadakis, H., Fragopoulou, P., Troisi, A., Zimeo, E.: A scalable architecture for discovery and composition in P2P service networks. In: Grid Computing: Achievements and Prospects. Springer, Heidelberg (2008)

The PLASTIC Framework and Tools for Testing Service-Oriented Applications

Antonia Bertolino[1], Guglielmo De Angelis[1], Lars Frantzen[1,2],
and Andrea Polini[1,3]

[1] Istituto di Scienza e Tecnologia della Informazione "Alessandro Faedo"
Consiglio Nazionale delle Ricerche, Pisa, Italy
{antonia.bertolino,guglielmo.deangelis}@isti.cnr.it
[2] Institute for Computing and Information Sciences
Radboud University Nijmegen, The Netherlands
lf@cs.ru.nl
[3] Department of Mathematics and Computer Science
University of Camerino, Italy
andrea.polini@unicam.it

Abstract. The emergence of the Service Oriented Architecture (SOA) is changing the way in which software applications are developed. A service-oriented application consists of the dynamic composition of autonomous services independently developed by different organizations and deployed on heterogenous networks. Therefore, validation of SOA poses several new challenges, without offering any discount for the more traditional testing problems. In this chapter we overview the PLASTIC validation framework in which different techniques can be combined for the verification of both functional and extra-functional properties, spanning over both off-line and on-line testing stages. The former stage concerns development time testing, at which services are exercised in a simulated environment. The latter foresees the monitoring of a service live usage, to dynamically reveal possible deviations from the expected behaviour. Some techniques and tools which fit within the outlined framework are presented.

1 Introduction

A widely used approach to validation in industrial software development is *testing*, which consists of observing the behavior of a program under some controlled executions [7]. Indeed, testing provides a feasible and effective strategy to check that a software implementation conforms to the specifications, or to evaluate its dependability and performance.

In the years, many different methods for test selection and execution have been proposed. As new software paradigms emerge, testers have to take into account many new features that in most cases make existing testing techniques no more sufficient or sometimes not even applicable. Therefore, testing methods and tools need to be continuously adapted and empowered to face the exigencies posed by the evolution of the development process and programming approaches.

A. De Lucia and F. Ferrucci (Eds.): ISSSE 2006–2008, LNCS 5413, pp. 106–139, 2009.
© Springer-Verlag Berlin Heidelberg 2009

The latest shift in software development is the *Service-oriented Architecture (SOA)*. All leading IT vendors, including IBM, SAP, Microsoft, Oracle, have already moved towards service-centric. Service-based technology promises to easily integrate software components deployed across distributed networks by different providers. Its great appeal derives from the announced flexibility and interoperability among heterogeneous platforms and operating systems, that is achieved by means of *loose coupling, implementation neutrality* and *flexible configurability* [22].

Loose coupling among services means that the mutual dependencies are minimized and maintained exclusively through standardized interfaces. The latter feature ensures implementation neutrality, in that the internal implementation details of a service must be totally uninfluential: a service must be seen as a "black box". But the most compelling feature of SOA is that its configuration can *change dynamically as needed and without loss of correctness* [22].

Unfortunately, these very same features that make SOA highly attractive to vendors and integrators, pose new difficult challenges to testers. Simplifying in a sentence, testing a program (or a subprogram) amounts at anticipating at development time a relevant and comprehensive sample of the potential program invocations in operation. Hence traditional testing presupposes that before a product is released, someone from the development organization or a third party is sufficiently acquainted with the intended system behavior and can control its configuration, so to select and launch an adequate executions sample (the test suite).

It is evident that in service integration such an assumption does not hold anymore: according to the SOA paradigm, services can discover each other at run-time and can select the partner to interact with based on parameters that are only defined at run-time. Therefore, new approaches and means for testing must be sought.

Interesting challenges for validation also stem from the great relevance of extra-functional requirements in SOA. As services are used in a pervasive way, in fact, ensuring adequate levels of their provided Quality of Service (QoS) becomes as important as guaranteeing their proper functional behavior. Therefore, an additional task that testers need to accomplish concerns the advance evaluation of the QoS characteristics of the System Under Test (SUT).

All the above issues are attracting great interest from researchers in industry and academia, and several techniques and tools have been proposed for SOA testing. A broad survey of such approaches is provided in Chapter 4 [9] of this book, and we refer to it for related work discussion. In this chapter we specifically focus on the framework for SOA testing developed in the European Project PLASTIC (Providing Lightweight and Adaptable Service Technology for pervasive Information and Communication) [12].

PLASTIC aims at facilitating the cost/effective development of adaptable context-aware services, with a special emphasis on enforcing service dependability. The project has been inspired by the vision that service development platforms for B3G (Beyond 3rd Generation) networks will be effective and successful only if the services they deliver are adaptive and offer Quality of Service (QoS) guarantees to users despite the uncontrolled open wireless environment. This vision is pursued via a development paradigm based on Service Level Agreements (SLAs) and resource-aware programming. The project, started in 2006 and now approaching its conclusion, has developed a SOA platform integrating:

- A development environment leveraging model-driven engineering for the rigorous development of SLA- and resource-aware services, which may be deployed on the various networked nodes, including handheld devices;
- A middleware leveraging multi-radio devices and multi-network environments for applications and services run on mobile devices, further enabling context-aware and secure discovery and access to such services;
- A validation framework enabling *off-line* and *on-line* testing of networked services, encompassing functional and extra-functional properties.

This chapter is meant as a brief summary of the PLASTIC validation framework and is not exhaustive of all research results and tools achieved in the project. Further information of the other PLASTIC tools and approaches can be found in the project deliverables and publications [12]. Indeed, another chapter in this volume [24] broadly discusses challenges for the software of the future, and in particular it illustrates possible solutions that have been investigated within PLASTIC. In this chapter we expand the discussion to challenges and solutions concerning testing activities.

Focusing on the validation framework, the above distinction between off-line and on-line approaches concerns the stage and the context in which the testing is carried on. In off-line testing, the system is still undergoing development or, in a wider-ranging view, it is already completed but not available for use yet. Hence, off-line validation implies a more traditional view that a system is tested in the laboratory, within an environment that reproduces or simulates possible real interacting situations. The advantage of off-line validation activities is that these are performed while no customer is using the service, thus avoiding undesired side-effects. On the other hand, on-line approaches concern a set of increasingly used techniques to monitor the system in its real working context after its deployment. A possible scenario is that while the end-users are using the service, real data are collected and sent back to the developers, e.g., for determining whether the service behavior is correct or for performing extra-functional analyses. Hence, on-line "test cases" consist of actual usage scenarios. Another scenario can be that the development organization performs on-line validation activities on a fielded service, with selected test cases, possibly during idle times.

In the following of this chapter we first provide (in Sect. 2) a brief overview of the whole PLASTIC validation framework. In Sect. 3 we provide some background information to the presented tools, and outline an example scenario on which the tools application is illustrated. Then, in Sect. 4 we present in more detail a set of testing tools proposed for testing a service before it is published, namely the tool JAMBITION (Sect. 4.1) for functional off-line testing, and the tool PUPPET (Sect. 4.2) for the generation of a testbed respecting both functional and extra-functional specifications. Sect. 5 presents and discusses the Audition framework (Sect. 5.1) that supports on-line testing before a service is published. Conclusions are drawn in Sect. 6.

2   The PLASTIC Validation Framework

The PLASTIC project aims at enabling the development and deployment of adaptable robust services for B3G networks. For this purpose, it has developed a comprehensive platform integrating both adequate software methodologies and tools, and the supporting middleware. The project has devoted special concern to equip the platform with suitable validation technology. A team of several partners has contributed with different approaches and tools for service analysis, testing and evaluation. Such approaches and tools are intended for usage at different phases of the lifetime of a service.

With reference to Fig. 1 below, a service life-cycle can include the following steps: after being developed, it must be installed and deployed for being made accessible to potential customers. To facilitate discovery, a service provider can then explicitly request to be registered with a registry (such as the UDDI [28]). We distinguish between the act of submitting the request for being included in the register, which we indicate as the "Admission" stage, and the actual inclusion of the service in the registry (publication), after which the service is made publicly accessible. Finally, the service enters live usage.

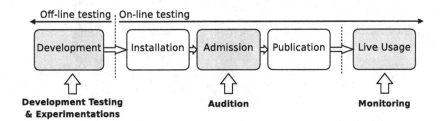

Fig. 1. PLASTIC Testing stages

Considering this service life-cycle model, three testing stages have been identified in the PLASTIC validation framework. They are shown in the figure with arrows pointing to the related life-cycle stages (Development, Admission, Live Usage), and include:

– Development Testing and Experimentation;
– Audition;
– Monitoring.

In principle, it is assumed that the three stages proceed in sequential order, since a service is first developed, then deployed, then used. There are however clear relationships among the stages. In particular the results of the analyses conducted off-line may be used to guide the on-line validation activities. Moreover, the results from analysis during the on-line validation might provide a feedback to the service developer or to the service integrator, highlighting necessary or desirable evolutions for the services, and therefore might be used for off-line validation of successive enhanced versions of services.

Having made clear the context for the three introduced stages for validation in PLASTIC, we describe in the following of this section the integrated framework in which all the PLASTIC developed approaches and tools fit together. An overall picture of the PLASTIC Validation Framework[1] is illustrated below in Fig. 2. Given the broad variety of PLASTIC target applications, this validation framework is not conceived as a fixed methodology, but rather as a set of techniques/tools that can be used alternatively, or in combination, depending on the constraints and exigencies of the considered application/scenario.

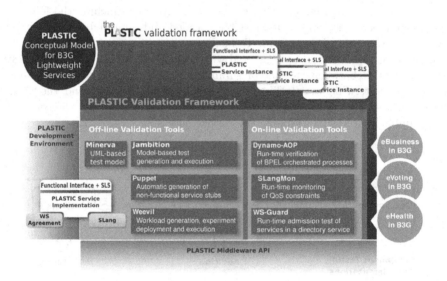

Fig. 2. PLASTIC Validation Framework

2.1   Development-Time Testing

As shown in Fig. 2, the PLASTIC off-line testing tools include: JAMBITION (with its library MINERVA), PUPPET and WEEVIL.

The JAMBITION tool relies on a model-based testing approach originating from a sound and well-established formal testing theory. The key idea of this tool is to exploit as much as possible the behavioral description often available for deployed services to automatically derive a conformance test suite for a service under development. Due to the extreme dynamicity of the service domain, many authors have suggested to augment the service WSDL description with operational specifications in order to characterize services in a richer way. JAMBITION

---

[1] All the PLASTIC test tools can be freely downloaded at [35].

assumes that such specifications are available in the Symbolic Transition System formalism, as introduced in Sect. 3.2, or through its UML interface, implemented via the MINERVA library. The JAMBITION tool is illustrated in Sect. 4.1.

As services are discovered and integrated only at run-time, it is difficult – if at all possible – to have advance guarantees on service behavior. This is particularly true when extra-functional properties are considered. Nevertheless, developers need tools and techniques to assess the quality of a service before its final deployment. Services in general may invoke other services in order to carry out the computation requested by the clients. If this invocation is directed to a service that does not refer to stateful resources, then for testing purposes it is possible to use existing and already running services. Conversely, if the invoked service accesses stateful resources, this option must be ruled out and the required services have to be simulated. Within PLASTIC the problems of reproducing predictable run-time environment is addressed providing two different tools, PUPPET and WEEVIL, which allow the developers to mock up different live usage scenarios.

In particular, PUPPET supports the automated derivation of the elements necessary to recreate a predictable "live" environment that is suitable for the evaluation of extra-functional properties. PUPPET allows testers to automatically generate the required services in such a way that they yield the "correct functional and extra-functional behavior" with respect to a given specification. As in the case of JAMBITION, we assume that the functional specification is given by means of Symbolic Transition System formalism. Concerning the extra-functional specification, we assume that it is based on the WS-Agreement language, as discussed in Sect. 3.3. How PUPPET works is further discussed in Sect. 3.3.

Finally, WEEVIL is meant to ease reproduction of distributed experimental environments. In particular it permits to recreate expected workload to stimulate the service under test, to remotely deploy the various element required by the experiment, and to collect data during the experiment. WEEVIL is not further discussed in this chapter, we refer to the PLASTIC project site [12] for more information and for getting the tool.

2.2 Admission Testing

The SOA foresees the existence of a service broker that is used by services to search and obtain references to each other. The idea of Admission testing is to have the service undergo a preliminary testing stage (also referred to as an audition) whose results will decide the actual registration of the service in the directory.

The intuition of Admission testing is that the quality of registered services can be increased by granting the registration only to those services that pass the audition testing phase. At the same time this should provide better confidence in the fact that services will interact in a correct way even if they discover each other at run-time.

Admission testing clearly raises issues regarding the invocations to fully-operating services (as opposed to services being auditioned). This may be particularly dangerous if the services invoked are related to stateful resources. In order to avoid side effects resulting from invocations fired in the process of auditing a service, suitable countermeasures must be taken. Sect. 5.1 introduces the issues behind admission testing, while Sect. 5.2 presents WS-GUARD, which is an implementation of a directory service conforming the UDDI specification that permits to test services before their registration.

2.3   Live Usage Verification

Difficulties in applying verification techniques before live usage suggest to extend the verification phase till run-time. The idea is to add suitable mechanisms to the SUT and the middleware so as to detect violations with respect to the expected behavior of services.

Within PLASTIC two different activities, aiming at the development of monitoring mechanisms, have been activated. The first of these approaches, called DYNAMO-AOP, focuses on functional behavior of orchestrated services, and provides support to augment orchestrating services with checks, in order to verify that the orchestrated services behave as expected.

Another approach in this category, called SLANGMON, supports the monitoring and logging of extra-functional properties for running services. In particular, SLANGMON implements a mechanism to automatically generate on-line checkers of Service Level Agreements (SLAs). The approach is founded on the timed automata theory.

DYNAMO-AOP and SLANGMON are not further discussed in this chapter, but are both extensively documented and made available in the PLASTIC web page.

3   Modelling Service Properties

In this section we introduce the modelling notations adopted by the tools presented in the chapter. The notations are exemplified on a simple case study, presented below.

3.1   An Example Service Scenario

We will exemplify the several testing approaches and tools on a common case study. It is a simplified variant of the scenario presented in [2], in which three services – the customer, the supplier, and the warehouse – cooperate to achieve the task of a trade. The customer service is interested in buying a certain amount of a given product, and queries the supplier service for a quote for the product of interest. Having received the request, the supplier queries the warehouse service to check if the requested quantity is in stock. The information provided by the warehouse is then returned to the customer service. If satisfied with the provided quote, the customer can proceed with the order. We will also look at advanced interactions like supplier authentication and bonus accounting. We can realistically assume that the three services are implemented and provided

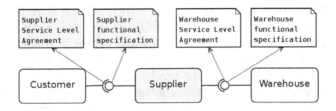

Fig. 3. The Customer-Supplier-Warehouse Case Study

by different stakeholders, and that their interactions are governed by functional specifications under agreed levels of QoS, as shown in Fig. 3.

3.2   Modeling Functional Behavior

The functional behavior of a stateful software entity like a class, component, or service, is commonly modelled using a state machine. There are many flavors of such machines defined. For model-based testing purposes there are two main classes of relevant models - *Labelled Transition Systems* (LTSs) [8] and *Mealy Machines* [26] (often just referred to as *Finite State Machines* (FSMs)). Most common model-based testing theories are based on either the LTS or the FSM model. One important feature of these models is their simplicity - labels on transitions correspond to basic actions like for instance PUSHING THE BUTTON, or INVOKING OPERATION SUCC(41) ON THE SERVICE. Whereas this simplicity is helpful in defining testing theories and algorithms, it is often hindering for modeling real-world systems. Instead of using just basic actions, one would like to use concepts known from programming languages like variables, conditional branching, etc. Such concepts are sometimes referred to as *symbolic concepts*. One prominent symbolic model is the UML 2.0 state machine [29]. To use the accessible and broadly accepted model of an UML state machine together with the precise and well-defined testing theories, one has to define a mapping from UML state machines to LTSs or FSMs.

A model which is somewhat similar to UML state machines is a *Symbolic Transition System* (STS). STSs are a well studied formalism in modeling and testing of reactive systems [16], and they can be mapped to LTSs. Still, also STSs could sound unfamiliar and difficult for practitioners. But since STSs are close to UML state machines we developed a library called MINERVA [35], which transforms UML state machines modelled with MAGICDRAW [19] – a commercial UML modeling tool – into STS representations understood by the tools we will present later. Thus, a developer can use MAGICDRAW to model the functionality of service interfaces in the common formalism of UML state machines. We do not describe this transformation here, but present instead directly the STS formalism. Finally, the important notion of a *testing relation*, which precisely defines when a system conforms to its specification, is introduced.

Symbolic Transition Systems. In our setting, STSs specify the functional aspects of a service interface. Firstly, there are the static constituents like types, messages, parameters, and operations. This information is commonly denoted in the WSDL [10]. Secondly, there are the dynamic constituents like states, and transitions between the states. STSs can be seen as a dynamic extension of a WSDL. They specify the legal ordering of the message flow at the service interface, together with constraints on the data exchanged via message parameters (called *parts* in the WSDL).

An STS can store information in STS-specific variables. Every STS transition corresponds to either a message sent to the service (input), or a message sent from the service (output). Furthermore, a transition can be guarded by a logical expression. After a transition has fired, the values of the variables can be updated. Due to its extent and generality we do not give here the formal definition of STSs, which can be found in [16]. Instead, we exemplify the concepts in the setting relevant for this paper.

We assume that data types in the WSDL are specified via XML Schema types, as commonly done. For our example scenario we first have a closer look at the warehouse service. Firstly, we need some complex types to represent quote requests, quotes, and addresses. We depict them in form of a class diagram:

QuoteRequest
product: String
quantity: Integer

Quote
status: Integer
product: String
quantity: Integer
price: Double
refNumber: Integer

Address
firstName: String
surname: String
...

The next table lists the operations we assume to be present in the WSDL of the warehouse:

Operation	Input Message	Output Message
checkAvail	?checkAvail(r : QuoteRequest)	!checkAvail(q : Quote)
auth	?auth(pw : String)	!auth(q : Quote)
cancelTransact	?cancelTransact(ref : Integer)	—
orderShipment	?orderShipment(ref : Integer, adr : Address)	—

Since the two operations `cancelTransact` and `orderShipment` do not have an output message, they are, in the WSDL jargon, *oneway* operations. The other operations have an input and an output message - they are *request-response* operations. Figure 4 shows an STS specifying the warehouse service. Initially, the warehouse is in state 1. Now a user of the service (in our example the supplier) can invoke the `checkAvail` operation by sending the `?checkAvail` message. This corresponds to the transition from state 1 to state 2. The guard of the transition [between square brackets] restricts the attribute `quantity` of parameter r (which is of type `QuoteRequest`) to be greater than zero. After the transition has fired, the requested quote object r is saved in the variable qr (which is

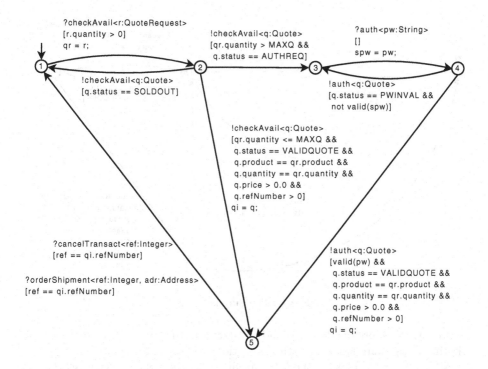

Fig. 4. The Warehouse STS

also of type `QuoteRequest`) via the update statement `qr = r;`. Next, the warehouse has to return a `Quote` object via the return parameter `q`. Three things can happen. Firstly, the requested product may not be in stock with the requested quantity. In this case a `Quote` object is returned with the status attribute being `SOLDOUT` (transition from state 2 to state 1). Secondly, if the product is in stock and the requested quantity is less than or equal some limit `MAXQ`, a `Quote` object is returned with status `VALIDQUOTE`, the same `product` and `quantity` as being requested, and a `price` and `refNumber` greater than zero (transition from state 2 to state 5). We save here the issued quote `q` in the variable `qi`. Thirdly, if the requested quantity exceeds `MAXQ`, a quote is returned with status `AUTHREQ` (transition from state 2 to state 3). This informs the supplier to provide a password string via the `auth` operation (transition from state 3 to state 4). If the password is invalid, a quote with status `PWINVAL` is returned (transition from state 4 to state 3), and the user has to invoke the `auth` operation again. Given a valid password, a valid quote is returned (transition from state 4 to state 5). Being in state 5, again two things can happen. Either the user of the service decides to reject the quote. He/she invokes the one-way operation `cancelTransact` by sending the message `?cancelTransact`. Here he/she must refer to the correct issued reference number `refNumber`. Or he/she decides to accept the quote. In this case, in addition to the correct reference number, an

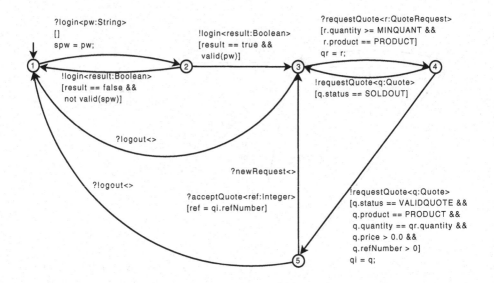

Fig. 5. The Supplier STS

address must be provided as a second parameter to the ?orderShipment message (both messages are labelled at the transition from state 5 to state 1).

Next we have a look at the STS specifying the supplier service, see Fig. 5. Its WSDL also specifies the QuoteRequest and Quote complex types, as shown above. The operations are as follows:

Operation	Input Message	Output Message
login	?login(pw : String)	!login(result : Boolean)
requestQuote	?requestQuote(r : QuoteRequest)	!requestQuote(q : Quote)
acceptQuote	?acceptQuote(ref : Integer)	—
newRequest	?newRequest()	—
logout	?logout()	—

The supplier interface is relevant for the customer service to request quotes at the supplier. After a customer service has passed the login procedure (transitions between states 1, 2, and 3), a quote can be requested (transition from state 3 to state 4). This supplier is specified to deal only with one specific product, represented by the constant PRODUCT. Only quote requests for this product are allowed by the guard r.product == PRODUCT. Furthermore, the requested quantity has to be at least MINQUANT. Also the supplier uses the quote status SOLDOUT to indicate to the customer that it could not reach a warehouse with the product in stock (transition from state 4 to state 3). If, instead, a warehouse could be reached with the product in stock, the corresponding quote is returned to the customer (transition from state 4 to state 5). Finally, the customer can either accept the quote, ignore the quote and request a new quote (both via transition from state 5 to state 3), or end the transaction (transition from state 5 to state 1).

Testing Relations. A *testing relation* precisely defines when a SUT conforms to its specification. Even though SUTs are not formal models, but physical systems, one can define this relation formally. The trick is to assume that the SUT can be represented by some formal model (like an LTS or FSM). Having this assumption, one can reason about the SUT by reasoning about the formal model it represents. This assumption is referred to as the *testing hypothesis*. Albeit this formal model is just assumed to exists, but not known for a given SUT, one can define a testing relation by relating the formal models representing SUTs with formal models representing the specifications. The gain of this effort is, that one can unambiguously express what a testing algorithm is testing for, since the notions of *passing* or *failing* a test case are formally defined. Furthermore, the testing algorithm itself can be proven to be sound and complete for a given testing relation, see also [36].

For the tools to be presented later in this paper two testing relations are specifically important – ioco [36] and eco [14]. Both relations originate from the domain of reactive systems. Such a reactive system is a more complex system than the services we deal with here. The main difference is that we assume services to be *passive*. What does that mean? Every service provides some operations via their WSDL to potential users, who can connect to the service and invoke those operations. If it is a *request-response* operation, the service will send a response message back, but it will never send a message to the user without being requested beforehand. Even though the WSDL allows in principle to specify *active* services via *solicit-response* and *notification* operations, such services are not in common use since they do not easily map to current programming paradigms and service deployment infrastructures. To overcome some issues related to the lack of active services, techniques like *asynchronous access* via *callback handlers* [27] are used.

Due to the restriction to passive services the testing relations simplify, concepts like *quiescence* [36] are not relevant here. We do not formally define the relations, but give instead their intuitive meaning, and some hints to implementation issues. For the precise definitions please refer to the cited papers.

ioco tests the provided interface of an SUT. For passive services it simplifies to the requirement: *If the Web Service produces a response message x after some specified trace σ, then the STS specification can also produce response message x after σ.* In other words, each observed response message must be allowed by the STS specification. For instance, a ioco-tester for the warehouse would play the role of the supplier, and test if the warehouse behaves conforming to its STS specification, given in Fig. 4. It requires that the requested quantity must be greater zero (transition from state 1 to state 2). Since this is an input message, it is under the control of the ioco-tester, which has to take care to respect this requirement by constructing a quote request with a positive quantity, and invoking the `checkAvail` operation with it. Which exact positive quantity is chosen, is at the discretion of the tester. We see here two tasks an automatic test tool must perform:

– construct input data which respects the given guard
– select a concrete input value in case of multiple solutions

Both problems can be difficult especially when dealing with symbolic models. We will come back to this when presenting the specific tools.

The STS does not specify what should happen when a zero or negative quantity is requested, we call this a *partial* specification since there are *underspecified inputs*[2]. Since it is not specified, it is also not tested for, the default interpretation is that everything is allowed after non-specified inputs.

After having requested the quote, the warehouse must response a `Quote` object. Here, the tester will receive the quote and check if it matches one of the three cases specified (transitions from state 2 to states 1, 3, and 5). A potential failure here is for instance a returned quote having status `AUTHREQ`, even though the requested quantity was less or equal `MAXQ`. Or, the returned quote has status `VALIDQUOTE`, but deals with a different product or quantity than requested – and so on. We will come back to ioco-based testing when explaining the JAMBITION tool in Sect. 4.1 and the WS-GUARD tool in Sect. 5.2.

ioco aims at testing if a service does conform to its interface specification. The question is: *Does the service give the specified responses?* The motivation of *eco* is to answer the question: *Is the service correctly invoked by other services?* The situation is somewhat dual to the ioco case. The starting point in both cases is an STS specification of some service S. A ioco-tester takes the STS, plays the role of a *user of* S, and generates requests to S as explained above. An eco tester, instead, takes the STS, plays the role of S *itself*, and checks if a user of S respects the STS specification. Again in simple words *eco* means here that each operation invocation to S must be allowed by its STS specification.

Taking again the warehouse STS specification given in Fig. 4, an eco-tester plays the role of the warehouse, and in doing so it can test if the supplier, while using the warehouse, does respect the STS specification. Initially, the STS is in state 1. The only allowed call here is `checkAvail` with a quantity greater zero. If the eco-tester receives a different call from the supplier, it will alert a detected failure of the supplier. If the call is correct, it moves to state 2. Now the tester can decide if it either returns a quote with status `SOLDOUT` (back to state 1), or if it checks the quantity and proceeds to state 3 or 5. We see here another choice a test tool has to make:

– choose a transition in case of multiple options

This choice, together with the choice of a concrete input value (see above) does affect the way the state space of the specification and the SUT is covered. Since specification- and code-coverage are basically the only means to measure test effectiveness, several approaches exist for making these choices. From simple random choices to sophisticated techniques based, for instance, on symbolic

---

[2] Underspecification of inputs has important consequences for the *compositionality* of ioco and its interpretation of non-determinism. This is out of the scope of this paper, please refer to [38].

execution of the model and/or the source-code of the SUT, exist, see for instance [31,34].

Let us further assume that the eco-tester decides to check the requested quantity and that the quantity is greater MAXQ. It then constructs a quote with status AUTHREQ, returns it to the supplier, and moves to state 3. Now it waits for the supplier to invoke the auth operation. Assuming that the supplier does provide a valid password here, the eco-tester moves the STS to state 4 and sees that the password is valid. Next it constructs a Quote object with status VALIDQUOTE. Also here the tester has many choices, every solution to the guard on the transition from state 4 to state 5 corresponds to a possible quote. After having made that choice the tester moves the STS to state 5. Now it waits again for the supplier to either cancel the transaction, or order the shipment. And so on.

One main observation here is, that an eco-tester for a service S does exactly what we demand from a functionally correct stub for S. It accepts invocations and always returns responses which are allowed by the given STS specification. We will come back to eco-based testing when explaining the PUPPET tool in Sect. 4.2 and the WS-GUARD tool in Sect. 5.2.

3.3 Modeling Extra-functional Behavior

In recent years both industry and academia have shown a great interest on expressing and modeling extra-functional properties by means of machine-readable artifacts. Specifically, several proposals on specification languages for SLAs exist (e.g. [23], [32], [17]).

Generally speaking, SLAs describe the agreements that a service commits to accomplish when processing a request from a client, starting from the moment it receives the request until the moment it replies [33]. QoS guarantees are usually defined only as a provider constraint, and do not include any kinds of events that the client may experience, for example due to the mobility of the devices or traffic congestion problems.

Nevertheless, in some scenarios it would be interesting to deal with the QoS perceived by the clients rather than the QoS offered by the services. Within PUPPET, we refer to a QoS testbed generator that can take into account also how the mobility of the devices hosting the services can affect the QoS provided at the service port (see Sect. 4.2).

In the rest of the section, we describe WS-Agreement [17], one widely used notation in modeling extra-functional behavior in the Web Service communities.

WS-Agreement [17] is a language defined by the Global Grid Forum aiming at providing a standard layer to build agreement-driven SOAs. The main ingredients of the language concern the specification of domain-independent elements of a simple contracting process. Such generic definitions can be augmented with domain-specific concepts. The top-level structure of a WS-Agreement is expressed via an XML document comprising the agreement descriptive information, the context it refers to and the definition of the agreement items. It includes the involved parties as well as other aspects such as its expiration date.

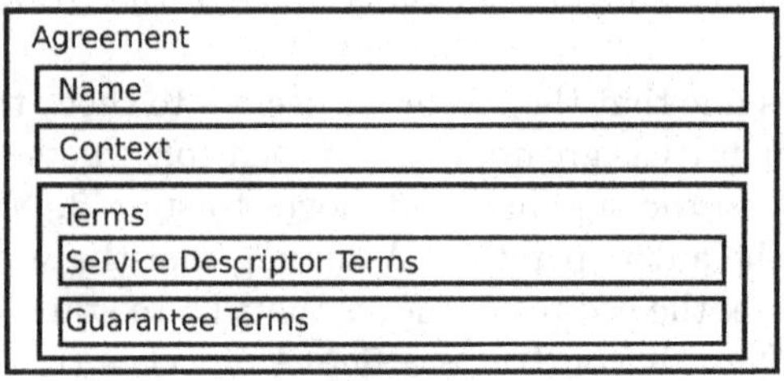

Fig. 6. WS-Agreement Structure

An agreement can be defined for one or more contexts. The defined consensus, or obligations, of a party core in a WS-Agreement specification are expressed by means of terms, organized in two logical parts. The **Service Description Terms** part specifies the involved services. It describes the reference to a description of a service, rather than describing it explicitly into the agreement. The second part of the terms definition specifies measurable guarantees associated with the other terms in the agreement. Such guarantees can be fulfilled or violated. A **Guarantee Term** definition consists of the obliged parties (i.e, *Service Consumer* and *Service Provider*), the list of services this guarantee applies to (**Service Scope**), a boolean expression that defines the condition under which the guarantee applies (**Qualifying Condition**), the actual assertions that have to be guaranteed over the service (**Service Level Objective - SLO**), and a set of business-related values (**Business Value List**) of the described agreement (i.e., importance, penalties, preferences). In general, the information contained in the fields of a **Guarantee Term** is expressed by means of domain-specific languages.

As introduced in Sect. 2.1, within PUPPET we use the QoS properties contained in an agreement specification in order to automatically derive the elements necessary to recreate a testbed that is suitable for predicting the extra-functional properties of the SUT.

Specifically, for each concept in the WS-Agreement (i.e., **SLO**, **Qualifying Condition**, **Service Scope**) we define an interpretation of it by means of a given operational semantics. Clearly, this can be a quite complex and effort-prone task, but given a specific language and an intended interpretation of the concepts, it has to be done only once and for all.

Precisely, such operational semantics is defined as a mapping from the declarative XML descriptions of the supported QoS properties to composable Java code segments. Such segments are then injected into the stubs composing the testbed in order to emulate the extra-functional behavior. The mapping is specified in a parametric format that is instantiated each time one occurrence of the concept appears. Within the scope of this paper, we deal with two QoS properties: latency and reliability. The remainder of this section introduces their characteristics. Please note that the specifications of such QoS properties conform to the definitions adopted within the PLASTIC Project [12]. Nevertheless, also other definitions can be adopted (e.g. as in [30]).

```
1   ...
2   <wsag:ServiceLevelObjective>
3    <puppetSLO:PuppetSLO>
4     <puppetSLO:Latency>
5      <value>25000</value>
6       <puppetSLO:Distribution>
7        <Gaussian>10</Gaussian>
8       </puppetSLO:Distribution>
9     </puppetSLO:Latency>
10    </puppetSLO:PuppetSLO>
11   </wsag:ServiceLevelObjective>
12   ...
```

```
1   ...
2   Density D = new Density();
3   long funcElapsedTime = puppet.ambition.Naturals.asNatural
        (aMbItIoNinvocationTime - System.currentTimeMillis()
        );
4   long maxSleepingPeriod = 25000 - funcElapsedTime;
5   Double sleepingPeriod = D.gaussian(maxSleepingPeriod,10);
6   try {
7     Thread.sleep(sleepValue.longValue());
8   } catch (InterruptedException e) {}
9   ...
```

–A–   –B–

Fig. 7. SLO Mapping for Latency

Latency is defined as a server-side constraint, and does not concern (just ignores) other kinds of delays that the client may experience, for example due to network failures or traffic congestion problems. Conditions on latency can be simulated generating *delay* instructions into the operation bodies of the services stubs. For each **Guarantee Term** in a WS-Agreement document, information concerning the maximum service latency is defined as a **Service Level Objective**. As an example, Fig. 7.A reports the XML code for a maximum latency declaration of $25000msec$ normally distributed, and Fig. 7.B shows the corresponding Java code that is automatically generated by PUPPET.

When dealing with latency constraints, PUPPET also has to deal with other computational tasks, like generating a functionally correct return message, taking care of reliability constraints, etc. Since these tasks also consume time, PUPPET has to adapt the generated latency sleeping period. For example, consider that the term in Fig. 7. A comes in combination with some functional computation statements. If at run time these computations take $2sec$, the delay of the service is adjusted to the range of $[0 \div 23000]msec$. In case the calculation of the functionally correct return message takes more than what is allowed by the latency constraint, the stub raises an exception and has failed its purpose. Since SLA latency constraints for services are commonly in the order of seconds, the computational tasks needed to generate the return messages only miss such deadlines in quite rare cases.

Reliability constraints are declared in the **Service Level Objective** of a **Guarantee Term**, stating the maximal admissible number of failures a service can raise in a given time window. Such kinds of QoS attributes can be reproduced introducing code that simulates a service failure. Within PUPPET, we map a reliability failure via an exception raised by the platform hosting the Web Service stub. An example of the PUPPET transformation for reliability constraints is shown in Fig. 8. Part A shows the XML code specifying a maximum allowed number of three failures over an observation window of 2 minutes; part B gives the corresponding Java translation, assuming that the Apache-Tomcat/Axis [3] platform is used.

A guarantee in a WS-Agreement document could also be stated under an optional condition expressed by means of some **Qualifying Condition** elements. Usually such optional constraints are defined in terms of accomplishments that

```
1   ...
2   <wsag:ServiceLevelObjective>
3     <puppetSLO:PuppetSLO>
4       <puppetSLO:Reliability>
5         <Reliabilitywindow>
6           120000
7         </Reliabilitywindow>
8         <MaxFailures>
9           3
10        </MaxFailures>
11        <puppetSLO:Distribution>
12          <Gaussian>
13            10
14          </Gaussian>
15        </puppetSLO:Distribution>
16      </puppetSLO:Reliability>
17    </puppetSLO:PuppetSLO>
18  </wsag:ServiceLevelObjective>
19  ...
```

–A–

```
1   ...
2   long winSize = 120000;
3   int maxFault = 3;
4   long currentTimeStamp = System.currentTimeMillis();
5   for (int i=0; i<faultBuffer.size();i++){
6     if (currentTimeStamp - faultBuffer.get(i) >= winSize){
7       faultBuffer.remove(i);
8     }
9   }
10  if (faultBuffer.size() < maxFault){
11    Density d = new Density();
12    double dv = d.gaussian(100);
13    if (dv > 50) {
14      String fCode = "Server.NoService";
15      String fString = "PUPPET␣EXCEPTION␣:␣No␣target␣
                         service␣to␣invoke!";
16      org.apache.axis.AxisFault fault = new org.apache.
                axis.AxisFault(fCode, fString, "", null);
17      aMbItIoNsim.undo();
18      faultBuffer.add(currentTimeStamp);
19      throw fault;
20    }
21  }
22  ...
```

–B–

Fig. 8. SLO Mapping for Reliability

the service consumer must meet. For instance, the latency of a service may depend on the value of some parameters provided at run-time. In these cases, the transformation function can wrap the simulating code obtained from the Service Level Objective part within a conditional statement. As mentioned, the scope for a guarantee term describes the list of services to which it applies. In these cases, for each listed service, the transformation function adds the behavior obtained from the Service Level Objective and Qualifying Condition transformations only to those operations declared in the scope.

4   Off-Line Testing Tools

In this section two tools for off-line testing will be introduced: JAMBITION and PUPPET. Whereas the former is a model-based functional testing tool, the latter is an automatic generator for service stubs respecting both a functional- and an extra-functional specification. The underlying models and theories have been explained in the preceding Sect. 3.

4.1   JAMBITION

JAMBITION [35] is a Java tool which automatically tests Web Services based on STS specifications, Fig. 9 shows a screen-shot. The underlying testing relation is ioco. Both STSs and the ioco relation have been introduced in Sect. 3.2.

The testing approach of JAMBITION is *random* and *on-the-fly*. This basically means that out of the set of specified input actions one input is chosen randomly, and then given to the service (i.e., an operation is invoked). Next, the returned

Fig. 9. The Jambition Testing Tool

message (if any) is received from the service. If that output message is not allowed by the STS, a failure is reported. Otherwise the next input is chosen – and so on. The *on-the-fly* approach differs from more classical testing techniques by not firstly generating a set of test cases, which are subsequently executed on the system. Instead, the test case generation, -execution, and -assessment happen in lockstep. So doing has the advantage of allaying the state space explosion problem faced by several conventional model-based testing techniques. The rationale here is that a test case developed beforehand has to consider all possible outputs the system might return, whereas the *on-the-fly* tester directly observes the specific output, and can guide the testing accordingly. Another cause of state space explosion is the transformation of symbolic models like STSs into semantic models like Labeled Transition Systems (LTSs). Several tools like TORX [37] and TGV [25] do this step to apply test algorithms which are defined on LTSs. JAMBITION also solves this issue by skipping this transformation step. Instead, its test algorithm, which is proven sound and complete for ioco, is dealing directly with the STS, see [15] for details. We have seen in Sect. 3.2 that a test tool has to perform three tasks:

1. construct input data which respects the given guard
2. select a concrete input value in case of multiple solutions
3. choose a transition in case of multiple options

To deal with the first task, JAMBITION consults the constraint solver of GNU Prolog [18] via a socket connection. That solver can compute solutions to constraints expressed over finite domain variables, which have a domain in the range [0..max_integer]. Since Web Services do not only deal with integer data, it would be quite restrictive to only allow integer message parameters. Fortunately, several types can be mapped to integers, so that constraint solving is still possible with them. In its current version, JAMBITION supports the *simple types* Integer, Boolean, String, and Enumeration. Furthermore, there is an experimental support for Double values having a fixed number of decimal places (to express for instance prices of products, as used in our example case study). Such "fake" doubles can also be mapped to integers. To express the STS transition guards, the most usual operators known from common programming languages can be used for integer- and boolean expressions. For enumerations and strings the only supported operator is (in)equality, see the manual for details [35]. Sometimes Web Services also deal with *complex types*, which store a sequence of data objects of arbitrary types, either simple or complex. Such a complex type is for instance used to represent struct data known from C, or objects of classes in OO languages. When explaining the warehouse service in Sect. 3.2 we have already seen three examples of complex types - *QuoteRequest*, *Quote*, and *Address*. JAMBITION also allows complex types, but not in a recursive manner, meaning that a complex type must not have a field of its own type. This excludes recursive types like *lists* and *trees*.

To deal with the second task, JAMBITION either selects a random value in case the input is not constrained by a guard. If it is constrained, four heuristics can be applied:

- **min:** choose the smallest solution
- **max:** choose the greatest solution
- **middle:** choose the solution in the middle
- **random:** choose a random solution

For instance, in Fig. 4 the transition from state 1 to state 2 requires r.quantity > 0. If we decide to choose the smallest solution, we get r.quantity = 1. But if MAXQ is greater 0, always choosing r.quantity = 1 will have the consequence that states 3 and 4 will never be reached. Thus, choosing a random solution is commonly good practice. To deal with the third task, a purely random choice is made. Being more sophisticated in these respects is one of our main future work goals.

To visualize the ongoing testing process, and to understand a reported failure, JAMBITION can display the messages exchanged with the service while being tested in real-time via the QUICK SEQUENCE DIAGRAM EDITOR [20], an external Java open-source visualizer for UML sequence diagrams. Figure 10 shows an excerpt of a sequence diagram representing the message exchange between JAMBITION and a warehouse service, being tested based on the STS specification from Fig. 4.

The left lifeline corresponds to JAMBITION, the right one to the warehouse service. The topmost message seen, sent from JAMBITION to the warehouse,

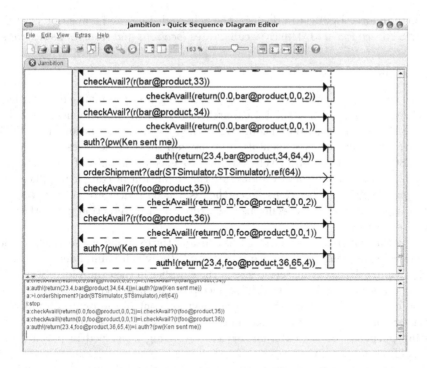

Fig. 10. The Quick Sequence Diagram Editor

invokes the `checkAvail` operation with the `QuoteRequest` object `r`. The `product` attribute of `r` is `bar`, and the `quantity` equals 33. The corresponding STS transition goes from state 1 to state 2. Since this is a *request-response* operation, the warehouse sends back a response message, depicted as the following return message (for technical reasons the returned `Quote` object is called `return`, not `q`, as in the STS). The last field of the offered quote is the `status` attribute, being 2, which is the encoding of `SOLDOUT`. `Jambition` receives the return message and moves the STS back to state 1. Now it again has to construct a quote request, this time it chooses a quantity of 34, also for the `bar` product, and the returned `status` is 1, which corresponds to `AUTHREQ` (transition from state 2 to 3. Next, `Jambition` sends a password string ("`Ken sent me`") via the `auth` operation (transition from state 3 to 4). Since the password string is not constrained, the probability that `Jambition` randomly chooses the right one is negligible. To still make it pick the right one once in a while, extra options can be set. The chosen password is correct in this case, and the warehouse returns a quote with `status` 4, meaning `VALIDQUOTE`. Here `Jambition` has to check the guard on the transition from state 4 to state 5, which is true, the warehouse behaves as specified: the `product` is `bar`, the `quantity` equals 34, the `price` is 23.4 > 0.0, and the `refNumber` is 64 > 0. Finally, `Jambition` decides to order the shipment via the *oneway* operation `orderShipment`, depicted as an asynchronous message. And so on.

Furthermore, JAMBITION displays the achieved state- and transition coverage of the STS, see Fig. 9 (JAMBITION calls states *locations* and transitions *switches*).

4.2   PUPPET

In this section, we introduce PUPPET illustrating first the main characteristics of the approach and then the logical architecture of the implemented tool. The idea of PUPPET is general and could be applied to any instantiation of the SOA. However, the current implementation focuses on the Web Services technology.

In SOAs, services collectively interact to execute a unit of programming logic [2]. Service composition allows for the definition of complex applications at higher levels of abstractions. Nevertheless, since services are always part of a larger aggregation, their executions often rely on the interaction with other/external services.

In such a cooperating scenario, let us consider the example of a service provider who develops a composite service (i.e., the SUT), which is intended to interact with several other existing services (e.g. the supplier in the example at Sect. 3.1). In general, we can suppose that the service provider needs to test the implementation of the SUT, but he/she does not own or control the externally invoked services: for example interactions may have a cost that is not affordable for testing purposes, or the external services are being developed in parallel with the SUT.

The approach proposed by PUPPET is to automatically derive stubs for the externally accessed services S_i from published functional and extra-functional specifications of the external services. PUPPET generates an environment (the services stubs) within which the composite service can be run and tested (see Fig. 11).

While various kinds of testbed can be generated according to the purposes of the validation activities, PUPPET aims specifically at providing a testbed for reliable estimation of the exposed QoS properties of the SUT. Concerning the externally accessed services, PUPPET is able to automatically derive stub services that expose a QoS behavior conforming to the extra-functional specifications such as agreements among the interacting services.

Once the QoS tested is generated, the service provider may test the SUT by deploying it on the real machine used at run-time. This would help in providing realistic QoS measures preventing the problem of recreating a fake deployment platform; in particular, the QoS evaluations will also take into account the other applications running on the same machine that compete for resources with the service under test (it is worth noting that handling this case would be extremely difficult using analytical techniques).

The stubs developed thus far include the set of operations they export and the emulation code for the extra-functional behaviors as specified in the WS-Agreement. Moreover, PUPPET includes a module to link each stub with code emulating the supposed functional behavior [5]. This module is optional, in the sense that is anyhow possible to skip it and still generate working stubs that only emulate the extra-functional behavior of the real services.

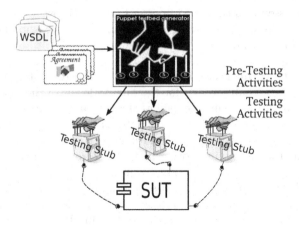

Fig. 11. General idea of PUPPET

The functional behavior of a service is modeled by means of the STS models as described in Sect. 3.2. PUPPET inserts into the stubs parametric code able to wrap an STS simulator we have developed [21]. The simulator simulates the STS according to the eco testing relation. Specifically, for each invocation to a service the stub can call the STS simulator package, choose one of the possible functionally correct results, and send it back to answer the service client request. The STS simulator can keep track of the symbolic states in which the STS can currently be. Thus, to supply the emulation of the functional behavior, PUPPET would demand that the external services carry on the STS specification corresponding to their provided interface.

In the following at Sect. 4.3 we will show an example on how the eco testing relation enhances the ability of the testbed in revealing extra-functional bugs in the SUT. Also, note that both the specification, and simulation of the STS are subject to the same restrictions as the ones given for the JAMBITION tool in Sect. 4.1 since the STS simulator is also used by JAMBITION as its underlying engine.

Latest works on PUPPET concerns the module that finally plugs into the obtained stubs the emulation of the mobility. The detailed description of this module is given in [6].

In the end, PUPPET generates service stubs that can be used by the testers in order to mock-up the deploying environment they would emulate. The architecture of PUPPET is structured in layered modules, whereby each module plays a specific role within the stub generation process. The detailed description of the architecture is reported in [5].

4.3 Combined Functional and Extra-functional Testing Mode

The two off-line approaches presented can be fruitfully combined, as functional testing can be influenced by extra-functional properties and vice-versa. We have previously discussed this combined approach in [5]. Below, we provide two examples extracted from [5], referring again to the customer, supplier, warehouse scenario introduced in Sect. 3.1.

Detecting Extra-functional Failures. This case refers to the task of the developer to derive reliable values for the quality levels of the newly developed service by taking into account the QoS of the external services.

As described in [5], a testbed that emulates the QoS features respecting also the functional protocols on the one hand it gives a more realistic model of the deployment environment; on the other hand it can reveal extra-functional leaks that can be closely related to functional values.

For example, the enforcement of its functional protocol by the warehouse stub may reveal failures in the extra-functional behavior of the supplier. Going in detail, let us assume that the supplier has to meet a given SLA on latency regarding the interactions with its clients, namely processing each request within $40000msec$. As defined in the agreement with the warehouse shown in Fig. 7, each interaction between the warehouse and the supplier service can take up to $25000msec$. Take also into account, as described in Sect. 3.2, that the warehouse service requires an additional authentication step in case the product quantity exceeds MAXQ (see Fig. 4).

A potential extra-functional failure here is, that when the authentication of the supplier is required, the time needed by the supplier to fulfill a client request may violate its SLA. Even if the first password provided is correct, the response of the warehouses to the availability request (the arc from state 2 to state 3 in Fig. 4), together with the response to the provided password (the arc from state 4 to state 5 in Fig. 4), may in the worst case sum up to $50000msec$, which respects for each invocation the SLA exposed by the warehouse, but breaks the supposed SLA between the supplier and the client. Given a warehouse stub which does not have any notion of the functional protocol might never notice the necessity of authentication for a supplier. Each request is considered stand-alone, and no relation to previous or following requests, including data interdependency, exist. Thus, in a mere extra-functional testbed this extra functional failure can easily be invisible.

Detecting Functional Failures. Similarly to what discussed above, in [5] it is shown how the extra-functional correctness of the stubs, can reveal further functional issues of the services under test.

To exemplify this, assume a supplier offering a special *welcome discount* to new clients for their first five purchases. Furthermore, let us consider that the supplier behaves as depicted in Fig. 12. For a given client, the supplier associates a counter FreeOrder, initially being five, which is decremented each time the client places an order. To fulfill the order request, the supplier invokes the orderShipment operation of the warehouse stub. In case a reliability failure occurs now, this is propagated to the client. Let us recall that the interactions between the supplier and the warehouse service is governed by an SLA containing a reliability clause as specified in Fig. 8. The supplier service is not prepared

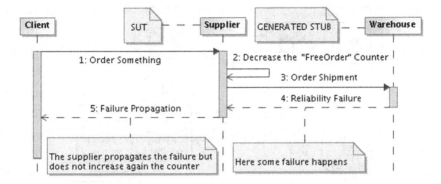

Fig. 12. Functional Fault Revealed by a Reliability Constraint

to deal functionally properties with such a reliability failure in the sense that it does not increase again the `FreeOrder` counter to its original value. This is necessary since the warehouse does not process the order due to its reliability failure - the products cannot be purchased by the client of the supplier. As a consequence, each reliability failure reduces the number of discounts by one, even though no goods have been purchased by the client. Such kinds of functional failures cannot be discovered using a testbed that only reproduces functionally correct behavior, ignoring the extra-functional specifications.

5   On-Line Testing Approaches

This section discuss on-line web-services testing strategies. Run-time testing can be a quite dangerous activity in particular when it involves stateful resources. Therefore in some cases run-time testing of services is not a valid option being monitoring a possible alternative solution for run-time verification. Obviously the drawback in this case is that observed fault are "real" i.e. they really exist on the running system. As a result monitoring approaches have to be combined with recovery strategies. In this paper we limit our discussion to testing strategies and in particular in this section with respect to the framework illustrated in Sect. 2 we discuss a suitable approach for the admission testing phase. The interested reader can refer to [4] for approaches to run-time monitoring.

5.1   The Audition Framework

The basic idea behind the audition framework is to test a service when it asks for registration within a directory service. Then in case the service fails to show the required behavior the registration in the directory is not granted. In this sense we called the framework "Audition", as if the service undergoes a monitored trial before being put "on stage".

It is worth noting that from a scientific point of view the implementation of the framework does not really introduce novel testing approaches. On the

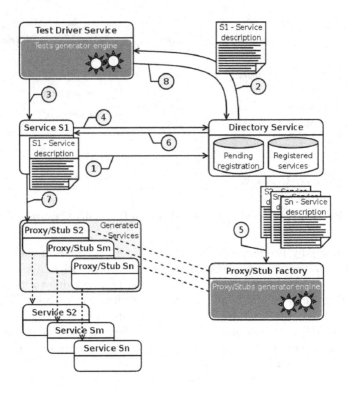

Fig. 13. The Audition Framework

contrary one of its target is just to reuse complex software tools (such as test generators) in a new context trying to take advantage of the new opportunities provided by the service oriented paradigm, such as for instance the existence of a "trusted party" corresponding to the service broker.

Nevertheless in order to automatically derive test cases for services asking for registration the framework requires the use of an increased service information model that should provide some description in a computer readable format of the service expected behavior. Such information model has to be provided to the service registry when a service asks for being included in the registry, and according to the framework the behavioral description has to be suitable for automatic test case derivation. Certainly this request has importance consequences on the applicability of the framework on a real setting. Nevertheless slightly different configuration of the framework can be derived for instance relaxing the part on automatic derivation of test cases with the usage of predefined and static test suites stored in the registry. This section will only discuss the framework when an automatic test generator is available. In particular Figure 13 shows the main elements of the framework. The figure intends to provide just a logical view, i.e., the arrows have not to be directly interpreted as invocations on methods provided by one of the elements. Instead they generally represent a logical step in the process and point to the elements that will take the responsibility of carrying on the associated task.

The process subsumed by the framework is activated by a request made by a service asking for being listed within the registry and is structured in eight main steps (the numbers in the list below correspond to the numbers in Figure 13):

1. a service S1 asks the registry (directory service in the figure) to be published among the services available to accept invocations. Contextually, S1 provides information concerning both the syntax (WSDL in the framework of the web service related technology) and a behavioral description of the offered service (expressing the protocol that a possible client should follow to correctly interact with the service). The behavioral description format has to be suitable for automatic test case generation.

2. the registry service stores S1 provided information marking them as "pending registration". At the same time S1 related information are sent to a Testing Driver Service (TDS). The provided behavioral description has to correspond to the one expected by the specific TDS. It is logically possible to accept different behavioral description for a service (contract based, automata based etc.); nevertheless for each accepted description a TDS able to automatically derive test cases from such a description has to be identified.

3. the TDS starts to make invocations on S1, acting as the driver of the test session, checking if the service behaves accordingly to the specification.

4. during the audition, unless S1 is a basic service, i.e. a service that does not require to cooperate with other services to fulfill its task, S1 will query the registry for references to other services necessary to complete the provision of its own service. Indeed S1 could use other services without asking to the registry since the references are hard coded in S1 definition. From the point of view of the framework in this case S1 is not different from a "basic service" since also at run-time it will continue to use the statically bound services.

5. the registry checks if the service asking for external references is in a pending state or not. If not, references for the required service description file and its relative access point are provided. Instead in case the service is in a pending state the registry provides the information, such as the interface and the behavioral description for the requested service to a Proxy/Stub Service factory. This Service starting from the syntactic and behavioral description is able to derive proxy or stubs for the requested service. In case of a proxy generation the generated service will implement the same interface of the "proxied" service, but at the same time it will check if the invocations made by S1 are in accordance to the ones defined in the specification and then expected by the invoked service. In case no errors are discovered the invocation is redirected to the real implementation of the service.

In some cases a testing invocation to a running service may not be an option, since it would result in permanent effects on a stateful resource. In such cases, in order to completely implement the framework, the factory has to be able to generate service stubs. Obviously this will increase the complexity of the framework and asks for the provisioning of service description models suitable for the automatic generation of service stubs. An STS specification could be for instance a model suitable for automatic stub derivation.

6. for each inquiry request made by S1 the registry service returns a binding reference to a Proxy/Stub version of the requested service.

7. on the base of the reference provided by the registry, S1 starts to make invocations on the Proxy/Stub versions of the required services in order to fulfill a request made by the test driver service. As a consequence the Proxy/Stub version of the service checks the content and the order of any invocation made by S1; In case a violation to the specification for the invoked service is detected, the Proxy/Stub informs the registry service that S1 is not suitable for being registered. As a consequence the directory service removes from the pending entries the service currently under test, and denies the registration;

8. finally in case one of the invocation made by the TDS results in the detection of an error the registry is informed. As for the previous case the registration will be denied.

Considerations on the Framework. The availability of a registry enhanced with testing capabilities, granting the registration only to "good" services, should reduce the risk of run-time failures and run-time interoperability mismatches. As described above, in our vision a service asking for registration will undergo two different kinds of check before being registered. The first concerns the ability of the service of behaving according to its specification and the second of being able to correctly interact with required services. Nevertheless some issues have to be considered in particular to derive a real implementation of the service and to better understand the applicability of the framework itself.

A first note concerns the reduced control over a service implementation by a third party such as the tester. In a SOA setting each organization has full control over the implementation of exposed services. This would mean that a service implementation could be changed by the organization to which it belongs, after its registration has been granted by the registry, and without informing the registry that otherwise would start another testing campaign. As a result a non-tested service will be considered as registered. Main consequence of this lack of control is that the framework can be fruitfully applied only within a semi-open environment, i.e. in an environment in which the participating organizations are known and interested in collaborating with the registry in order to guarantee that no "bad" services will enter the "stage".

Another relevant request posed by the framework concerns the fact that each interaction with the registry has to permit the identification of the sender. This constraint directly derives from the fact that the registry has to recognize the status of the registration for the invoking service when it asks for references to external services. At the same time it is worth mentioning that a service asking for registration has to know that it will undergo a testing session. Therefore during the testing session, and until the registration is not confirmed, the invocations should not lead to permanent effects.

A final interesting note concerns the automatic generation of stubs and proxies. Stubs intend to simulate the behavior of an invoked service. However the automatic generation of a service stub asks for the storing in the registry of a complex service model such as for instance the one discussed in Sect. 3.2. Indeed in case the registered service model does not permit the automatic derivation of a suitable stub the framework foresees the generation of proxy services instead of stub services. A proxy service will check and log incoming invocations with respect to the model and then it will redirect the invocation to a real implementation of the service in order to generate a meaningful answer. However this option is only acceptable in case the invoked service does not refer to a stateful resource; or otherwise in case the platform provides specific support for run-time testing purpose.

Next section shows a partial implementation of the framework that we derived within the Web Service domain.

5.2   WS-Guard

This section describes some relevant detail of a real implementation of an enhanced version of a UDDI registry able to apply the "audition phases". The resulting registry shows a standard UDDI web service interface and has been called WS-Guard(Guaranteeing Uddi Audition at Registration and Discovery) [11].

The first decision to take concerns the different technologies can be used for SOA. In developing WS-Guard we decided to use Apache related technologies and in particular the Axis2 SOAP container. This permitted us to easily derive, using the WSDL2Java tool, skeleton classes from the WSDL definitions for the two interfaces foreseen by the UDDI 2.0 specification : one for publishing services and the other for inquiring registered services.

Concerning the registry, we adopt an open source version of a UDDI registry that is provided by the Apache foundation under the project called jUDDI [13]. jUDDI consists of a set of servlets that are able to handle SOAP messages formatted according to the message format defined by the UDDI specification. To store the information related to registered services jUDDI requires to be linked to a suitable database, being MySQL one of the possible options (and the one we took).

Figure 14 describes the basic elements necessary to set-up a UDDI server using jUDDI.

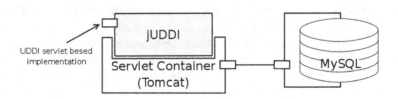

Fig. 14. jUDDI environment setting and technology

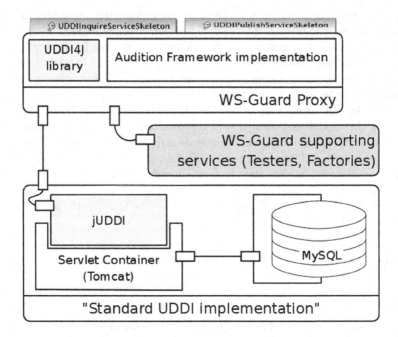

Fig. 15. WS-GUARD service logical structure

Another tool that can be usefully adopted in this setting is UDDI4J [1]. This is a java based library providing an API that permits to directly interact with a remote servlet based implementation of the UDDI specification. As a result using UDDI4J it is possible to interact with a jUDDI server just making local calls to suitable objects derived from the UDDI4J library.

The availability of all these tools permitted to us to drastically reduce the required implementation effort, making also natural the choice of implementing our enhanced "UDDI server" as a Proxy service. This means that we were able to completely decouple the "audition enhancements" from a standard UDDI implementation. So within WS-GUARD the functionalities required by the audition framework are enclosed in the skeletons derived by the UDDI WSDL specification using the WSDL2Java tool. At the same time the skeletons act as proxy implementation for a real UDDI implementation derived using jUDDI. Within the proxy the interactions with jUDDI are defined through the use of classes made available by the UDDI4J library.

Figure 15 shows the logical structure of the implementation we derived. The picture reports the main elements of the WS-GUARD implementation and in particular it shows a supporting services element whose implementation is detailed in the next subsection.

5.3   WS-GUARD Usage: Issues and Solutions

In this section we illustrate the various implementation choices we took to develop the WS-GUARD registry and how the various issues posed by the framework have been solved. For the sake of presentation we illustrate the various steps reusing the scenario highlighted in Sect. 3.1 assuming that a supplier service provider wants to register its service on a audition enhanced directory service.

Modeling and Testing Web Services. WS-GUARD requires that a service asking for registration provides a specification of its external behavior (also a reference to an URL from which such specification can be retrieved). The formalism we have adopted for such step is the one described in Sect. 3.2. In order to store such information we had to change the data structure used by UDDI and the WSDL-UDDI mapping in order to be able to associate a WSDL description to an STS specification. So with reference to the Supplier service it is required that the service provides a reference to a suitable representation of the STS shown in Figure 5. Such model will be then stored in the registry.

Having services represented as STSs, we could exploit the JAmbition "engine" illustrated in 4.1 in order to implement a tester service. So JAmbition has been wrapped within a web service that is then invoked by our WS-GUARD proxy service after receiving a publish request. WS-GUARD provides the tester with the endpoint of the service to be tested and the corresponding STS representation.

Web Services Identification. The Audition framework foresees the ability of recognizing if a service performing an inquiry corresponds to a service under test. In such a case the registry returns a reference to a proxy version of the requested service instead of a direct reference.

To uniquely identify a Web service we decided to choose the service endpoint reference as an identifier. To gather the endpoint reference, we mandate the usage of messages compliant to the WS-Addressing specification [39] when interacting with the registry. Indeed this specification provides a means to the receiver to identify the service endpoint from which a Web service message request comes from. Moreover Axis 2 provides mechanisms to support communications and message generation according to this standard.

Pending Data Structures. A Java HashSet data structure is used to store identification information of services under test (pending state). The data structure is maintained in memory in order to make faster the check that have to be carried on for each incoming inquiry request in order to verify the status of the sender. All the other service related information are directly inserted in the database and marked as pending. This is necessary in order to avoid that the service endpoint is returned as result of inquiry made by already registered services. So with reference to the example, the supplier service reference will not be returned to any other service until it is marked as pending. All the entries related to a service under audition will be deleted in case the service does not overtake the audition phase.

Discovery of Services and Generation of Proxies. One key point of the Audition process is the replies to inquires made by services in a pending state. Going to our example this is the case of the supplier that needs to access to retrieve and access to warehouse services. According to the framework in this case WS-GUARD must returns, to the supplier service, a reference to a proxy version of the warehouse and not a direct access point. Moreover the proxy service should be able to identify wrong calls made by the supplier on the warehouse. To do this we automatically generate proxies that can check received invocations against the STS defined for the requested service (warehouse in our case). In case of an error the registry is then informed.

Finally to cope with stateful services WS-GUARD make the assumption that services are deployed in two copies. One copy is the regular service accessible at the endpoint `http://www.mycompany.com/service` and that have been registered in the registry. The second copy is made available only for testing purpose at `http://www.mycompany.com/service_test`. In order to avoid dangerous usage of stateful services WS-GUARD generate proxies that only interact with services at endpoints with extension "_test".

6   Conclusions

This chapter has overviewed several issues and recent results in the field of SOA testing, with a special focus on the PLASTIC project, which is also discussed in Chapter 1 [24].

We have presented several new testing methods facing the exigencies of flexibility posed by SOAs. Such flexibility is mainly expressed in terms of the dynamic interactions among "black-box" software, provided by different organizations. We have also addressed the evaluation of extra-functional properties, which are of outmost importance in pervasive SOAs.

Summarizing, the described PLASTIC framework spans over the whole service life-cycle, covering with a coherent set of tools both off-line and on-line stages, and addressing both functional and QoS concerns. Given the broad variety of PLASTIC applications, the validation framework is not conceived as a fixed methodology, but rather as a set of techniques/tools that can be used alternatively, or in combination, depending on the constraints/requirements on each considered application/scenario.

Although verification and validation of SOA is a very active research topic, as shown by the many works surveyed in Chapter 4 [9], solutions that can be found in the literature generally address a specific limited objective. The concerted effort for service validation in PLASTIC provided the opportunity for developing a consistent methodology which is unique in terms of comprehensiveness and flexibility. The platform integrates several approaches that can be applied during the whole service life-cycle: after being developed, when published on a new environment, and during the actual live usage.

In particular: JAMBITION, PUPPET, and WEEVIL allow service developers to rigorously test a service (using the original STS model) before deployment in a realistic reproduction of the deployment context (as opposed to testing in the real environment or to manually mocking it). SLANGMON and DYNAMO-AOP support monitoring against the defined properties with an improved efficiency with respect to existing solutions, and directly deriving the monitor from the SLA contracts.

Further work on experimentation on realistic testbeds and on real applications is required. At the current stage, a set of prototype tools have been released and are publicly available for download, but their usage on PLASTIC industrial case studies is still ongoing. Usage of the tools requires some adaptation/modeling effort and a major open issue is the lack of realistic testbeds on which to perform experiments that can provide realistic validation.

Acknowledgement

This paper reports about the work carried on in the 32 months European STREP IST-26955 PLASTIC. All the partners in the project have in different measures and ways inspired our ideas and collaborated with us. The PLASTIC validation framework has been mainly developed within Workpackage 4, and we would like to thank the many colleagues who contributed to it, and in particular Domenico Bianculli, Franco Raimondi, Antonino Sabetta and Alexander Wolf. Section 2 of this paper is an excerpt of joint discussions and writings for the WP4 deliverables. Lars Frantzen is further supported by the Marie Curie Network TAROT (MRTN-CT-2004-505121) and by the Netherlands Organization for Scientific Research (NWO) under project STRESS.

References

1. UDDI4J (accessed on June 3rd, 2008), http://uddi4j.sourceforge.net/
2. Alonso, G., Casati, F., Kuno, H., Machiraju, V.: Web Services–Concepts, Architectures and Applications. Springer, Heidelberg (2004)
3. Basha, S.J., Irani, R.: AXIS: the next generation of Java SOAP. Wrox Press (2002)
4. Bertolino, A., Bianculli, D., De Angelis, G., Frantzen, L., Kiss, Z.G., Ghezzi, C., Polini, A., Raimondi, F., Sabetta, A., Toffetti Carughi, G., Wolf, A.: Test Framework: Assessment and Revision. Technical Report Deliverable D4.3, PLASTIC Consortium. IST STREP Project (May 2008)
5. Bertolino, A., De Angelis, G., Frantzen, L., Polini, A.: Model-based Generation of Testbeds for Web Services. In: Proc. of the 20th IFIP Int. Conference on Testing of Communicating Systems (TESTCOM 2008). LNCS. Springer, Heidelberg (2008)
6. Bertolino, A., De Angelis, G., Lonetti, L., Sabetta, A.: Let The Puppets Move! Automated Testbed Generation for Service-oriented Mobile Applications. In: Proc. of the 34rd EUROMICRO CONFERENCE on Software Engineering and Advanced Applications. IEEE, Los Alamitos (2008)
7. Bertolino, A., Marchetti, E.: A brief essay on software testing. In: Thayer, R.H., Christensen, M.J. (eds.) Software Engineering, 3rd edn. Development process, vol. 1, pp. 393–411. Wiley-IEEE Computer Society Press (2005)

8. Brinksma, E., Tretmans, J.: Testing transition systems: An annotated bibliography. In: Cassez, F., Jard, C., Rozoy, B., Dermot, M. (eds.) MOVEP 2000. LNCS, vol. 2067, pp. 187–195. Springer, Heidelberg (2001)

9. Canfora, G., Di Penta, M.: Service Oriented Architectures Testing: A Survey. In: De Lucia, A., Ferrucci, F. (eds.) ISSSE 2006–2008, University of Salerno, Italy. LNCS, vol. 5413, pp. 78–105. Springer, Heidelberg (2009)

10. Christensen, E., et al.: Web Service Definition Language (WSDL) ver. 1.1 (2001), http://www.w3.org/TR/wsdl/

11. Ciotti, F.: Ws-guard - enhancing uddi registries with on-line testing capabilities. Master's thesis, Department of Computer Science, University of Pisa (April 2007)

12. PLASTIC european project homepage, http://www.ist-plastic.org

13. Apache Foundation. JUDDI (accessed on June 3rd, 2008), http://ws.apache.org/juddi/

14. Frantzen, L., Tretmans, J.: Model-Based Testing of Environmental Conformance of Components. In: de Boer, F.S., Bonsangue, M.M., Graf, S., de Roever, W.-P. (eds.) FMCO 2006. LNCS, vol. 4709, pp. 1–25. Springer, Heidelberg (2007)

15. Frantzen, L., Tretmans, J., Willemse, T.A.C.: Test generation based on symbolic specifications. In: Grabowski, J., Nielsen, B. (eds.) FATES 2004. LNCS, vol. 3395, pp. 1–15. Springer, Heidelberg (2005)

16. Frantzen, L., Tretmans, J., Willemse, T.A.C.: A Symbolic Framework for Model-Based Testing. In: Havelund, K., Núñez, M., Roşu, G., Wolff, B. (eds.) FATES 2006 and RV 2006. LNCS, vol. 4262, pp. 40–54. Springer, Heidelberg (2006)

17. Global Grid Forum. Web Services Agreement Specification (WS–Agreement), version 2005/09 edn. (September 2005)

18. GNU Prolog homepage, http://www.gprolog.org/

19. MagicDraw homepage, http://www.magicdraw.com

20. Quick Sequence Diagram Editor homepage, http://sdedit.sourceforge.net/

21. STSimulator homepage, http://www.cs.ru.nl/~lf/tools/stsimulator/

22. Huhns, M.N., Singh, M.P.: Service-Oriented Computing: Key Concepts and Principles. IEEE Internet Computing 9(1), 75–81 (2005)

23. IBM. WSLA: Web Service Level Agreements, version: 1.0 revision: wsla-2003/01/28 edn. (2003)

24. Inverardi, P., Tivoli, M.: The future of Software: Adaptation and Dependability. In: De Lucia, A., Ferrucci, F. (eds.) ISSSE 2006–2008, University of Salerno, Italy. LNCS, vol. 5413, pp. 1–31. Springer, Heidelberg (2009)

25. Jard, C., Jéron, T.: TGV: theory, principles and algorithms. In: IDPT 2002. Society for Design and Process Science (2002)

26. Lee, D., Yannakakis, M.: Principles and methods of testing finite state machines - A survey. Proceedings of the IEEE 84, 1090–1126 (1996)

27. NetBeans Tutorial on Asynchronous JAX-WS Web Service Client End-to-End Scenario, http://www.netbeans.org/kb/55/websvc-jax-ws-asynch.html

28. OASIS consortium. Universal Description, Discovery, and Integration (UDDI) (accessed on June 3rd, 2008), http://www.oasis-open.org/committees/tc_home.php?wg_abbrev=uddi-spec

29. Object Management Group. UML 2.0 Superstructure Specification, ptc/03-08-02 edn. Adopted Specification

30. Sahner, R.A., Trivedi, K.S., Puliafito, A.: Performance and Reliability Analysis of Computer Systems An Example-Based Approach Using the SHARPE Software Package. Kluwer Academic Publishers, Dordrecht (1995)

31. Sen, K., Agha, G.: CUTE and jCUTE: Concolic Unit Testing and Explicit Path Model-Checking Tools. In: Ball, T., Jones, R.B. (eds.) CAV 2006. LNCS, vol. 4144, pp. 419–423. Springer, Heidelberg (2006)

32. Skene, J., Lamanna, D.D., Emmerich, W.: Precise Service Level Agreements. In: Proc. of ICSE 2004, pp. 179–188. IEEE Computer Society Press, Los Alamitos (2004)

33. Skene, J., Skene, A., Crampton, J., Emmerich, W.: The Monitorability of Service-Level Agreements for Application-Service Provision. In: Proc. of WOSP 2007, pp. 3–14. ACM Press, New York (2007)

34. Tillmann, N., de Halleux, J.: Pex–White Box Test Generation for.NET. In: Beckert, B., Hähnle, R. (eds.) TAP 2008. LNCS, vol. 4966, pp. 134–153. Springer, Heidelberg (2008)

35. PLASTIC tools homepage, `http://plastic.isti.cnr.it/wiki/tools`

36. Tretmans, J.: Test generation with inputs, outputs and repetitive quiescence. Software—Concepts and Tools 17(3), 103–120 (1996)

37. Tretmans, J., Brinksma, E.: TorX : Automated Model Based Testing. In: Hartman, A., Dussa-Zieger, K. (eds.) First European Conference on Model-Driven Software Engineering, December 11-12 2003, Imbuss, Möhrendorf, Germany (2003)

38. van der Bijl, M., Rensink, A., Tretmans, J.: Compositional Testing with ioco. In: Petrenko, A., Ulrich, A. (eds.) FATES 2003. LNCS, vol. 2931, pp. 86–100. Springer, Heidelberg (2004)

39. W3C. WS-Addressing (accessed on June 3rd, 2008), `http://www.w3.org/Submission/ws-addressing/`

Architecture Reconstruction
Tutorial on Reverse Engineering to the Architectural Level

Rainer Koschke*

Universität Bremen
Fachbereich Mathematik und Informatik
Arbeitsgruppe Softwaretechnik
koschke@informatik.uni-bremen.de

Abstract. Software architectures are described by different views which depend upon the concerns of the respective stakeholders. Far too often, software architectures are not documented sufficiently. In such cases, an architecture description must be reconstructed when changes to the system are to be made.

This article summarizes the current state of the art of techniques and methods for software architecture reconstruction and relates them to the viewpoints that have been proposed in architecture design. The article identifies research opportunities based on the comparison.

Keywords: Reverse engineering, architecture reconstruction, software architecture, bibliography.

1 Introduction

All but the trivial changes in software systems require a global understanding of the system to be changed. Such non-trivial task include migrations, auditing, application integration, or impact analysis. A global understanding cannot be achieved by looking at every single statement. The source code provides a huge amount of details in which we cannot see the forest for the trees. Instead, to understand large systems, we need a more coarse-grained map. This map is called the software architecture.

Only in very few cases, the software architecture is described sufficiently in practice. In software engineering classes, we teach to document all the relevant architectural decisions and their rationales and to update this information whenever these decisions are revised. Yet in practice, architecture descriptions are—if available at all—often outdated and incorrect, or inappropriate for the task at hand. If information on the architecture is lost, it must be recovered.

Software architecture reconstruction is the form of reverse engineering in which architectural information is reconstructed for an existing system. Typically, the information is gathered from the source code, the system's execution,

---

* With contributions of Arie van Deursen, Christine Hofmeister, Leon Moonen, and Claudio Riva.

A. De Lucia and F. Ferrucci (Eds.): ISSSE 2006–2008, LNCS 5413, pp. 140–173, 2009.
© Springer-Verlag Berlin Heidelberg 2009

available documentation, stakeholder interviews, and domain knowledge. Architecture reconstruction typically involves three steps: extract raw data on the system, apply the appropriate abstraction technique, and present or visualize the information obtained.

In this paper, a conceptual framework for architecture reconstruction is introduced. The framework, known as the *Symphony* framework, is an amalgamation of common patterns and best practices reported in the reverse engineering literature [1]. Symphony is based on the concept of architectural views and viewpoints. We will introduce these concepts, the Symphony method and techniques and tools that support this method.

2 Architectural Descriptions

The intent of architecture reconstruction is to reconstruct architectural information to be documented by architectural descriptions. One widely accepted definition for software architecture is given by the standard *IEEE Recommended Practice for Architectural Descriptions*: *Software architecture* is the fundamental organization of a system embodied in its components, their relationships to each other and to the environment, and the principles guiding its design and evolution [2].

One organization, for instance, is the hierarchical decomposition of a system into subsystems. Yet, software—like every complex engineering product—consists of many distinct organizations (also known as structures). As early as 1974, Parnas wrote that there are several organizations beyond the hierarchical decomposition of a software system [3]. Since then, a large number of architectural structures has been proposed in the literature.

Rather than defining a fixed set of architectural structures to be described, the *IEEE Standard P1471* has recommended to describe a system by several views [2]. A view describes an architecture from the perspective of a particular audience (called stakeholders) sharing common interests. For an unambiguous interpretation, the content of views must be defined precisely. Views are specified by so called viewpoints, so that their interpretation and use is clear.

2.1 Views and Viewpoints

A *view* is a representation of a whole system from the perspective of a related set of concerns [2]. In IEEE P1471, a view conforms to a viewpoint. While a view describes a particular system, a viewpoint describes the rules and conventions used to create, depict, and analyze a view based on this viewpoint [2]. A viewpoint specifies the kind of information that can be put in a view. It is the specification of the type of view used to document a particular system or several systems. If a view is considered a model of a software system, a viewpoint would be its meta model.

In forward design, different architectural viewpoints are useful for separating engineering concerns, which reduces the complexity of design activities. When the resulting design is captured in separate views, this separation of concerns helps stakeholders and architects understand the architecture. For architecture reconstruction, different viewpoints specify what information should be reconstructed and help to structure the reconstruction process.

2.2 Source, Target, and Hypothesis Views

A software reconstruction process may be structured as a sequence of activities. Each is specified by the kind of information it expects, the kind of information it produces, and the resources and mechanisms it uses to produce this information from the available information. Consequently, reconstruction activities can be specified by a set of *source views* which are expected to exists and a set of *target views* which ought to be the result of the activity. The target views describe aspects of the architecture as implemented.

Some of the source views can be extracted directly from artifacts of the system, such as source code, build files, configuration information, documentation, or execution traces. Some of these views are so close to the source code or its execution that they would not be considered architectural views. Some others are the result of previous activities and may already be rather high level and abstract.

A *target view* is a view of a software system that describes the as-implemented architecture and contains the information needed to solve the problem/perform the tasks for which the reconstruction process was carried out.

Based on the source and target view, the reconstruction activity can be viewed as a *mapping* activity that takes the information in the source view to infer the target view. Most often this mapping requires involvement of a human expert although some aspects may be automated. In as much as the forward engineering process is a creative experience-based activity, we cannot expect that the reverse of this process can be fully automated.

Often, a *hypothetical view* is used during the reconstruction. It represents the working hypothesis for the target view. Because it is just a hypothesis gathered from the information gathered so far, it may describe the architecture of the system inaccurately. Such hypothetical views are always used at least informally and implicitly by the reverse engineer, but they may also be used explicitly and systematically. If used systematically, the reverse engineer follows a scientific process in which he or she formulates a hypothesis, determines appropriate measures to validate the hypothesis, gathers empirical evidence for or against the hypothesis, and finally falsifies, accepts, or refines the hypothesis based on the result of the validation.

2.3 Viewpoints in Forward Engineering

Viewpoints used in forward engineering are often also target views in architecture reconstruction. Among the first authors explicitly proposing several viewpoints is J. A. Zachman. His viewpoints are meant to describe the architecture of information system; yet, these viewpoints are generic enough to apply to other software systems as well.

Zachman observed from civil engineering that the process of building houses creates several (interim) products that describe the house from the perspectives of different stakeholders [4,5]. For houses, we have bubble charts in the first negotiations between the architect and the customer, an architect's drawing for the contract between the architect and the customer, an architect's plan that elaborates the drawing, a contractor's plan representing the building from the builder's perspective, the shop plans for the individual manufacturers (i.e., subcontractors), and the final building. Zachman notes that each of the architectural descriptions differs from the others in *essence*, not merely in level of detail; that is, they describe different concepts.

Zachman concludes that an analogous set of architectural descriptions is likely to be produced in building any complex product—including software systems. The different artifacts created in the process of developing information systems Zachman observed are scope description (bubble chart), model of the business (architect's drawing), model of the information system (architect's elaborate plan), technology model (contracter's plan), detailed description (shop plan), and the actual system (building).

Orthogonally to the different levels of conceptual descriptions, any product created in the process of engineering can be described, for different purposes, in different ways, resulting in different types of descriptions. Zachman suggests that the following aspects need to be addressed at the same relative level of description [6]:

- **Data:** *What* the thing is being made of.
- **Function:** *How* the thing works.
- **Network:** *Where* the flows (connections) exist.
- **People:** *Who* is building.
- **Time:** *When* it is happening.
- **Motivation:** *Why* it is built

The combination of the six different conceptual levels and the six different aspects at each level results in 36 different architectural viewpoints.

Influenced by Zachman's work, Perry and Wolf suggest three viewpoints in their classical paper [7]: the viewpoints of data, processing, and connections. The data viewpoint highlights the data elements and their processing flow. The processing viewpoint, in contrast, shows the processing elements and the data flow in between. The connection viewpoint shows how data and processing elements are connected. These three viewpoints actually contain the same information but with different emphasis (similarly to UML collaboration and sequence diagrams). The similarity of Perry and Wolf's three different viewpoints to the data, function, and network viewpoints by Zachman is obvious.

In another classical paper, Kruchten [8] proposes four viewpoints (logical, process, development, and physical) that cover more distinct aspects of a system. Kruchten proposes another redundant viewpoint to show how these four different viewpoints relate to each other by way of usage scenarios.

Table 1. Viewpoint categorization by Clements et al. [11]

- **M**: Module viewpoints
  - **M1**: Decomposition: module is-part-of module
  - **M2**: Uses: module uses module
  - **M3**: Generalization: module specializes module
  - **M4**: Layering: module belongs-to layer, layer may-use layer
- **CC**:Component-connector viewpoints (C&C)
  - **CC1**: Pipe-and-filter
  - **CC2**: Shared-data
  - **CC3**: Publish-Subscribe
  - **CC4**: Client-server
  - **CC5**: Peer-to-peer
  - **CC6**: Communicating processes
- **A**: Allocation viewpoints
  - **A1**: Deployment: software entity is-allocated-to/migrates-to physical entity
  - **A2**: Implementation: module is-allocated-on configuration unit, configuration unit is-contained-in configuration unit
  - **A3**: Work assignment: software element has-responsible developer

Soni, Nord, and Hofmeister have found four similar viewpoints from field observations in industry [9]. These four viewpoints have later been elaborated in their book on applied software architecture [10].

Clements and colleagues categorize many of these viewpoints and describe how to document them [11]. The categories they consider—without claiming completeness—are module, component-and-connector, and allocation viewpoints. *Module viewpoints* describe the decomposition, layering, and generalization of modules and their use dependencies. A module is a static code unit that implements a set of responsibilities. *Component-and-connector viewpoints* express runtime behavior described in terms of components and connectors. A component is one of the principal processing units of the executing system; a connector is an interaction mechanism for the components. Component-and-connector viewpoints resemble architectural styles [12]. *Allocation viewpoints* describe mappings of software units onto elements of the environment (the hardware, the file systems, or the development team). Table 1 summarizes the categories and viewpoints by stating the entities and their relations that are part of the viewpoint.

Because the different viewpoint categories are related to each other, mappings are required that map viewpoints in one category to viewpoints in another category. For instance, modules in a programming viewpoint are mapped onto files in a code viewpoint. These mappings are themselves viewpoints—viewpoints that anchor in two categories.

3 Architecture Reconstruction Process

The previous sections has introduced the concepts of views and viewpoints and described example viewpoints proposed in the forward engineering literature.

This section describes the process of architecture reconstruction which is based on views and viewpoints.

Architecture reconstruction may be conducted in two major phases. The first one attempts to determine the problem, to set the context, and to plan the reconstruction by defining source and target views using viewpoints along with the mapping rules. This phase is called *Reconstruction Design*. The next major phase executes the plan. In this phase, the reverse engineer analyzes the system, extracts the source views, and applies the mapping rules to populate the target views. This phase is called the *Reconstruction Execution*.

These two phases are highly incremental and iterative. The reconstruction execution may reveal new reconstruction opportunities, which then lead to a refined understanding of the problem and a refined reconstruction design. The source viewpoints, target viewpoints, and mapping rules may evolve throughout the process.

The outcomes of the reconstruction process are twofold: Reconstruction Design results in a well-defined procedure for reconstructing the architecture of the system. This procedure may be useful beyond the scope of the current reconstruction: it can play a role in continuous architecture conformance checking and in future reconstructions. Reconstruction Execution yields the architecture description needed to solve the problem that triggered the original reconstruction activity.

In the following, we describe the two phases in more detail.

3.1 Reconstruction Design

During reconstruction design we distinguish problem elicitation in which the problem triggering the reconstruction is analyzed and discussed with stakeholders, and concept determination, in which the architectural concepts relevant to the problem at hand and a recovery strategy are identified.

Problem Elicitation. All stakeholders of an architecture must be involved in reconstructing architectures. Stakeholders may be testers, developers, management, representatives of the business owning the system, and system users. Because it is difficult to get so many busy people aboard, there must be a compelling reason to start a reconstruction. Rarely, the reason is to improve just the maintainability of the system. Typically, there are external drivers experienced as a pain of the customers such as performance problems, poor reliability, need for migration, and considerations concerning system replacement or system extensions. It is important that all stakeholders define their problem explicitly and in written form. Stakeholders must reach a consensus on the goals and priorities, otherwise the reconstruction project is doomed to fail.

This list of problems triggers the a software reconstruction activity. The first step is then to elaborate the problem statement. This is the purpose of the *Problem Elicitation* step and requires the involvement of more technical people in the problem analysis.

There are several techniques that can be used during problem elicitation, such as structured workshops, checklists, role playing, and scenario analysis.

Outcomes of the Problem Elicitation step include summaries of interviews, workshop sessions, and relevant discussions; summaries of available high-level relevant documentation, if available; an elaboration and refinement of the problem statement based on these summaries; and an initial list of documentation and other resources that can be used during the reconstruction.

Observe that the original list of problems, the collected summaries and the refined problem statement may very well be "architecture-agnostic": they must be expressed in terms familiar to the stakeholders. The translation of the problems-as-perceived to software architecture concepts is the purpose of the *Concept Determination* step.

Concept Determination. Once the problem is understood, the *Concept Determination* step is used to determine the architectural information needed to solve the problem and the way to derive this information. In this step, the reverse engineer is a process designer, defining the architectural reconstruction that will take place in the final three steps.

There are five outcomes of this step, each of which is described in the remainder of this section. The UML diagram in Figure 1 summarizes the relationships involving the viewpoints and mapping rules produced in this step.

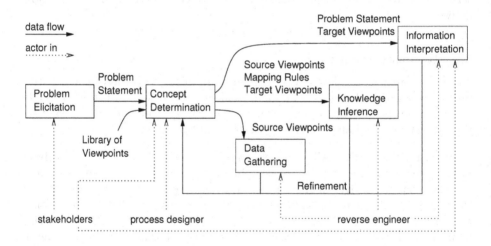

Fig. 1. Activities in Reconstruction Design

Identify Potentially Useful Viewpoints. The first step towards defining the target viewpoint is to identify a set of viewpoints that contain the information the stakeholders believe will be needed to solve the problem as described in *Problem Elicitation*. These viewpoints serve as the initial goal of the reconstruction project.

Typically, technical Stakeholders know which viewpoints will be useful, or have at least some initial ideas. In most cases, one can at least use some of the viewpoints described in Section 2.3 as a starting point. After getting input from

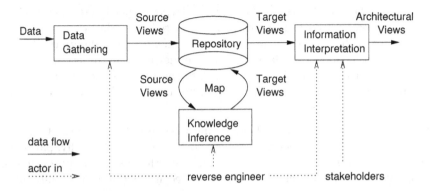

Fig. 2. Activities in Reconstruction Execution

the stakeholders, the reverse engineer should review the problems and questions, looking for additional useful viewpoints. Although the reverse engineer is responsible for producing the list of viewpoints, ultimately the stakeholders must agree to them.

These viewpoints can come from a library of well-known viewpoints such as the one by Clements et al. [11], or a new viewpoint can be created for a specific reconstruction. If the problem is not understood well enough to identify viewpoints of interest, the Problem Elicitation step should be re-applied.

One of the most commonly used viewpoints for architecture reconstruction is the Module viewpoint [10]. It identifies the layers, subsystems, and modules in the system and describes relationships (e.g. usage-dependency and decomposition) among them. Other common viewpoints are the Code architecture viewpoint, which describes the directory structure and build relationships, and the Execution viewpoint, which describes the runtime entities and their mapping to physical resources [10]. The Conceptual viewpoint [10], describing the functionality of the system in terms of components and connectors, is less commonly used for reconstruction because it is a more abstract view and is therefore more difficult to reconstruct.

One useful approach for creating the target viewpoint is to use the Stakeholder/View tables described by Clements et al. [11], adapted somewhat for reconstruction. In its original form this is a three-step process culminating in a prioritized list of views needed for documenting a software system.

In Symphony, the first step, producing a candidate view list, begins with the potentially useful viewpoints already identified. Each of these should be listed along with the extent to which it is important for solving the problem. The second step is to identify the specific relationships of each viewpoint that are needed. The third step is to prioritize these relationships and eliminate any duplicates. During this process the reverse engineer should be thinking about similarities among the relationships, which can be derived from others, which are most critical to solving the overall problem, and should try to consolidate them to arrive at the set of relationships in the target viewpoint.

Define/Refine Source Viewpoint. The source viewpoint specifies the source view. The source view will contain information extracted from the source code and gathered from other sources; the source viewpoint formally describes this information. The challenge in defining a source viewpoint is to determine what information will be needed in order to create the target views. Thus defining the source viewpoint needs to be done in conjunction with defining the mapping from source to target viewpoint.

Define/Refine Mapping Rules. The mapping rules are ideally a formal description of how to derive a target view from a source view. Realistically, parts will often be in the form of heuristics, guidelines, or other informal approaches. If a mapping can be completely formalized, the reconstruction can be fully automated. As said earlier, this is not typically possible for software architecture, thus we expect the mapping to contain both formal and informal parts.

Figure 3 shows that the mapping rules specify the map. The 'mapping rules' entity is an association class connecting the target viewpoint and source viewpoint. Thus it describes the 'maps to' association between these two entities. The map, as the instantiation of the mapping rules, describes how specific implementation facts in the source view are abstracted to architectural facts in the target view.

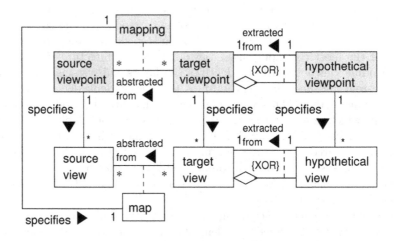

Fig. 3. Views and Viewpoints in Symphony

Determine Role and Viewpoint of Hypothetical Views. In addition to the above activities, the stakeholders and reverse engineers must determine whether a hypothetical view is needed and what its role will be. This role depends on the purpose of the reconstruction. The most common roles of a hypothetical view are as a guide during the reconstruction activity and as a baseline to compare with the system's current architecture.

When serving as a baseline there are two ways the comparison can be done. One is to create an explicit comparison view, with the comparison embodied in the target view. The second way to use a hypothetical view as a baseline is informally. In this case it is used in the last step, Information Interpretation. Typically the reverse engineer browses both the target view and hypothetical view, compares them, and based on the results may decide to perform another iteration of the reconstruction process, modifying the target viewpoint, source viewpoint, mapping, or some combination of these.

The hypothetical view also has a viewpoint that must be defined. If the hypothetical view is embedded in the target view (as in the Reflexion example) then its viewpoint is defined as part of the target viewpoint. This is shown as the containment relationship between the two viewpoints in Figure 3. If the hypothetical view is not embedded, then typically its viewpoint is very similar to the target viewpoint so that the comparison is straightforward. In Figure 3, this is shown as the 'extracted from' relationship between the two viewpoints.

3.2   Reconstruction Execution

During reconstruction execution, an extract—abstract—present approach is used, tailored towards the specific needs of architecture reconstruction. The three steps populate the source view, apply the mapping rules to create the target views, and interpret the results to solve the problem at hand. The activities to be carried out were designed in the earlier phase Reconstruction Design.

Data Gathering. The goal of the *Data Gathering* step is to collect the data that is required to recover selected architectural concepts from a system's artifacts. The motivation is that a large part of the truth about the actual (concrete) architecture is in the source code. However, in general, one can look at other artifacts of the system than just its source code. These other artifacts include a system's buildfiles/makefiles, (unit) tests, configuration files, etc. The data gathered are stored in a repository and processed in the Knowledge Inference step. A complementary approach is to gather information by observing the execution of the program. In Section 4, we will elaborate on such techniques in more detail.

Note that these kinds of analyses do not necessarily have to be developed by the team that is using them to recover the architecture. Suitable results can be imported from a wide range of reverse engineering tools (such as clustering tools, data flow analysis tools, etc.). In practice, often a pragmatic mix-and-match approach for data gathering is applied, combining the results from various extraction tools using scripting and glueing, for example, based on UNIX utilities such as join, split, awk and perl.

The output of the data gathering stage is a populated repository containing the extracted source views.

Knowledge Inference. The goal of the *Knowledge Inference* step is to derive the target view from the source view (typically a large relational data set describing the implementation of the system). The reverse engineer creates the target view by condensing the low-level details of the source view and abstracting them into architectural information. The mapping rules and domain knowledge are used to define a map between the source and target view. For example, if the mapping contains a rule about using naming conventions to combine classes into modules, the resulting map lists each class and the module to which it belongs. This activity may require either interviewing the system experts in order to formalize architecturally-relevant aspects not available in the implementation or to iteratively augment the source view by adding new concepts to the source viewpoint.

Depending on the degree of formalization of the mapping, this step can be fully or partly automated. The Knowledge Inference step is conducted initially in close cooperation with the system experts and, as more domain knowledge becomes formalized, more automation is added. This step can be summarized in the following activities: (1) create the map (containing the domain knowledge), and (2) combine the source view with the map to produce the target view. In practice, the map is often created iteratively, with each iteration refining the map or raising its level of abstraction until it can produce a satisfactory target view.

Existing techniques for the mapping can be categorized as manual, semi-automatic, or automatic. Manual approaches typically use simple, general-purpose tools and manual inspection of the system. While they may use reconstruction-specific tools such as SHRiMP, Rigi, PBS, or Bauhaus to help visualize intermediate results, there is no automated support for the process.

Semi-automatic approaches help the reverse engineer create architectural views in an interactive or formal way. They typically rely on the manual definition of the map. Differences among the approaches concern the expressiveness of the language used for defining the transformations, support for calculating transitive closures of relations, degree of repeatability of the process, amount of interaction required by the user, and the types of architectural views that can be generated.

Relational algebra approaches allow the reverse engineer to define a repeatable set of transformations for creating a particular architectural view. In the work of Holt et al.[13], relational algebra is used for creating a hierarchical module view of the source code (by grouping source files into modules and calculating the module dependencies). The reverse engineer must manually prepare the containment relations, but new relationships can also be inferred using algebra propositions. Postma [14] uses relational partition algebra (RPA) [15] to calculate module dependencies from dependencies extracted from code. RPA is also used to check the conformance of an extracted target view with a hypothetical view (established in the design phase). The process is repeatable and is part of the build process.

Riva has proposed a method for inferring the architectural information based on relational algebra and Prolog [16]. Mens [17] uses logic meta programming (Prolog) for mapping implementation artifacts to high-level design and for checking conformance of architectural rules.

More light-weight examples are the Reflexion Model [18], Tcl scripts for defining graph transformations in Rigi, SQL queries for defining grouping rules (Dali), or the ad-hoc graph query language (GReQL) of GUPRO.

Fully automatic approaches are based on different kinds of clustering algorithms based on coupling and cohesion (e.g., the Bunch tool) or file names.

Formal concept analysis and type inference are also used. A more detailed overview on specific techniques is given in Section 4.

For the creation of the map, technological, organizational, and often historical background knowledge as well as domain knowledge is required. Moreover, the mapping is often difficult because of hidden dependencies. Obviously, the quality of the data gathering is key to a successful knowledge inference. The realization of poor data quality forces us to reiterate the data gathering with different means.

The output of the Knowledge Inference step is an enriched and structured repository where the source view and the domain knowledge has been combined to create the target view.

Information Interpretation. The target views–selected to address a particular problem–are inspected, interpreted, and eventually applied to solve the problem. To these ends, the target views need to be made accessible both physically and mentally to all stakeholders.

The views that result from Knowledge Inference are not the answer to the problem but provide a foundation to address the problem. In the Information Interpretation, conclusions are drawn from the reconstructed views. These conclusions then lead to measures to be taken to remedy the problem. The measures themselves are not part of the reconstruction process.

Ideally, the viewpoints were selected to allow an immediate use of the views; however, even if the viewpoints are carefully tailored, it might become difficult to get an answer at the level of the target views because they may span a huge information space. In such cases, presentations are required that make this information space amenable to all stakeholders. The presentation must be readable and traceable. Readability relates to the ability to easily find and grasp relevant information in the views; traceability allows us to trace the inferred knowledge back to the original data. Visualization and interaction techniques can be used to support readability and traceability.

For all presentation techniques, we need to determine the scope, the viewers, and the task to be achieved. The scope of the presentation (i.e., the artifacts and their aspects to be presented) is already given in form of the selected viewpoints and target views. The viewers and task to be achieved are stated in the Problem Elicitation. We focus on presentation and interaction issues in the following.

Although the selected viewpoints define the vocabulary and semantics for the representation, they do not define how to present the information. Information presentation addresses this problem, where we take presentation quite liberally: any means to communicate information to a viewer, be it textually, graphically, or through other forms of human perception including any form of interaction with the presentation. Sight is the most often addressed form of human perception by information presentation in the software architecture domain; that is why we are using the narrower term visualization instead of perception in the following.

Presentation issues have to do with effective visual communication including the visual vocabulary, the use of the specific visual elements to convey particular kinds of information, the organization of visual information, and the order in which material is presented to the viewer. Most application domains have their own conventions and symbology that should be used for the visual vocabulary and elements.

Due to lack of space, the reader is referred to overviews on software visualization in the literature [19,20,21]. Yet, at least I want to point out that graphs seem to be a "natural" visualization of architecture elements and their (often binary) relations, as confirmed by independent surveys that indicate their popularity [19,22] (in the end, class and object diagrams in UML are just graphs with predefined semantics and rendering characteristics).

The aspect of interaction refers to the way the visualization is constructed. Visualizations range from "hard-wired", where the viewer has no influence on the presentation, to arbitrary redefinition by the viewer. Visualizations should not be static pictures, but should offer querying, zooming in and out, navigation along cross-references and hierarchies, selective hiding, and gathering of transitive relations.

Many architecture reconstructions in practice could have benefited from more advanced and carefully selected means of visualization. Visualization issues are often brought up as an afterthought and, hence, the potential of visualization is only partially leveraged. The reason for this shortcoming is simply that the means of presentation chosen are often opportunistically selected from available tools. The focus is to solve the problem quickly with available tools. As the initial processes are repeated more often, we expect that their maturity will improve by a more careful consideration of presentation issues.

A particular problem of software architecture is the need to understand a combination of multiple views, which is further complicated when the views are of conceptually different viewpoints. There have been several suggestions to the "view fusion" problem. If the views overlap in some of their entities, one can use certain inferences to map entities with no immediate correspondence to entities in the other view. For instance, Kazman and Carriere use "lifting" operations along containment relations to fuse views [23]. If the entities may be mapped onto source code, one could leverage overlapping source code regions to identify correspondences between entities [24]. If there is no such simple correspondence, the mapping is typically manual. Hillard, Rice, and Schwarm [25], for instance, systematically cross reference related entities from distinct views and use Ross's model tie process from Structured Analysis to integrate the views [26]. These cross-references are created as part of Symphony's Knowledge Inference in the form of the maps and stored so that the connection among views is made explicit. The cross-references may be implemented and inserted into the views by available frameworks [27,28].

The output of the Information Interpretation is a hyperstructure offering a holistic perspective on the software system as a foundation for investigating the concrete architecture's impact on the problems signaled. This hyperstructure includes traceability links between views and links to other software artifacts, such as the source text, relevant documentation, etc. The ideal hyperstructure allows you to explore the system at various levels of abstraction: it lets you zoom in and zoom out between sources and architecture and navigate between views.

4   Architecture Reconstruction Techniques

This section describes techniques to reconstruct architectural views proposed in the literature. Another comprehensive summary of existing architecture reconstruction techniques was written by Pollet et al. [29]. The focus in this section is on concrete techniques rather than methods. We consider techniques to be approaches that are (semi-)automated with one particular concrete set of views as target, whereas we use the term *method* for approaches that are more general process descriptions with little focus on particular views (e.g., [1,30,31,32,33,34,35,36,37,38]).

The techniques can be described as a mapping from source views to target views. The following description is based on this distinction. Unfortunately, source and target views are often only implicit in the literature.

4.1   Source Views

Base source views are views that can be extracted immediately from the system's code or execution, people, or existing documentation. Typically, we would not consider them architectural because they lack abstraction. These views yield the basic facts upon which the architectural reconstruction can be started.

There are two distinct approaches to analyzing a system. One can either observe its behavior at runtime or study its static description, that is, its source code. The former is a dynamic analysis, the latter a static analysis. There are pros and cons for both approaches and in some cases they can be reasonably combined.

There are many different types of static analysis to gather architectural knowledge varying in effort, precision, scalability, prerequisites etc. Moreover, source code is not the only artefact that can be analyzed statically. Other examples include build files, scripts, configuration files, emails, natural language text, or version control repositories. The more formal the analyzed document, the easier can it be processed automatically.

The spectrum of static analyses is as follows:

- Manual analysis: Here, the reverse engineer analyzes the system without any automated support by reading the code. He or she can examine the directory structure or the hierarchical structure imposed by the programming language or by exploring the source code for beacons that signal aspects of interest.
- Lexical analysis: Several tools are available that perform lexical analysis of textual files. The most well-known is probably `grep` that searches text for strings matching a regular expression. Tools like `grep` generally give little support to process the matched strings, they just print matching lines. Such support is available in more advanced text-processing tools such as `awk`, `perl`, and `lex` that allow one to execute certain actions when a specific expression is matched.
- Syntactic analysis: Parser-based approaches are used to increase the accuracy and level of detail that can be expressed. These typically create a syntax tree of the input and allow the users to traverse, query, or match the tree to look

for certain patterns. This relieves them from having to handle all aspects of a language and focus on interesting parts.

– Semantical analysis: Additional techniques such as name and type resolution, control and data flow analysis and points-to analysis can be used to improve the results from other analyses.

Abstract syntax trees, control and data flow graphs are often used to represent aspects of a program at the detailed level. More coarse-grained graphs are used to represent the global declarations such as classes, modules, etc. as nodes and their dependencies such as inheritance, use, etc. as edges.

The problem of static analysis is that many questions related to the possible behavior are undecidable in general. Safe static analyses are forced to make conservative assumption and, hence, yield an overapproximation of the real behavior. In particular, if it comes to large systems, one has to sacrifice precision to achieve scalability.

While conservative static analyses yield every possible behavior and likely more, dynamic analyses yield only actual behavior but not necessarily every possible behavior. It may be objectionable to draw general conclusions from only dynamic information. Also, often one collects a huge amount of events at runtime and the observation of the program may interfere with the program's execution.

Analyzing only the system does not answer all relevant questions. For instance, we cannot know infer how the system should have been nor can we tell why something is the way it is. Analyzing the system may be complemented by interviewing developers, studying existing documents and the development process, or analyzing the version history available in version control systems such as CVS or Subversion. This additional analysis may create hypotheses for the reconstruction process which can then be validated under some circumstances by investigating the system.

4.2   Target Views

Target views are the result of reconstruction activities. This section classifies existing reconstruction techniques into the target viewpoint categories outlined in Table 1 in Section 2.3. Table 2 gives an overview using the abbreviations introduced in Table 1. Some of the target viewpoints cannot be classified to one particular viewpoint in Table 1, but at least to a viewpoint category therein.

There are some papers addressing multiple viewpoints, in which case they appear several times in Table 2. The view integration and combination does not match with Clements et al.'s categorization. Rather they can be viewed as a meta view connecting different views specified by different viewpoints.

5   Reconstructing Module Viewpoints

Most published techniques address module viewpoints because they are closest to the source. For this reason, we will focus on these techniques in this paper. References to techniques addressing other viewpoint categories can be found in Table 2.

Table 2. Categorized published techniques

Cat.	Viewp.	Content	References
M1	decomposition	part-of	[39,40,41,42,43,44,45,46] [47,48,49,50,51,52,53,54] [55,56,57,58,59,60,61,62] [63,64,65,66,67,68,69,70] [71,72,73,74,75,76,77,78] [79,80,81]
M3	class hierarchies	inherits, attribute-of, method-of	[82,83]
M2	class diagrams	association, aggregation	[84,85,86,87,88,89,90] [91,92,93]
M2	interfaces	provides, requires	[94,95,96]
M	design pattern	element participates-in pattern	[97,98,99,100,101,102,103] [104,105,106,107,108]
M	conformance	conforms-to, diverges-from	[109,110,111,112,113,114] [115]
M	feature location	implemented-by	[116,117,118,119,120,121] [122,123,124,125,126,127] [128,129,130,131]
M	use cases	implemented-by	[132,133]
M	configuration	varies-with	[134,135]
CC	object traces	receives-message	[136,137]
CC	component interaction	interacts-with	[138,139,140]
CC	process interaction	interacts-with	[141,142,143,144,145,146] [147,148,80,81]
CC	object interaction	interacts-with	[149,150,151,152,153,154] [155,156,157,158,159,160]
CC	conceptual	implemented-by	[161,162,80]
A3.	responsibility	responsible-for	[163]
A2	build process	generated-from, generated-by	[164]
A2	files	described-in, saved-in	[80]
Meta	View integration/combination	element corresponds-to element	[165,166,167,168,169]

5.1 Decomposition

The most dominating research area in architecture reconstruction is the inference of the structural decomposition. At the lower level, one groups global declarations such as variables, routines, types, and classes into modules. At the higher level, modules are clustered into subsystems and layers. The result are flat or hierarchical modules. Examples for flat modules are abstract data types and objects [170,171,172,173,174,175,176,177,178,179,180,181,182,183,184].

Hierarchical modules are often called subsystems [185,47,186,57]. While earlier research focused on flat modules for procedural systems, newer research addresses hierarchical modules.

Typically, static dependencies such as calls, variable accesses, and type relations are used to determine the grouping. In some cases, similarity of identifiers are also used [60,40,187,188]. Gall et al. proposed to explicitly model the application domain to get more application-oriented concepts [79]. Only one approach groups using dynamic information gathered through executing use cases [43].

Different techniques are used for the grouping. Software clustering is the most popular one and leverages existing clustering techniques developed in other fields, for instance in biology, to categorize animals [58,64,70,78,189,186,187,188]. In many cases a hierarchical agglomerative similarity clustering is used. The approaches differ mostly in the underlying definition of similarity that decides which elements to group.

Other techniques view grouping as a partitioning problem that attempts to minimize coupling and maximize cohesion between software entities. Because finding the best partition is NP hard, approximative techniques are used, for instance, based on generative programming [57] or more traditional search techniques such as hill climbing [55,57].

Also, methods from graph theory are used, as for instance, search for cycles or dominance analysis [185,47,61] and graph pattern matching [66,67,68,69]. Other techniques are based on mathematical methods for binary relations, such as formal concept analysis [43,45,52,72,73,74,181,175]. The result of formal concept analysis is a concept lattice, which describes a hierarchy of concepts. The techniques using formal concept analysis differ in the definition of the so called formal context that defines the objects, attributes, and relation used as input to concept analysis and also in the use of the resulting lattice. Data mining techniques [62,65,69] and spectral analysis [71] are also used.

In general, these fully automated techniques are part of an interactive process [61,189] because the criteria for logically cohesive elements are not defined exactly. In iterative processes, incremental techniques play a prominent role. These incremental techniques need to group new elements and not yet grouped elements into existing groups [76,189].

The intensive analysis of these techniques have lead to comparative studies reflecting about them. For instance, their stability against minor changes in the input dependencies [75] and the influence of different approaches to generate call graphs [63] were analyzed. Differences in call graphs can arise from different techniques used to resolve function pointers and dynamic dispatching. Moreover, competing approaches to validate the results of clustering techniques were developed [48,190,49,51,54,59,77,189].

5.2   Class Hierarchies

Reverse engineering class hierarchies from object-oriented programs seems trivial at first sight because the inheritance relation can be retrieved syntactically from object-oriented programming languages. Yet, the syntactic inheritance yields only class hierarchies as specified and not how the classes are actually used in the code. More advanced analyses yield the optimal class hierarchy as mirrored in using code. Optimal means that a class has only those properties that all of its instances actually require [82,83]. The optimal hierarchy is a refinement of the actual hierarchy where unnecessary properties are removed and where classes as declared are split into subclasses so that a declared instance of such a class has all properties that are used through this instance and only those. The means to obtain the optimal class hierarchy is formal concept analysis.

5.3 Interfaces

Syntactic export interfaces describe all types, operations, and attributes provided by a module whereas syntactic import interfaces list all types, operations, and attributes the module requires from other module in order to work correctly. Syntactic export interfaces can be specified in most languages; in C, it is conventional to specify this type of interface by header files with external declarations while in more advanced languages such as Java, C#, and C++ there exist syntactic means for the specification. Syntactic import interfaces can typically not be specified directly, or at least only at a relatively coarse level by import or include statements. Here, at least one specifies upon which other modules a module depends. Yet, more interesting is usually what is really used and not just exported and which other interface elements of other modules are actually used by a module. This type of information can be reconstructed by global name resolution, in the compiler domain known as semantic analysis. While direct references can be detected relatively easily by name resolution (although it is still complicated enough when it comes to overloaded methods in C++ or Ada, for instance) since the names are explicitly mentioned. Indirect references through function pointers, dispatching calls, or reflection in Java are much more difficult to obtain. For function pointers, we can use a pointer analysis to obtain the potential targets of a function pointer call. For dispatching calls, we need a data flow analysis that tells us which dynamic types an object can take on at runtime in order to determine which redefined method is called within a class hierarchy.

As soon as we know all references, we can determine the provided and required interfaces of a module. A generic approach for that is described by Mancoridis [94]. Viljamaa describes a method how the interface of an object-oriented framework (variation points and call interface) is obtained from different instantiations of this framework [96]. Once again, formal concept analysis plays a role in this process.

Yet, interfaces are much more than just references and syntax. An interface is the set of assumptions a modules makes on its client modules and the modules it requires. Preconditions and postconditions and constraints on the allowable sequences of operations offered by the interface are additional aspects one needs to specify for an interface. In particular, in embedded real-time systems we also need to specify nonfunctional properties such as memory consumption and timing of the operations. Preconditions may be retrieved from code as path conditions that yield to statements that explicitly raise exceptions as proposed by Whaley et al. [191] in cases where programmers used the strategy of defensive programming.

5.4 Class Models

Class models describe the dependencies between classes beyond inheritance. Essentially, they reconstruct complete UML class diagrams with associations, aggregations, and compositions. The techniques range from lightweight techniques analyzing byte code [85,86] to more advanced data flow analyses that determine which objects may be referenced [87].

The extraction for large systems may yield very detailed yet also overwhelming data. In order to cope with these data, rules for abstraction may be useful [84].

In class diagrams, we distinguish aggregation and composition from the more general associations. These types of relations cannot be distinguished syntactically in ordinary programming languages. To distinguish them in the source code is difficult. There are some approaches that are based on the static lifetime of objects or the propagation by operations [93]. Class models may even be extracted for procedural languages [91] where the programming language gives even fewer hints on the intended class model.

5.5   Design Patterns

A relatively new line of research is the detection of design pattern implementations in source code. In the beginning, structural patterns were the main focus. They may be detected as structural patterns in class models. Today's research tackles behavioral and creational patterns as well using static and dynamic analysis.

Static techniques are based on pattern matching for graphs representing class models or abstract syntax trees [97,98,99,101,102,104,105,106]. Once these patterns are detected, one can filter these candidates by dynamic analysis on execution traces of the operations involved in the matched pattern [100]. Data mining may be used as well [103].

The problem of pattern matching in graphs is to circumvent the combinatorial explosion of the possible ways to instantiate a pattern. In essence, the underlying problem here is the NP hard problem of finding isomorphic subgraphs. The existing approaches are using heuristics and yield approximative solutions. Some approaches attempt to explicitly model uncertainty of the matching using fuzzy-set theory [105].

A very different approach to design pattern detection was proposed by Tonella and Antoniol [107,108]. All other approaches require a library of known pattern implementations to detect pattern instantiations in code. They are able to find only patterns which are assumed to exist but cannot find new patterns. Tonella and Antontiol's technique attempts to detect new unknown patterns by using formal concept analysis. Potential patterns are detected in the resulting concept lattice as frequent occurrences of collaborations of classes. These patterns are then validated by a reverse engineer.

5.6   Conformance

All manual approaches to architecture reconstruction use hypotheses on the expected architecture at least implicitly. Theses hypotheses guide the reconstruction process. Some approaches offer to specify these hypotheses explicitly. These approaches may also be used to check conformance of the implementation with the architecture or to track the evolution of the architecture [114].

The conformance viewpoint is a particularity in architecture reconstruction. It does not exist in forward engineering because it requires two models: an intended architecture model and a model of the architecture as implemented.

The reflexion model by Murphy et al. [112,113,192,111,193,194] is the most prominent hypothesis-driven approach. It consists of several steps. In the first step, an architecture model is specified on the expected components and their dependencies. Then the implementation components and their dependencies are extracted from the code. The implementation components are mapped onto the architecture components by a reverse engineer. Given this mapping, the commonalities and differences between these two models can be determined as three types of relations:

- a *convergence* is found when the architecture specifies a dependency that really exists in the code
- an *absence* is found when the architecture specifies a dependency that does not exist in the code
- a *divergence* is found when the architecture specifies a dependency that does exist in the code but not in the architecture

Frenzel, Koschke et al. have later extended this technique to reconstructing the architectures of software variants incrementally [195].

A variation of this technique that does not compare dependencies but coupling metrics derived from these was proposed by Tvedt et al. [115]. While Murphy et al. specify the hypothesized architecture model as a separate graph, Aldrich et al. [109] embed this specification directly in the source code.

5.7   Feature Location

Modules take on responsibilities to implement a coherent set of product functions, also known as *features*. In many cases, it is not known which feature is implemented by which module. In these cases, traceability links from features onto modules must be reconstructed. This can be done through static or dynamic analysis.

Static approaches extract a global static dependency graph, which can be browsed by a reverse engineer for the relevant features [117,127]. Dedicated browsing tools can be used to support the systematic search. Some familiarity with the code is required for an efficient and effective search. Otherwise the whole dependency graph must be investigated. Other static approaches use information retrieval techniques to compare significant words in a requirement specification or change request to identifiers and words in comments in the source code [126,128,131].

Dynamic analyses observe which routines are executed when the feature of interest is executed [116,119,125,196]. The reverse engineer can inspect the trace execution detecting visual patterns of the feature execution.

Other dynamic analyses compute the set difference between the set of routines when the feature was invoked and the set of routines when the program was executed without invoking the feature [118,129,197].

An extension to this binary comparison was proposed by Eisenbarth, Koschke and Simon using formal concept analysis [120,123]. Beyond that they developed ideas to combine static and dynamic analysis and to apply formal concept analysis incrementally [121,122,124]. A case study of feature location based on formal concept analysis for programs with a complex and large feature set was reported by Quante and Koschke [198].

Wilde and Rajlich compared their distinct static and dynamic techniques in a controlled experiment [130]. The experiment suggests that the dynamic approach is more suited for large programs that are changed rarely because it gives only a partial understanding whereas the static approach is better suited for a more manageable program often changed since it gives a more complete understanding.

5.8   Use-Cases

Related to feature location is the reconstruction of use cases. A use case can combine several features to obtain a result meaningful to a user. Again, static and dynamic approaches can be applied. The dynamic technique by El-Ramly et al. [133] reconstructs use cases by re-occurring patterns in recorded interactions with user dialogs and their succession.

In the static technique by Lucca et al. [132] those sequences of static calls between classes are followed that start with an input statement and end in an output statement. All such paths yield a method-message graph (MM-graph). A use case corresponds to a path in the MM-graph. Use cases that are part of another use case can be detected in the MM-graph as inner paths between forking and joining nodes in the MM-graph.

5.9   Configuration

Source code is often configured using preprocessor directives. At the architectural level, such preprocessor directives indicate variant components. The code that is actually analyzed by the compiler depends upon macros. These configurations are analyzed by Krone and Snelting using formal concept analysis [134,135]. The resulting concept lattice shows which lines of code depend upon which macro values and which macros control jointly which code lines.

6   Summary and Future Research

The comparison of viewpoints in architecture reconstruction and viewpoints in forward engineering in Table 2 shows a large overlap but also a discrepancy. Largely, module viewpoints are addressed in architecture reconstruction and to some extent component-and-connector viewpoints. The allocation viewpoints are hardly addressed.

Consequently, future research should better address the discrepancies. The effort disproportionately spent on the structural decomposition could be redirected to the lesser addressed viewpoints. The discovery of new design patterns in the component-connector-viewpoints also deserves more research.

Current research focuses on the reconstruction of the status quo of a system. A newer trend is the analysis of evolutionary aspects based on the analysis of version control systems such as CVS or Subversion. Evolutionary analyses may detect the underlying drivers for design decisions. Yet, even this work is able to look back only on what actually happened but not on what should have happened. That is, we see the consequences of design decisions but not the influencing factors and alternatives that were ignored along with the rationales for these decisions.

While there are a few papers on the process of reconstruction, a comprehensive catalogue of techniques with detailed process descriptions when and how the techniques can be applied is missing. There is a lack of cost models for architecture reconstruction and knowledge when to prefer one technique over other techniques. Beyond that an embedding of architecture reconstruction in the normal development process is missing in order to monitor the evolution and to take countermeasures against architectural erosion early. Such an embedding would allow to take measures at the first signs of architectural erosion and would avoid more expensive large-scale refactorings after the fact.

Another challenge for the future is the reconstruction of architectures of highly dynamic and adaptive systems. These kinds of systems are gaining more and more currency.

References

1. van Deursen, A., Hofmeister, C., Koschke, R., Moonen, L., Riva, C.: Symphony: View-driven software architecture reconstruction. In: IEEE/IFIP Working Conference on Software Architecture, pp. 122–132. IEEE Computer Society Press, Los Alamitos (2004)
2. IEEE P1471: IEEE recommended practice for architectural description of software-intensive systems—std. 1471-2000 (2000)
3. Parnas, D.L.: On a 'buzzword': Hierarchical structure. In: Proc. IFIP Congress, North Holland Publishing Company, Amsterdam (1974)
4. Zachman, J.A.: A framework for information systems architecture. IBM Systems Journal 26(3) (1987)
5. Sowa, J.F., Zachman, J.A.: Extending and formalising the framework for information systems architecture. IBM Systems Journal 31(3), 590–616 (1992)
6. Zachman, J.A.: A framework for information systems architecture. IBM Systems Journal 38(2&3), 454–470 (1999)
7. Perry, D.E., Wolf, A.L.: Foundations for the study of software. ACM SIGSOFT 17(4), 40–52 (1992)
8. Kruchten, P.: The 4+1 view model of architecture. IEEE Software 12(6), 42–50 (1995)
9. Soni, D., Nord, R.L., Hofmeister, C.: Software architecture in industrial applications. In: International Conference on Software Engineering, pp. 196–206. ACM Press, New York (1995)
10. Hofmeister, C., Nord, R., Soni, D.: Applied Software Architecture. Object Technology Series. Addison-Wesley, Reading (2000)
11. Clements, P., Bachmann, F., Bass, L., Garlan, D., Ivers, J., Little, R., Nord, R., Stafford, J.: Documenting Software Architecture. Addison-Wesley, Boston (2002)

12. Shaw, M., Garlan, D.: Software Architecture: Perspectives on an Emerging Discipline. Prentice Hall, Englwood Cliffs (1996)
13. Holt, R.C.: Structural manipulation of software architecture using tarski relational algebra. In: Blaha, M., Verhoef, C. (eds.) Working Conference on Reverse Engineering, pp. 210–219. IEEE Computer Society Press, Los Alamitos (1998)
14. Postma, A.: A method for module architecture verification and its application on a large component-based system. Information and Software Technology 45, 171–194 (2003)
15. Feijs, L., Krikhaar, R., van Ommering, R.: A relational approach to support software architecture analysis. Software—Practice and Experience 28(4), 371–400 (1998)
16. Riva, C.: Architecture reconstruction in practice. In: IEEE/IFIP Working Conference on Software Architecture. IEEE Computer Society Press, Los Alamitos (2002)
17. Mens, K.: Automating architectural conformance checking by means of logic meta programming. Phd thesis, Departement Informatica, Vrije Universiteit Brussel (2000)
18. Murphy, G.C., Notkin, D.: Reengineering with reflexion models: A case study. IEEE Computer 30(8), 29–36 (1997)
19. Bassil, S., Keller, R.K.: Software visualization tools: Survey and analysis. In: International Workshop on Program Comprehension, pp. 7–17. IEEE Computer Society Press, Los Alamitos (2001)
20. Knight, C., Munro, M.: Mediating diverse visualisations for comprehension. In: International Workshop on Program Comprehension, pp. 18–25. IEEE Computer Society Press, Los Alamitos (2001)
21. Wiggins, M.: An overview of program visualization tools and systems. In: 36th Annual Southeast Regional Conference, pp. 194–200. ACM Press, New York (1998)
22. Koschke, R.: Software visualization in software maintenance, reverse engineering, and reengineering: A research survey. Journal on Software Maintenance and Evolution 15(2), 87–109 (2003)
23. Kazman, R., Carriere, S.: View extraction and view fusion in architectural understanding. In: International Conference on Software Reuse (1998)
24. Chase, M.P., Harris, D., Yeh, A.: Manipulating recovered software architecture views. In: International Conference on Software Engineering, pp. 184–194. ACM Press, New York (1997)
25. Hillard II, R.F., Rice, T.B., Schwarm, S.C.: The architectural metaphor as foundation for system engineering. In: Annual Symposium of the International Council on Systems Engineering (1995)
26. Ross, D.T.: Removing the limitations of natural languages (with the principles behind the rsa language). In: Proceedings of the Software Engineering Workshop. Academic Press, London (1980)
27. Anderson, K.M., Taylor, R.N., Whitehead Jr., E.J.: Chimera: hypertext for heterogeneous software environments. In: Proceedings of the European conference on Hypermedia technology. ACM Press, New York (1994)
28. Devanbu, P., Chen, R., Gansner, E., Müller, H., Martin, A.: Chime: Customizable hyperlink insertion and maintenance engine for software engineering environments. In: International Conference on Software Engineering. ACM Press, New York (1999)

29. Pollet, D., Ducasse, S., Poyet, L., Alloui, I., Cîmpan, S., Verjus, H.: Towards a process-oriented software architecture reconstruction taxonomy. In: European Conference on Software Maintenance and Reengineering, pp. 137–148. IEEE Computer Society Press, Los Alamitos (2007)

30. Ivkovic, I., Godfrey, M.: Enhancing domain-specific software architecture recovery. In: International Workshop on Program Comprehension, may 2003, pp. 266–270. IEEE Computer Society Press, Los Alamitos (2003)

31. Liu, K., Alderson, A., Qureshi, Z.: Requirements recovery from legacy systems by analyzing and modelling behavior. In: International Conference on Software Maintenance. IEEE Computer Society Press, Los Alamitos (1999)

32. Riva, C., Yang, Y.: Generation of architectural documentation using XML. In: Working Conference on Reverse Engineering, pp. 161–169. IEEE Computer Society Press, Los Alamitos (2002)

33. Riva, C.: Architecture reconstruction in practice. In: IEEE/IFIP Working Conference on Software Architecture, pp. 159–173. IEEE Computer Society Press, Los Alamitos (2002)

34. Bril, R.J., Postma, A., Krikhaar, R.L.: Embedding architectural support in industry. In: International Conference on Software Maintenance, pp. 348–357. IEEE Computer Society Press, Los Alamitos (2003)

35. Stoermer, C., O'Brien, L., Verhoef, C.: Practice patterns for architecture reconstruction. In: Working Conference on Reverse Engineering, pp. 151–160. IEEE Computer Society Press, Los Alamitos (2002)

36. Stoermer, C., O'Brien, L., Verhoef, C.: Moving towards quality attribute driven software architecture reconstruction. In: Working Conference on Reverse Engineering, pp. 46–56. IEEE Computer Society Press, Los Alamitos (2003)

37. Stoermer, C., O'Brien, L.: MAP—mining architectures for product line evaluations. In: IEEE/IFIP Working Conference on Software Architecture, pp. 35–44. IEEE Computer Society Press, Los Alamitos (2001)

38. Ding, L., Medvidovic, N.: Focus: A light-weight, incremental approach to software architecture recovery and evolution. In: IEEE/IFIP Working Conference on Software Architecture, pp. 191–200. IEEE Computer Society Press, Los Alamitos (2001)

39. Andritsos, P., Tzerpos, V.: Software clustering based on information loss minimization. In: Working Conference on Reverse Engineering, pp. 334–343. IEEE Computer Society Press, Los Alamitos (2003)

40. Anquetil, N., Lethbridge, T.: Extracting concepts from file names: a new file clustering criterion. In: International Conference on Software Engineering, pp. 84–93. ACM Press, New York (1998)

41. Baniassad, E.L.A., Murphy, G.C.: Conceptual module querying for software reengineering. In: International Conference on Software Engineering, pp. 64–73. ACM Press, New York (1998)

42. Bauer, M., Trifu, M.: Architecture-aware adaptive clustering of oo systems. In: European Conference on Software Maintenance and Reengineering, pp. 3–12. IEEE Computer Society Press, Los Alamitos (2004)

43. Bojic, D., Velasevic, D.: A use-case driven method of architecture recovery for program understanding and reuse reengineering. In: European Conference on Software Maintenance and Reengineering. IEEE Computer Society Press, Los Alamitos (2000)

44. Chiricota, Y., Jourdan, F., Melançon, G.: Software components capture using graph clustering. In: International Workshop on Program Comprehension, pp. 217–226. IEEE Computer Society Press, Los Alamitos (2003)

45. van Deursen, A., Kuipers, T.: Identifying objects using cluster and concept analysis. In: International Conference on Software Engineering, pp. 246–255. IEEE Computer Society Press, Los Alamitos (1999)
46. Embley, D.W., Woodfield, S.N.: Assessing the quality of abstract data types written in Ada. In: International Conference on Software Engineering, pp. 144–153. ACM Press, New York (1988)
47. Girard, J.F., Koschke, R.: Finding components in a hierarchy of modules: a step towards architectural understanding. In: International Conference on Software Maintenance. IEEE Computer Society Press, Los Alamitos (1997)
48. Girard, J.F., Koschke, R., Schied, G.: Comparison of abstract data type and abstract state encapsulation detection techniques for architectural understanding. In: Working Conference on Reverse Engineering. IEEE Computer Society Press, Los Alamitos (1997)
49. Koschke, R., Eisenbarth, T.: A framework for experimental evaluation of clustering techniques. In: International Workshop on Program Comprehension. IEEE Computer Society Press, Los Alamitos (2000)
50. Krikhaar, R.: Reverse architecting approach for complex systems. In: International Conference on Software Maintenance. IEEE Computer Society Press, Los Alamitos (1997)
51. Lakhotia, A., Gravley, J.: Toward experimental evaluation of subsystem classification recovery techniques. In: Working Conference on Reverse Engineering, pp. 262–271. IEEE Computer Society Press, Los Alamitos (1995)
52. Lindig, C., Snelting, G.: Assessing modular structure of legacy code based on mathematical concept analysis. In: International Conference on Software Engineering, pp. 349–359. IEEE Computer Society Press, Los Alamitos (1997)
53. Lung, C.H.: Software architecture recovery and restructuring through clustering techniques. In: Proceedings of the third international workshop on Software architecture, pp. 101–104. ACM Press, New York (1998)
54. Tzerpos, V., Holt, R.C.: Mojo: A distance metric for software clustering. In: Working Conference on Reverse Engineering, pp. 187–196. IEEE Computer Society Press, Los Alamitos (1999)
55. Mahdavi, K., Harman, M., Hierons, R.M.: A multiple hill climbing approach to software module clustering. In: International Conference on Software Maintenance, pp. 315–324. IEEE Computer Society Press, Los Alamitos (2003)
56. Mancoridis, S., Holt, R.C.: Recovering the structure of software systems using tube graph interconnection clustering. In: International Conference on Software Maintenance. IEEE Computer Society Press, Los Alamitos (1996)
57. Mancoridis, S., Mitchell, B., Rorres, C., Chen, Y., Gansner, E.: Using automatic clustering to produce high-level system organizations of source code. In: International Workshop on Program Comprehension. IEEE Computer Society Press, Los Alamitos (1998)
58. Maqbool, O., Babri, H.A.: The weighted combined algorithm: A linkage algorithm for software clustering. In: European Conference on Software Maintenance and Reengineering, pp. 15–24. IEEE Computer Society Press, Los Alamitos (2004)
59. Mitchell, B.S., Mancoridis, S.: Craft: A framework for evaluating software clustering results in the absence of benchmark decompositions. In: Working Conference on Reverse Engineering, pp. 93–102. IEEE Computer Society Press, Los Alamitos (2001)
60. Müller, H.A., Klashinsky, K.: Rigi—a system for programming-in-the-large. In: International Conference on Software Engineering, pp. 80–86. ACM Press, New York (1985)

61. Müller, H.A., Tilley, S.R., Orgun, M.A., Corrie, B.D., Madhavji, N.H.: A reverse engineering environment based on spatial and visual software interconnection models. In: Proceedings of the Fifth ACM SIGSOFT Symposium on Software development environments, pp. 88–98. ACM Press, New York (1992)

62. de Oca, C.M., Carver, D.L.: A visual representation model for software subsystem decomposition. In: Working Conference on Reverse Engineering. IEEE Computer Society Press, Los Alamitos (1998)

63. Rayside, D., Reuss, S., Hedges, E., Kontogiannis, K.: The effect of call graph construction algorithms for object-oriented programs on automatic clustering. In: International Workshop on Program Comprehension. IEEE Computer Society Press, Los Alamitos (2000)

64. Saeed, M., Maqbool, O., Babri, H., Hassan, S., Sarwar, S.: Software clustering techniques and the use of combined algorithm. In: European Conference on Software Maintenance and Reengineering, pp. 301–310. IEEE Computer Society Press, Los Alamitos (2003)

65. Sartipi, K., Kontogiannis, K., Mavaddat, F.: Architectural design recovery using data mining techniques. In: European Conference on Software Maintenance and Reengineering. IEEE Computer Society Press, Los Alamitos (2000)

66. Sartipi, K., Kontogiannis, K.: A graph pattern matching approach to software architecture recovery. In: International Conference on Software Maintenance, pp. 408–417. IEEE Computer Society Press, Los Alamitos (2001)

67. Sartipi, K., Kontogiannis, K.: On modeling software architecture recovery as graph matching. In: International Conference on Software Maintenance, pp. 224–234. IEEE Computer Society Press, Los Alamitos (2003)

68. Sartipi, K., Kontogiannis, K., Mavaddat, F.: A pattern matching framework for software architecture recovery and restructuring. In: International Workshop on Program Comprehension. IEEE Computer Society Press, Los Alamitos (2000)

69. Sartipi, K.: Alborz: A query-based tool for software architecture recovery. In: International Workshop on Program Comprehension, pp. 115–117. IEEE Computer Society Press, Los Alamitos (2001)

70. Schwanke, R.W.: An intelligent tool for re-engineering software modularity. In: International Conference on Software Engineering. ACM Press, New York (1992)

71. Shokoufandeh, A., Mancoridis, S., Maycock, M.: Applying spectral methods to software clustering. In: Working Conference on Reverse Engineering, pp. 3–12. IEEE Computer Society Press, Los Alamitos (2002)

72. Siff, M., Reps, T.: Identifying modules via concept analysis. In: International Conference on Software Maintenance, pp. 170–179. IEEE Computer Society Press, Los Alamitos (1997)

73. Siff, M., Reps, T.: Identifying modules via concept analysis. IEEE Computer Society Transactions on Software Engineering 25(6), 749–768 (1999)

74. Tonella, P.: Concept analysis for module restructuring. IEEE Computer Society Transactions on Software Engineering 27(4), 351–363 (2001)

75. Tzerpos, V., Holt, R.C.: On the stability of software clustering algorithms. In: International Workshop on Program Comprehension. IEEE Computer Society Press, Los Alamitos (2000)

76. Tzerpos, V.: The orphan adoption problem in architecture maintenance. In: Working Conference on Reverse Engineering. IEEE Computer Society Press, Los Alamitos (1997)

77. Wen, Z., Tzerpos, V.: An optimal algorithm for mojo distance. In: International Workshop on Program Comprehension, pp. 227–236. IEEE Computer Society Press, Los Alamitos (2003)

78. Abreu, F., Pereira, G., Sousa, P.: A coupling-guided cluster analysis approach to reengineer the modularity of object-oriented systems. In: European Conference on Software Maintenance and Reengineering. IEEE Computer Society Press, Los Alamitos (2000)

79. Gall, H., Klösch, R.: Finding objects in procedural programs: an alternative approach. In: Working Conference on Reverse Engineering, pp. 208–217. IEEE Computer Society Press, Los Alamitos (1995)

80. Han, M., Hofmeister, C., Nord, R.L.: Reconstructing software architecture for J2EE web applications. In: Working Conference on Reverse Engineering, pp. 67–76. IEEE Computer Society Press, Los Alamitos (2003)

81. Mendonca, N.C., Kramer, J.: Developing an approach for the recovery of distributed software architectures. In: International Workshop on Program Comprehension. IEEE Computer Society Press, Los Alamitos (1998)

82. Dekel, U., Gil, Y.: Revealing class structure with concept lattices. In: Working Conference on Reverse Engineering, pp. 353–362. IEEE Computer Society Press, Los Alamitos (2003)

83. Snelting, G., Tip, F.: Reengineering class hierarchies using concept analysis. In: Proceedings of the ACM SIGSOFT sixth international symposium on Foundations of software engineering, pp. 99–110. ACM Press, New York (1998)

84. Egyed, A.: Automated abstraction of class diagrams. ACM Transactions on Software Engineering and Methodology 11(4), 449–491 (2002)

85. Jackson, D., Waingold, A.: Lightweight extraction of object models from bytecode. In: International Conference on Software Engineering, pp. 194–202. ACM Press, New York (1999)

86. Jackson, D., Waingold, A.: Lightweight extraction of object models from bytecode. IEEE Computer Society Transactions on Software Engineering 27(2), 159–169 (2001)

87. Milanova, A., Rountev, A., Ryder, B.: Constructing precise object relation diagrams. In: International Conference on Software Maintenance, pp. 586–595. IEEE Computer Society Press, Los Alamitos (2002)

88. Richner, T., Ducasse, S.: Using dynamic information for the iterative recovery of collaborations and roles. In: International Conference on Software Maintenance, pp. 34–43. IEEE Computer Society Press, Los Alamitos (2002)

89. Richner, T., Ducasse, S.: Recovering high-level views of object-oriented applications from static and dynamic information. In: International Conference on Software Maintenance. IEEE Computer Society Press, Los Alamitos (1999)

90. Riva, C., Rodriguez, J.V.: Combining static and dynamic views for architecture reconstruction. In: European Conference on Software Maintenance and Reengineering, pp. 47–56. IEEE Computer Society Press, Los Alamitos (2002)

91. Subramaniam, G.V., Byrne, E.J.: Deriving an object model from legacy fortran code. In: International Conference on Software Maintenance. IEEE Computer Society Press, Los Alamitos (1996)

92. Tonella, P., Potrich, A.: Reverse engineering of the interaction diagrams from C++ code. In: International Conference on Software Maintenance, pp. 159–168. IEEE Computer Society Press, Los Alamitos (2003)

93. Yeh, D., Kuo, W.Y.: Reverse engineering aggregation relationship based on propagation of operations. In: European Conference on Software Maintenance and Reengineering, pp. 223–231. IEEE Computer Society Press, Los Alamitos (2002)

94. Mancoridis, S.: Toward a generic framework for computing subsystem interfaces. In: Joint Proceedings of the Second International Software Architecture Workshop (ISAW-2) and International Workshop on Multiple Perspectives in Software Development (Viewpoints 1996) on SIGSOFT 1996 Workshops, pp. 106–110. ACM Press, New York (1996)

95. Whaley, J., Martin, M.C., Lam, M.S.: Automatic extraction of object-oriented component interfaces. In: Proceedings of the International Symposium on Software Testing and Analysis (July 2002)

96. Viljamaa, J.: Reverse engineering framework reuse interfaces. In: Proceedings of the 9th European Software Engineering Conference held jointly with 10th ACM SIGSOFT International Symposium on Foundations of Software Engineering, pp. 217–226. ACM Press, New York (2003)

97. Antoniol, G., Fiutem, R., Cristoforetti, L.: Design pattern recovery in object-oriented software. In: International Workshop on Program Comprehension. IEEE Computer Society Press, Los Alamitos (1998)

98. Asencio, A., Cardman, S., Harris, D., Laderman, E.: Relating expectations to automatically recovered design patterns. In: Working Conference on Reverse Engineering, pp. 87–96. IEEE Computer Society Press, Los Alamitos (2002)

99. Balanyi, Z., Ferenc, R.: Mining design patterns from C++ source code. In: International Conference on Software Maintenance, pp. 305–314. IEEE Computer Society Press, Los Alamitos (2003)

100. Heuzeroth, D., Holl, T., Högström, G., Löwe, W.: Automatic design pattern detection. In: International Workshop on Program Comprehension, pp. 94–103. IEEE Computer Society Press, Los Alamitos (2003)

101. Keller, R.K., Schauer, R., Robitaille, S., Page, P.: Pattern-based reverse-engineering of design components. In: International Conference on Software Engineering, pp. 226–235. ACM Press, New York (1999)

102. Kramer, C., Prechelt, L.: Design recovery by automated search for structural design patterns in object-oriented software. In: Working Conference on Reverse Engineering. IEEE Computer Society Press, Los Alamitos (1996)

103. Michail, A.: Data mining library reuse patterns using generalized association rules. In: International Conference on Software Engineering, pp. 167–176. ACM Press, New York (2000)

104. Niere, J., Schäfer, W., Wadsack, J.P., Wendehals, L., Welsh, J.: Towards pattern-based design recovery. In: International Conference on Software Engineering, pp. 338–348. ACM Press, New York (2002)

105. Niere, J., Wadsack, J.P., Wendehals, L.: Handling large search space in pattern-based reverse engineering. In: International Workshop on Program Comprehension, pp. 274–283. IEEE Computer Society Press, Los Alamitos (2003)

106. Seemann, J., von Gudenberg, J.W.: Pattern-based design recovery of java software. In: Proceedings of the ACM SIGSOFT sixth international symposium on Foundations of software engineering, pp. 10–16. ACM Press, New York (1998)

107. Tonella, P., Antoniol, G.: Object oriented design pattern inference. In: International Conference on Software Maintenance. IEEE Computer Society Press, Los Alamitos (1999)

108. Tonella, P., Antoniol, G.: Inference of object-oriented design patterns. Journal of Software Maintenance and Evolution: Research and Practice 13(5), 309–330 (2001)

109. Aldrich, J., Chambers, C., Notkin, D.: Archjava: Connecting software architecture to implementation. In: International Conference on Software Engineering, pp. 187–196. ACM Press, New York (2002)

110. Gannod, G.C., Murthy, S.: Verification of recovered software architectures. In: International Workshop on Program Comprehension, pp. 258–267. IEEE Computer Society Press, Los Alamitos (2003)
111. Koschke, R., Simon, D.: Hierarchical reflexion models. In: Working Conference on Reverse Engineering, pp. 36–45. IEEE Computer Society Press, Los Alamitos (2003)
112. Murphy, G.C., Notkin, D., Sullivan, K.: Software reflexion models: Bridging the gap between source and high-level models. In: Proceedings of the Third ACM SIGSOFT Symposium on the Foundations of Software Engineering, pp. 18–28. ACM Press, New York (1995)
113. Murphy, G.C., Notkin, D., Sullivan, K.J.: Software reflexion models: Bridging the gap between design and implementation. IEEE Computer Society Transactions on Software Engineering 27(4) (April 2001)
114. Rötschke, T., Krikhaar, R.: Architecture analysis tools to support evolution of large industrial systems. In: International Conference on Software Maintenance, pp. 182–191. IEEE Computer Society Press, Los Alamitos (2002)
115. Tvedt, R., Costa, P., Lindvall, M.: Does the code match the design? a process for architecture evaluation. In: International Conference on Software Maintenance, pp. 393–403. IEEE Computer Society Press, Los Alamitos (2002)
116. Chan, K., Liang, Z.C.L., Michail, A.: Design recovery of interactive graphical applications. In: International Conference on Software Engineering, pp. 114–124. ACM Press, New York (2003)
117. Chen, K., Rajlich, V.: Case study of feature location using dependence graph. In: International Workshop on Program Comprehension. IEEE Computer Society Press, Los Alamitos (2000)
118. Deprez, J.C., Lakhotia, A.: A formalism to automate mapping from program features to code. In: International Workshop on Program Comprehension. IEEE Computer Society Press, Los Alamitos (2000)
119. Egyed, A.: A scenario-driven approach to traceability. In: International Conference on Software Engineering, pp. 123–132. ACM Press, New York (2001)
120. Eisenbarth, T., Koschke, R., Simon, D.: Derivation of feature component maps by means of concept analysis. In: European Conference on Software Maintenance and Reengineering, pp. 176–180. IEEE Computer Society Press, Los Alamitos (2001)
121. Eisenbarth, T., Koschke, R., Simon, D.: Aiding program comprehension by static and dynamic feature analysis. In: International Conference on Software Maintenance, pp. 602–611. IEEE Computer Society Press, Los Alamitos (2001)
122. Eisenbarth, T., Koschke, R., Simon, D.: Incremental location of combined features for large-scale programs. In: International Conference on Software Maintenance, pp. 273–282. IEEE Computer Society Press, Los Alamitos (2002)
123. Eisenbarth, T., Koschke, R., Simon, D.: Feature-driven program understanding using concept analysis of execution traces. In: International Workshop on Program Comprehension, pp. 300–309. IEEE Computer Society Press, Los Alamitos (2001)
124. Eisenbarth, T., Koschke, R., Simon, D.: Locating features in source code. IEEE Computer Society Transactions on Software Engineering 29(3) (2003)
125. Lukoit, K., Wilde, N., Stowell, S., Hennessey, T.: Tracegraph: Immediate visual location of software features. In: International Conference on Software Maintenance. IEEE Computer Society Press, Los Alamitos (2000)
126. Marcus, A., Maletic, J.I.: Recovering documentation-to-source-code traceability links using latent semantic indexing. In: International Conference on Software Engineering, pp. 125–134. IEEE Computer Society Press, Los Alamitos (2003)

127. Murphy, G.C., Lai, A., Walker, R.J., Robillard, M.P.: Separating features in source code: An exploratory study. In: International Conference on Software Engineering, pp. 275–284. ACM Press, New York (2001)

128. Pashov, I., Riebisch, M., Philippow, I.: Supporting architectural restructuring by analyzing feature models. In: European Conference on Software Maintenance and Reengineering, pp. 25–34. IEEE Computer Society Press, Los Alamitos (2004)

129. Wilde, N., Scully, M.: Software reconnaissance: Mapping from features to code. Journal on Software Maintenance and Evolution 7, 49–62 (1995)

130. Wilde, N., Buckellew, M., Page, H., Rajlich, V.: A case study of feature location in unstructured legacy fortran code. In: European Conference on Software Maintenance and Reengineering, pp. 68–77. IEEE Computer Society Press, Los Alamitos (2001)

131. Zhao, W., Zhang, L., Liu, Y., Sun, J., Yang, F.: Sniafl: Towards a static non-interactive approach to feature location. In: International Conference on Software Engineering, pp. 293–303. IEEE Computer Society Press, Los Alamitos (2004)

132. Lucca, G.A.D., Fasolino, A.R., Carlini, U.D.: Recovering use case models from object-oriented code: A thread-based approach. In: Working Conference on Reverse Engineering. IEEE Computer Society Press, Los Alamitos (2000)

133. El-Ramly, M., Stroulia, E., Sorenson, P.: Mining system-user interaction traces for use case models. In: International Workshop on Program Comprehension, pp. 21–30. IEEE Computer Society Press, Los Alamitos (2002)

134. Krone, M., Snelting, G.: On the inference of configuration structures from source code. In: International Conference on Software Engineering, pp. 49–57. ACM Press, New York (1994)

135. Snelting, G.: Reengineering of configurations based on mathematical concept analysis. ACM Transactions on Software Engineering and Methodology 5(2), 146–189 (1996)

136. Eisenbarth, T., Koschke, R., Vogel, G.: Static object trace extraction for programs with pointers. Journals of Systems and Software (2005)

137. Eisenbarth, T., Koschke, R., Vogel, G.: Static trace extraction. In: Working Conference on Reverse Engineering. IEEE Computer Society Press, Los Alamitos (2002)

138. Ivkovic, I., Godfrey, M.W.: Architecture recovery of dynamically linked applications: A case study. In: International Workshop on Program Comprehension, pp. 178–184. IEEE Computer Society Press, Los Alamitos (2002)

139. Marburger, A., Herzberg, D.: E-cares research project: Understanding complex legacy telecommunication systems. In: European Conference on Software Maintenance and Reengineering, pp. 139–147. IEEE Computer Society Press, Los Alamitos (2001)

140. Moe, J., Carr, D.A.: Understanding distributed systems via execution trace data. In: International Workshop on Program Comprehension, pp. 60–69. IEEE Computer Society Press, Los Alamitos (2001)

141. Chase, M.P., Christey, S.M., Harris, D.R., Yeh, A.S.: Recovering software architecture from multiple source code analyses. In: Program Analysis for Software Technology, pp. 43–50. ACM Press, New York (1998)

142. Chase, M.P., Christey, S.M., Harris, D.R., Yeh, A.S.: Managing recovered function and structure of legacy software components. In: Working Conference on Reverse Engineering. IEEE Computer Society Press, Los Alamitos (1998)

143. Fiutem, R., Tonella, P., Antoniol, G., Merlo, E.: A cliche-based environment to support architectural reverse engineering. In: International Conference on Software Maintenance. IEEE Computer Society Press, Los Alamitos (1996)

144. Harris, R., Reubenstein, H.B., Yeh, A.S.: Reverse engineering to the architectural level. In: International Conference on Software Engineering, pp. 186–195. ACM Press, New York (1995)

145. Harris, D., Reubenstein, H., Yeh, A.: Recognizers for extracting architectural features from source code. In: Working Conference on Reverse Engineering, pp. 252–261. IEEE Computer Society Press, Los Alamitos (1996)

146. Holtzblatt, L., Piazza, R., Reubenstein, H., Roberts, S., Harris, D.: Design recovery for distributed systems. IEEE Computer Society Transactions on Software Engineering 23(7), 461–472 (1997)

147. Pinzger, M., Gall, H.: Pattern-supported architecture recovery. In: International Workshop on Program Comprehension, pp. 53–62. IEEE Computer Society Press, Los Alamitos (2002)

148. Tonella, P., Fiutem, R., Antoniol, G., Merlo, E.: Augmenting pattern-based architectural recovery with flow analysis: Mosaic—a case study. In: Working Conference on Reverse Engineering. IEEE Computer Society Press, Los Alamitos (1996)

149. De Pauw, W., Jensen, E., Mitchell, N., Sevitsky, G., Vlissides, J., Yang, J.: Visualizing the execution of java programs. In: Diehl, S. (ed.) Dagstuhl Seminar 2001. LNCS, vol. 2269, pp. 151–162. Springer, Heidelberg (2002)

150. Briand, L., Labiche, Y., Miao, Y.: Towards the reverse engineering of uml sequence diagrams. In: Working Conference on Reverse Engineering, pp. 57–66. IEEE Computer Society Press, Los Alamitos (2003)

151. Jerding, D.F., Stasko, J.T., Ball, T.: Visualizing interactions in program executions. In: International Conference on Software Engineering, pp. 360–370. IEEE Computer Society Press, Los Alamitos (1997)

152. Jerding, D., Rugaber, S.: Using visualization for architectural localization and extraction. In: Working Conference on Reverse Engineering. IEEE Computer Society Press, Los Alamitos (1997)

153. Kollmann, R., Gogolla, M.: Capturing dynamic program behaviour with UML collaboration diagrams. In: European Conference on Software Maintenance and Reengineering, pp. 58–67. IEEE Computer Society Press, Los Alamitos (2001)

154. Krikhaar, R., Feijs, L., de Jong, R., Medema, J.: Architecture comprehension tools for a PBX system. In: European Conference on Software Maintenance and Reengineering. IEEE Computer Society Press, Los Alamitos (1999)

155. Systä, T., Koskimies, K., Müller, H.: Shimba—an environment for reverse engineering java software systems. Software—Practice and Experience 31(4), 371–394 (2001)

156. Systä, T.: Understanding the behavior of java programs. In: Working Conference on Reverse Engineering, pp. 214–223. IEEE Computer Society Press, Los Alamitos (2000)

157. Systä, T.: On the Relationships between Static and Dynamic Models in Reverse Engineering Java Software. In: Proceedings of the 6th Working Conference on Reverse Engineering, Atlanta, GA, USA, pp. 304–313. IEEE Computer Society Press, Los Alamitos (1999)

158. Souder, T., Mancoridis, S., Salah, M.: Form: A framework for creating views of program executions. In: International Conference on Software Maintenance, pp. 612–621. IEEE Computer Society Press, Los Alamitos (2001)

159. Yan, H., Garlan, D., Schmerl, B., Rich, J.A., Kazman, R.: Discotect: A system for discovering architectures from running systems. In: International Conference on Software Engineering, pp. 470–479. ACM Press, New York (2004)

160. Wu, J., Hassan, A.E., Holt, R.C.: Using graph patterns to extract scenarios. In: International Workshop on Program Comprehension, pp. 239–248. IEEE Computer Society Press, Los Alamitos (2002)
161. Biggerstaff, T.J., Mitbander, B.G., Webster, D.: The concept assignment problem in program understanding. In: International Conference on Software Engineering, pp. 482–498. ACM Press, New York (1993)
162. Gall, H., Jazayeri, M., Klösch, R., Lugmayr, W., Trausmuth, G.: Architecture recovery in ares. In: Joint Proceedings of the Second International Software Architecture Workshop (ISAW-2) and International Workshop on Multiple Perspectives in Software Development (Viewpoints 1996) on SIGSOFT 1996 Workshops, pp. 111–115. ACM Press, New York (1996)
163. Bowman, I.T., Holt, R.C.: Reconstructing ownership architectures to help understand software systems. In: International Workshop on Program Comprehension. IEEE Computer Society Press, Los Alamitos (1999)
164. Tu, Q., Godfrey, M.W.: The build-time software architecture view. In: International Conference on Software Maintenance, pp. 398–407. IEEE Computer Society Press, Los Alamitos (2001)
165. Chase, M.P., Harris, D.R., Roberts, S.N., Yeh, A.S.: Analysis and presentation of recovered software architectures. In: Working Conference on Reverse Engineering. IEEE Computer Society Press, Los Alamitos (1996)
166. Issarny, V., Saridakis, T., Zarras, A.: Multi-view description of software architectures. In: ISAW 1998, Proceedings of the Third International Workshop on Software Architecture, pp. 81–84 (1998)
167. Kazman, R., Carriere, S.J.: View extraction and view fusion in architectural understanding. In: Proceedings of the Fifth Internation Conference on Software Reuse. IEEE Computer Society Press, Los Alamitos (1998)
168. Waters, R., Abowd, G.D.: Architectural synthesis: Integrating multiple architectural perspectives. In: Working Conference on Reverse Engineering. IEEE Computer Society Press, Los Alamitos (1999)
169. Yeh, A.S., Harris, D.R., Chase, M.P.: Manipulating recovered software architecture views. In: International Conference on Software Engineering, pp. 184–194. ACM Press, New York (1997)
170. Canfora, G., Cimitile, A., Munro, M., Taylor, C.J.: Extracting abstract data types from C programs: A case study. In: International Conference on Software Maintenance, pp. 200–209. IEEE Computer Society Press, Los Alamitos (1993)
171. Canfora, G., Cimitile, A., Munro, M.: An improved algorithm for identifying objects in code. Journal of Software Practice and Experience 26(1), 25–48 (1996)
172. Canfora, G., Cimitile, A., Lucia, A.D., Lucca, G.A.D.: A case study of applying an eclectic approach to identify objects in code. In: International Workshop on Program Comprehension, pp. 136–143. IEEE Computer Society Press, Los Alamitos (1999)
173. Choi, S., Scacchi, W.: Extracting and restructuring the design of large systems. IEEE Software 7(1), 66–71 (1990)
174. Belady, L.A., Evangelisti, C.J.: System partitioning and its measure. Journal of Systems and Software 2(1), 23–29 (1982)
175. Graudejus, H.: Implementing a concept analysis tool for identifying abstract data types in C code. Diplomarbeit, University of Kaiserslautern, Germany (1998)
176. Hutchens, D.H., Basili, V.R.: System structure analysis: Clustering with data bindings. IEEE Computer Society Transactions on Software Engineering 11(8), 749–757 (1985)

177. Liu, S.S., Wilde, N.: Identifying objects in a conventional procedural language: An example of data design recovery. In: International Conference on Software Maintenance, pp. 266–271. IEEE Computer Society Press, Los Alamitos (1990)
178. Livadas, P., Johnson, T.: A new approach to finding objects in programs. Journal on Software Maintenance and Evolution 6, 249–260 (1994)
179. Ogando, R.M., Yau, S.S., Wilde, N.: An object finder for program structure understanding in software maintenance. Journal on Software Maintenance and Evolution 6(5), 261–283 (1994)
180. Patel, S., Chu, W., Baxter, R.: A measure for composite module cohesion. In: International Conference on Software Engineering, pp. 38–48. ACM Press, New York (1992)
181. Sahraoui, H., Melo, W., Lounis, H., Dumont, F.: Applying concept formation methods to object identfication in procedural code. In: International Conference on Automated Software Engineering, pp. 210–218. IEEE Computer Society Press, Los Alamitos (1997)
182. Valasareddi, R.R., Carver, D.L.: A graph-based object identification process for procedural programs. In: Working Conference on Reverse Engineering, pp. 50–58. IEEE Computer Society Press, Los Alamitos (1998)
183. Weidl, J., Gall, H.: Binding object models to source code: An approach to object-oriented re-architecturing. In: Proc. of the 22nd Computer Software and Applications Conference. IEEE Computer Society Press, Los Alamitos (1998)
184. Yeh, A.S., Harris, D., Reubenstein, H.: Recovering abstract data types and object instances from a conventional procedural language. In: Working Conference on Reverse Engineering, pp. 227–236. IEEE Computer Society Press, Los Alamitos (1995)
185. Cimitile, A., Visaggio, G.: Software salvaging and the call dominance tree. Journal of Systems and Software 28, 117–127 (1995)
186. Schwanke, R.W., Hanson, S.J.: Using neural networks to modularize software. Machine Learning 15, 136–168 (1994)
187. Girard, J.F., Koschke, R., Schied, G.: A metric-based approach to detect abstract data types and state encapsulations. In: International Conference on Automated Software Engineering. IEEE Computer Society Press, Los Alamitos (1997)
188. Girard, J.F., Koschke, R., Schied, G.: A metric-based approach to detect abstract data types and state encapsulations. Journal on Automated Software Engineering 6(4) (1999)
189. Koschke, R.: Atomic Architectural Component Recovery for Program Understanding and Evolution. Ph.d. thesis, University of Stuttgart (October 1999), http://www.iste.uni-stuttgart.de/ps/rainer/thesis
190. Girard, J.F., Koschke, R.: A comparison of abstract data type and objects recovery techniques. Journal Science of Computer Programming 6(2–3), 149–181 (2000)
191. Whaley, J., Martin, M.C., Lam, M.S.: Automatic extraction of object-oriented component interfaces. In: Proceedings of the International Symposium on Software Testing and Analysis (July 2002)
192. Murphy, G.C., Notkin, D.: Reengineering with reflexion models: A case study. IEEE Computer 30(8), 29–36 (1997)
193. Christl, A., Koschke, R., Storey, M.A.: Equipping the reflexion method with automated clustering. In: Working Conference on Reverse Engineering, pp. 89–98. IEEE Computer Society Press, Los Alamitos (2005)
194. Christl, A., Koschke, R., Storey, M.A.: Automated clustering to support the reflexion method 49(3), 255–274 (2007)

195. Frenzel, P., Koschke, R., Breu, A.P.J., Angstmann, K.: Extending the reflection method for consolidating software variants into product lines. In: Working Conference on Reverse Engineering, pp. 160–169. IEEE Computer Society Press, Los Alamitos (2007)
196. Kuhn, A., Greevy, O.: Exploiting the analogy between traces and signal processing. In: International Conference on Software Maintenance. IEEE Computer Society Press, Los Alamitos (2006)
197. Greevy, O.: Enriching Reverse Engineering through Feature Analysis. Ph.d. thesis, University of Berne, Switzerland, Software Composition Group (May 2007)
198. Koschke, R., Quante, J.: On dynamic feature location. In: International Conference on Automated Software Engineering, pp. 86–95. ACM Press, New York (2005)

Collaboration in Distributed Software Development

Filippo Lanubile

Dipartimento di Informatica, University of Bari
Via Orabona 4, 70126 Bari, Italy
lanubile@di.uniba.it

Abstract. Software development is an intense collaborative process where success depends on the ability to create, share and integrate information. Given the trend towards globalization in the software development industry, distance creates an additional challenge to development processes, as fewer opportunities for rich interaction and lower frequencies of direct communication. The chapter introduces a taxonomy of software engineering tools for distributed projects and presents collaborative development environments, ranging from classic platforms for dispersed developers in open source software projects to modern environments for flexible and distributed processes. Moreover, it introduces computer-mediated communication theories which reveal some patterns of tool usage to overcome the challenges of distance. Building upon the theoretical background of media selection, the chapter summarizes research activities aimed to build an evidence-based model of task-technology fit for communication-intensive activities such as distributed requirements workshops.

Keywords: Distributed software development, global software development, computer-supported cooperative work, collaborative development environments.

1 Introduction

Working across distances has become commonplace for software projects today. Nevertheless, distance creates an additional challenge to development processes, because of fewer opportunities for rich interaction and lower frequencies of direct communication [27].

In order to support collaborative work on their projects, software engineers communicate both directly, through meetings and informal conversations, and indirectly, by means of software artifacts. Adequate tool support is paramount to enable collaboration in distributed software development. However, most work in collaborative environments for distributed development has focused on code-specific tasks rather than on other software engineering activities at a higher level of abstraction like requirements engineering or software design [35].

This chapter focuses on requirements engineering as an appropriate domain for studying distributed engineering teams. In fact requirements engineering is essentially a collaborative endeavor which involves a large pool of stakeholders processing significant amount of information about the problem domain and solution space. Hence requirements engineering involves a complex set of communication-intensive tasks

A. De Lucia and F. Ferrucci (Eds.): ISSSE 2006–2008, LNCS 5413, pp. 174–193, 2009.

that are significantly affected by the stakeholders' geographical distribution which impedes collocated meetings. Videoconferencing is generally considered the first choice communication medium to conduct requirements workshops between remote stakeholders. However, while videoconferencing sessions come with an additional overhead (e.g., the costs of infrastructure setup and maintenance), even when everything runs smoothly, it is still hard to conduct a long-running and productive discussion during a videoconference, especially when more than a few people are involved.

There is a need to further our knowledge of what is the most appropriate collaboration toolset to achieve a shared understanding among distributed project stakeholders. Distributed software development thus can benefit from an interdisciplinary approach in which the research areas of software engineering and computer-supported cooperative work (CSCW) converge.

This chapter is organized as follows. In Section 2 we provide first the motivation for distributed software development and then we introduce the challenges which rise from the negative effects of distance. Section 3 introduces a taxonomy of software engineering tools for distributed projects and presents collaborative development environments, ranging from classic platforms for dispersed developers in open source software projects to modern environments for flexible and distributed processes. Next, in Section 4 we present computer-mediated communication (CMC) theories from the field CSCW. Building upon the theoretical background of media selection, Section 5 summarizes our research activities aimed to build an evidence-based model of task-technology fit for communication-intensive activities such as distributed requirements workshops. The chapter concludes with a brief summary and some remarks.

2 Distributed Software Development

Distributed software development (DSD; or GSD for global software development; or GSE for global software engineering) means splitting the development of the same product or service among globally distributed sites.

In his seminal book [6], Erran Carmel lists the six main 'catalyst' factors, or potential benefits, which have driven to distributed software development.

Mergers and acquisitions. The global demand for software products and services that began in the 80s lead to a rush for mergers and acquisitions, as ICT firms strived to penetrate new markets and adjust or complement their products lines. As a result, software teams, no longer independent but yet in their own sites, are forced to collaborate as an overall global software team.

Position as global organizations. Software firms also began in the 80s to position themselves as 'global players,' to increase business opportunities with other global organizations that prefer comprehensive software suppliers for all their global subsidiaries rather than an heterogeneous network of vendors in different countries.

Increase proximity to the market. The business advantages of proximity to the market includes knowledge of customers and local conditions, such as localization, customization, and after-sale services, as well as the goodwill engendered by local investments such as a favorable tax treatment from governments.

Access the most talented developers. The quality of the programmers is mentioned as the most important factor in software work [25]. This statement is supported by multiple sources of empirical evidence other than common wisdom. The implication is that organizations that want to deploy market-winning software products have to hire the most talented developers throughout the world, regardless of their geographical location.

Reduce development costs. Software companies in high-cost countries try to reduce development costs by outsourcing development work to programmers in low-cost countries (e.g., India, China, Brazil, and East Europe). Most managers mention cost reduction by offshoring (i.e., global outsourcing to contracting staff located offshore) as the first driving factor for GSD.

Reduce time to market. Since programmers are scattered across multiple sites, dispersion allows for 'round-the-clock', or 'follow-the-sun', development, which has the potential to permit the reduction of development cycles by increasing the amount of time in a day that software is being developed. However, there are very few studies on the effects of time separation [21] and then the benefits of follow-the-sun development are more a claim than a fact based on empirical evidence.

In spite of the benefits described above, the success of a globally distributed project is not guaranteed by just opening a development center in another region of the world [17]. Developing software as a team is a challenging task, but developing as a global software team is even more challenging due to distance [26]. Distance has an impact on the three main forms of cooperation within a team [7]: communication coordination, and control. *Communication* is the exchange between the members of information, whether formal or informal, occurring in planned or impromptu interaction. *Coordination* is that act of orchestrating each task and organizational unit, so that they all contribute to the overall objective. *Control* is the process of adhering to goals, policies, standards or quality levels, set either formally (e.g., formal meetings, plans, guidelines) or informally (e.g., team culture, peer pressure). Distributed teams create further burdens on communication, coordination and control mechanisms, primarily the informal ones.

Because of distance, people cannot coordinate and control by just visiting the other team members. The absence of management-by-walking can result in coordination and control issues, like misalignment and rework. When control and coordination needs of distributed software teams rise, so does the load on all communication channels available. In fact, software projects have two complementary communication needs. First, the more formal, official communications is used for crucial tasks like updating project status, escalating project issues, and determining who has responsibility for particular work products. Secondly, informal 'corridor talk' allows team members to keep a 'peripheral awareness' of what is going on around them, what other people are working on, what states the various parts of the project are in, and many other essential pieces of background information that enable developers to work together efficiently. In collocated settings, communication is taken for granted and then, its importance often goes unnoticed. When developers are not located together, they have much less opportunities of communication. There is empirical evidence that the frequency of communication drops off with the physical separation among developers' sites [27]. As Fig. 1 shows, distance exacerbates coordination and control problems directly or indirectly through its negative effects on communication. In other words, communication disruption due to distance further increases and aggravates coordination and control breakdowns [7].

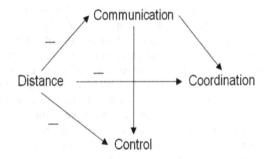

Fig. 1. Impact of distance on distributed software development (from [7])

Table 1. GSD threats and dimensions of distance (adapted from [1])

	Temporal Distance	Geographical Distance	Sociocultural Distance
Communication	- Reduced opportunities for synchronous communication	- Face-to-face meetings difficult	- Cultural misunderstandings
Coordination	- Typically increased coordination costs	- Reduced informal contact can lead to lack of critical task awareness	- Inconsistent work practices can impinge on effective coordination - Reduced cooperation arising from misunderstandings
Control	- Management of project artifacts may be subject to delays	- Difficult to convey vision and strategy - Perceived threat from training low-cost "rivals"	- Different perceptions of authority can undermine morale - Managers must adapt to local regulations

Table 1 summarizes the impact of the three dimensions of distance: geographical, temporal, and socio-cultural. *Geographical distance* is a measure of the spatial dispersion, occurring when team members are scattered across different sites. It can be operationalized as the cost or effort required to exchange visits from one site to another. *Temporal distance* is a measure of the temporal dispersion, occurring when team members wishing to interact. It can be caused by time-zone differences or just time shifting work patterns (e.g., one site having a quick lunch break at noon and another site a two-hour lunch time at 1:00 pm). *Socio-cultural distance* is a measure of the effort required by team members to understand the organizational and national cultures (e.g., norms, practices, values, spoken languages) in remote sites.

3 Collaboration Tools and Environments

Tools provide a considerable help to software development activities. Software engineering tools to assist distributed projects may fall into the following categories:

Software Configuration management. A software configuration management (SCM) tool includes the ability to manage change in a controlled manner, by checking components in and out of a repository, and the evolution of software products, by storing multiple versions of components, and producing specified versions on command. SCM tools also provide a good way to share software artifacts with other team members in a controlled manner. Rather than just using a directory to exchange files with other people, with an SCM tool developers can make sure that interdependent files are changed together and control who is allowed to make changes. Further, SCM tools make it possible to save messages about what changed and why. Open-source SCM tools, such as Subversion and its predecessor CVS, have become indispensable tools for coordinating the interaction of distributed developers.

Bug and change tracking. This function is centered around a database, accessible by all team members through a web-based interface. Other than an identifier and a description, a recorded bug includes information about who found it, the steps to reproduce it, who has been assigned on it, which releases the bug exists in and it has been fixed in. Bug tracking systems also define a life cycle for bugs to help team members to track the resolution of defects. Fig. 2 shows the life cycle of a defect in Bugzilla [3], the bug tracking system originally developed and used by the Mozilla project. Trackers are a generalization of bug tracking systems to include the management of other issues such as feature requests, support requests, or patches.

Build and release management. It allows projects to create and schedule workflows that execute build scripts, compile binaries, invoke test frameworks, deploy to production systems and send email notifications to developers. The larger the project, the greater the need for automating the build and release function. Build and release management tools can also provide a web-based dashboard to view the status of current and past builds (see Fig. 3). Build tools, such as CruiseControl and its ancestor like the UNIX make utility, are essential tools to perform Continuous Integration [22], an agile development practice which allows developers to integrate daily thus reducing integration problems.

Product and process modeling. This function encompasses the core features of what was called Computer Aided Software Engineering (CASE), from requirements management to visual modeling of both software artifacts and customized software processes. Collaboration in software development tends to be around the creation of formal or semiformal software artifacts. According to [38], model-based collaboration is what distinguishes software engineering collaboration from more general collaboration activities which lack the focus on using the models to create shared meanings.

Knowledge center. This function is mostly document-driven and web-enabled, and allows team members to share explicit knowledge across a work unit. A knowledge center includes technical references, standards, frequently asked questions (FAQs) and best practices. Recently wiki software for collaborative web publishing has emerged as a practical and economical option to consider for creating and maintaining group documentation. Wikis are particularly valuable in distributed projects as global teams may use them to organize, track, and publish their work [30]. Fig. 4 shows the home page of the Fedora project wiki where both developers and users may contribute other than find information. Knowledge centers may also include sophisticated knowledge management activities to acquire tacit knowledge in explicit forms, such as expert identification and skills management [34].

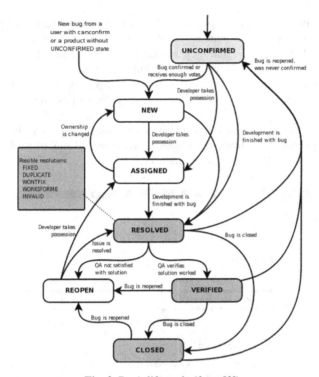

Fig. 2. Bug's life cycle (from [3])

Fig. 3. Project build information within a dashboard (from [12])

Communication tools. Software engineers have adopted a wide range of mainstream communication technologies for project use in addition or replacement of communicating face-to-face by speech. Asynchronous communication tools include email, mailing lists, newsgroups, web forums and, more recently blogs; synchronous tools include the classic telephone and conference calls, chat, instant messaging, voice over IP, and videoconferencing. Email is the most-widely used and successful collaborative application. Thanks to its flexibility and ease of use, email can support conversations, but also operate as a task/contact manager. However, one of the drawbacks of email is that, due to its success, people tend to use email for a variety of purposes and often in a quasi-synchronous manner. In addition, email is 'socially blind' [20] in that it does not enable users to signal their availability. Nevertheless, before becoming an indispensable tool ubiquitous in every workplace, email was initially used by the niche of research community and opposed by management. Currently, chat and instant messaging are following a similar evolution path. At first mostly used by young people for exchanging 'social' messages, these synchronous tools have been recently spreading more and more in the workplace. While email is socially blind, these tools, in contrast, provide a lightweight means to ascertain availability of remote team members and contact them in a timely manner.

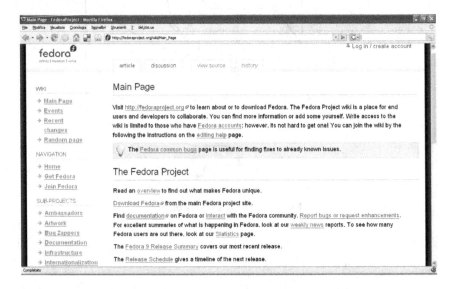

Fig. 4. Fedora Project documentation based on wiki

General communication tools (i.e., non software engineering specific) fall in the category of 'groupware' which refers to the class of applications that support groups of people engaged in performing a common task [19]. However, the term groupware is nowadays almost disused in favor of preferred wordings such as 'collaborative software', 'social software,' or 'Web 2.0' [32] which also include systems used outside the workplace (e.g., blogs, wikis, instant messaging).

Interoperability and a familiar user interface provide strong motivations to integrate task-specific solutions and generic groupware into collaborative development environments (CDE). A *CDE* provides a project workspace with a standardized toolset to be used by the global software team. Earliest CDE were developed within open source software (OSS) projects because OSS projects, from the beginning, have been composed of dispersed individuals. Today a number of CDE are available as commercial products, open source initiatives or research prototypes to enable distributed software development.

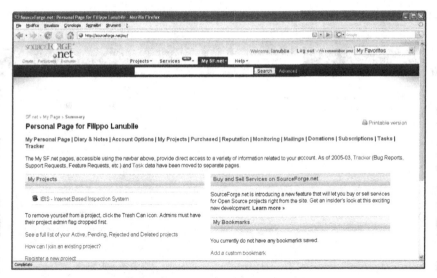

Fig. 5. Personal SourceForge portal

SourceForge, from CollabNet, is the most popular CDE with over 170.000 hosted projects and 1.800.000 registered users [11]. The original mission of SourceForge was to enrich the open source community by providing a centralized place for developers to control and manage OSS projects. SourceForge offers a variety of free services: web interface for project administration, space for web content and scripts, trackers (for reporting bugs, submitting support requests or patches to review, and posting feature requests), mailing lists and discussion forums, download notification of new releases, shell functions and compile farm, and CVS-based as well as Subversion-based configuration management. Fig. 5 shows the personal page of the author which provides access to a standard toolset which can be used on every project. The commercial versions for corporate use, called SourceForge Enterprise Edition and CollabNet Enterprise Edition, add features for tracking, measuring and reporting on software project activities.

GForge [24] is a fork of the 2.61 SourceForge.net project. It has been downloaded and configured as in-house server by many industrial and academic organizations (see Fig. 6 from [10]. Like SourceForge it also offers a commercial version, called GForge Advanced Server.

Trac [18] provides an integrated wiki, an issue tracking system and a front-end interface to SCM tools, usually Subversion. Project overview and progress tracking is allowed by setting a roadmap of milestones, which include a set of so-called "tickets" (i.e., tasks, feature requests, bug reports and support issues), and by viewing the timeline of changes. Trac also allows team members to be notified about project events and ticket changes through email messages and RSS feeds. Fig. 7 shows a screenshot of a research project at University of Bari with active tickets grouped by milestone and colored to indicate different priorities.

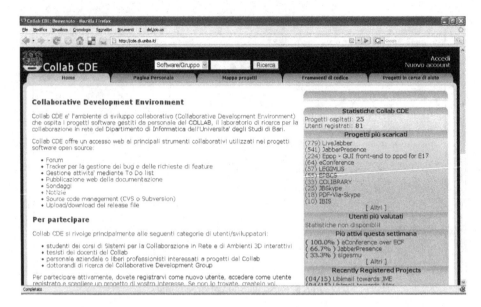

Fig. 6. A GForge-based CDE

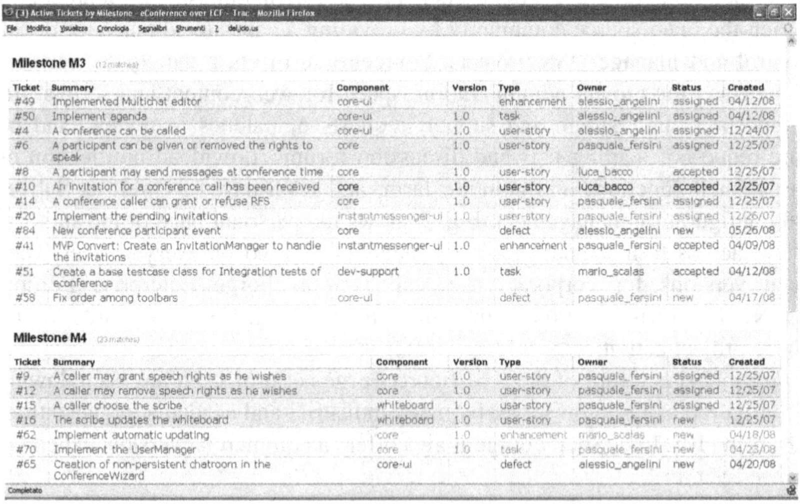

Fig. 7. Active tickets in Trac grouped by milestone

ADAMS is a CDE developed at University of Salerno [15]. ADAMS puts a great emphasis on creating and storing traceability links among software artifacts for the purpose of impact analysis and change management during software evolution. Events concerning changes to an artifact are automatically propagated along traceability links to other artifacts which have been impacted directly or indirectly by the change, and then to developers who have been assigned the responsibility of those artifacts.

Jazz [23] is an extensible platform which leverages the Eclipse's notion of plug-ins to build specific CDE products like the IBM Rational Team Concert. The present version has a wide-ranging scope but in the former version of Jazz [8, 28] the goal was to integrate synchronous communication and reciprocal awareness of coding tasks into the Eclipse IDE. The development of Jazz has been inspired to the Booch and Brown's vision of a "frictionless surface" for development [2], which was motivated by the observation that much of the developers' effort is wasted in switching back and forth between different applications to communicate and work together. According to this vision, collaborative features should be available as components that extend core applications (e.g., the IDE), thus increasing the users' comfort and productivity. Fig. 8 shows two Jazz client-side plug-ins installed into the Eclipse IDE.

Fig. 8. Jazz plugins

4 Computer-Mediated Communication

Communication media are usually classified in the classic time/space matrix, according to both the spatial dimension (collocated/distributed, i.e., where the interaction occurs) and the temporal dimension (synchronous/asynchronous, i.e., when the interaction occurs). Media can also be classified according to another dimension, 'richness', which can be defined as the ability of media to convey a large amount of information in different forms. Fig. 9 shows the media within the time/space matrix and along the media richness continuum. Face-to-face (F2F) is the richest form of communication, since it conveys information via audio and video channels, but also through cues like gesture and posture. Consequently, videoconference is richer than telephone, since the latter lacks video as information channel, whereas email is richer than letter, since electronic mail can also attach multimedia content.

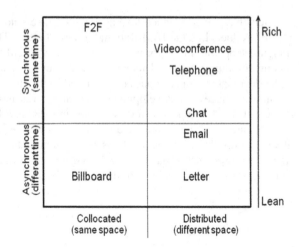

Fig. 9. Media-Richness continuum in the Time/Space Matrix (adapted from [19])

Some CMC theories have agreed on the inadequateness of text-based communication for complex, collaborative tasks, arguing that, as complexity increases, so should the level of richness of the media used, thus suggesting the use of a video link in distributed contexts. Nevertheless, the last decade has witnessed the success of many open-source projects which are coordinated through the almost-exclusive use of text-based technologies, such as wikis, email, and instant messaging. Further, nowadays the practicality of organizing videoconferencing sessions still remains low due to the additional overhead (e.g, infrastructure expensive to setup and maintain at the remote sites).

In the following we review the most prominent, and often conflicting, CMC theories.

The *Social Presence* (SP) [36] and *Media Richness* (MR) [13] theories posit group effectiveness to decrease when media other than F2F are used to accomplish equivocal tasks that require relational cues to be exchanged. Compared to rich media like F2F and video, 'lean' media like email and instant messaging lack the ability of conveying nonverbal cues (e.g., gaze, tone of voice, facial expressions) that contribute to the level of social presence, which in turns fosters individuals' motivation and mutual understanding. Hence, rich media are recommended for accomplishing equivocal tasks (i.e., when multiple and conflicting interpretations exist about a situation), for which also communicating relation content is relevant. In contrast, lean media are sufficient for executing tasks of uncertainty (i.e., the difference between the amount of information required and already possessed about a situation), which need only task-focused communication.

Common Ground (CG) theory [9] posits that people should attempt to achieve common ground (i.e., mutual understanding) with techniques available in a communication medium that lead to the least collaborative effort. CG theory presents eight properties that a medium may impose as constraints on the grounding process: copresence, visibility, audibility, cotemporality, simultaneity, sequentiality, reviewability, revisability. No medium has all the attributes at the same time. When a medium lacks one of these characteristics, it forces people to use alternative grounding techniques with different costs for the speaker, the receiver or both. Participants in a F2F conversation usually establish common ground on the fly, as they have access to cues like facial expression, gestures and voice intonation. Instead, when participants communicate over media, the fewer cues they have, the harder to construct it. As a consequence, people who do not share mutual knowledge largely benefits from using audio/video channels for completing collaborative tasks, whereas those who have an extensive preexisting common ground can communicate effectively also on lean media such as email.

The *Time-Interaction-Performance* (TIP) theory [31] hypothesizes that communication that occurs in four tasks categories (generating, intellective, judgment, and negotiation) can be ordered by complexity and the amount of information required. Fig. 10 illustrates the task-media fit attempted by the theory, with respect to the communication media. TIP theory argues that rich media do not always provide the best-fitting combination regardless of the task type. There are in fact two possible types of poor fit: when a task requires more information that the medium can deliver and when the medium provides more information than the task requires (i.e., information overload).

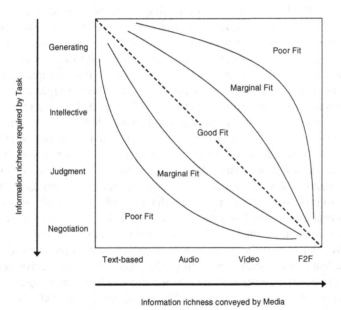

Fig. 10. Task-media fit as suggested by TIP theory (adapted from [31])

Media Synchronicity (MS) theory [16] distinguishes between the interplay of two different communication processes (the conveyance of additional information, and the convergence to shared views), which vary with the degree of synchronicity of the medium. The level of 'medium synchronicity' measures the extent to which it supports two inversely proportional properties, that is, immediacy of feedback (i.e., the ability of a medium to have rapid bidirectional communication) and parallel input (i.e., the ability of a medium to allow for more simultaneous conversations at one time). F2F conversation and audio/video conference are high-synchronicity media because they grant high immediacy of feedback, but no parallel input (i.e., just one speaker at a time). In contrast, email, chat and instant messaging are low-synchronicity media because they ensure high input parallelism and low immediacy of feedback. MS theory suggests that when extra-information (i.e., conveyance) is needed, low-synchronicity media are to be preferred due to the support of input parallelism, whereas high-synchronicity media are better able to support convergence because of the higher degree of immediacy of feedback ensured. However, in media selection one must take into account that most tasks require individuals to both convey information and converge on shared meanings, and media that excel at information conveyance are often not those that excel at convergence. Thus, choosing one single medium for any task may prove less effective than choosing a medium, or set of media, which the group uses at different times in performing the task, depending on the current communication process (convey or converge).

Cognitive-Based View (CBV) [33] looks at communication as a cognitive process: Not only must the sender's comfort with the communication medium be taken into account, but also the motivation of receivers and, above all, their ability to process the message properly. Rich media, require participants to be present at the same time, if not at a same place. This requires a high level of commitment to participate in the communication process, which in turn provides the ability to reciprocally monitor attention. In contrast, lean media allow a receiver to gain time for thinking at their will, as well as finding additional information sources, until comprehension is fully achieved. However, lean media must compete with other activities on the receiver's side and can be easily ignored with no feedback for the sender. As a result, rich media ensure that motivation and attention stays up, while lean media provides a higher ability to process information. On the other hand, when faced with highly complex messages sent with high social presence, a receiver can be overwhelmed with information, thus delaying or biasing the decision. Fig. 11 shows the so-called 'media richness paradox', that is the inverse relationship between motivation/attention and the ability to process. CBV argues that different media are needed for complex tasks where information overload may be generated. In such cases, the use of mixed media, or 'media switching', is motivated by the need to balance attention and motivation required by senders with the ability to process information of receivers. Depending on the task at hand, when senders want to get the attention of the receiver and motivate them for an immediate response, they should use a rich medium, high in social presence. In contrast, when deep thought and deliberation are needed to process the information, the sender should use a lean medium, low in social presence, to give the receiver time to objectively elaborate on messages.

The common denominator of the many existing CMC theories is that the interaction of individuals is deeply influenced not only by media characteristics, but also by other factors such as tasks requirements. Drawing upon these theories, we argue that, by understanding the driving factors of CMC, groups may be better able to select and use the most appropriate sets of media to accomplish their goals.

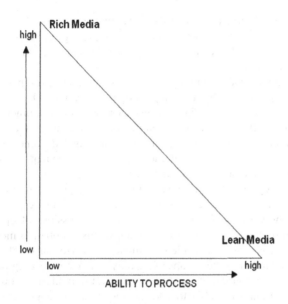

Fig. 11. Media richness paradox according to CBV (adapted from [33])

5 Media Switching in Distributed Requirements Engineering

Recent CMC theories from the literature suggest that relying on rich media alone may not yield the best results in terms of performance, and that a combination with lean media would facilitate a more rational approach to decision making. These theories form the theoretical basis for our central thesis: a mix of lean and rich media is needed to improve requirements engineering activities when stakeholders are geographically dispersed.

The rest of this section describes a family of empirical studies [4, 14] in distributed requirements engineering which have been conducted jointly by the Collaborative Development Group (CDG) at University of Bari, Italy, and the Software Engineering Global interAction Laboratory (SEGAL) at University of Victoria, Canada.

Asynchronous Discussions as a Complement to Videoconference Requirements Negotiation Meetings
To improve the effectiveness of distributed requirements engineering, drawing upon the postulates of modern theories on media selection, we have investigated ways to increase the effectiveness of videoconference requirements negotiation meetings by means of asynchronous text-based discussions as a useful complement for the preparation of such meetings.

We conducted a replicated case study of six academic global projects with the participation of students from three universities of three different countries: Australia, Canada, and Italy. Cross-university student projects were structured as outsourcing projects in which work was allocated to a developer group in a different organization and country. The project outcome was a requirements specification (RS) as a negotiated software contract between the developer group and the outsourcing company (client group). Teamwork was critical in completing the software project as the developer group had to frequently interact with the client group to understand the required software features.

Reaching a mutual understanding between clients and developers mean reducing equivocality and uncertainty by resolving all open issues found by clients in an evolving RS throughout the process. Fig. 12 illustrates the RS development workflow over a period of 7 weeks. It consisted of eleven phases of continuous requirements discovery and validation through which the understanding and documentation of requirements had to be improved. Each of these stages consisted of tasks for either the client/developer groups, or project team tasks.

Project teams negotiated requirements during one-hour synchronous videoconferencing meetings. In our research design, we created two process variants in which half of the groups were involved in asynchronous discussions of open issues, using the IBIS inspection tool [29], prior to the synchronous negotiation meeting, while the other half was not. We were thus able to compare the performance of the groups using a mix of media with that of the groups using only videoconferencing meetings.

Fig. 13 provides empirical evidence for our main hypothesis: groups in the mixed media process variant were able to end the requirements engineering process with significantly fewer open issues than the groups that were not involved in the asynchronous discussion. More uncertainties than ambiguities were clarified and then closed in the asynchronous discussions. Consequently, when participants had already discussed asynchronously, they began the videoconference negotiation meetings with a shorter list of open issues to be discussed.

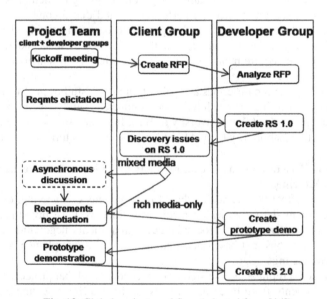

Fig. 12. Global project workflow (adapted from [14])

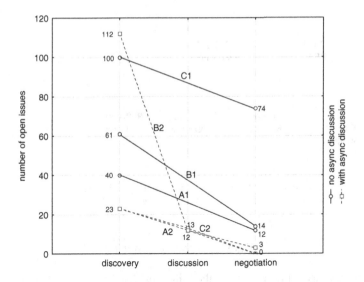

Fig. 13. Open issues in the six projects throughout three stages (from [14])

Comparing Text-Based Synchronous Communication and Face-to-Face Meetings in Distributed Requirements Workshops

Requirements workshops, whether for eliciting or negotiating requirements, are complex tasks that require a constant interplay between idea generation, decision making, and conflict resolution activities, although in different measure: requirements elicitation is more a generative task, whereas requirements negotiation is more oriented to decision making.

To build a body of knowledge about task/technology fit, rooted in the software engineering field, we evaluated the support of synchronous text-based communication for conducting distributed requirements workshops. In particular we investigated two research questions: (1) how synchronous text-based requirements workshops vary from F2F counterparts, and (2) whether both synchronous text-based elicitation and synchronous text-based negotiation represent an appropriate task-technology fit.

The empirical study involved six academic groups, playing the role of stakeholders while completing the project work of a requirements engineering course held at the University of Victoria. Analogously to the previous study, the goal of each project was to develop a Requirements Specification (RS) document through the interaction of a client and a developer team over a period of about ten weeks. Fig. 14 shows the workflow of the requirements development process. In order to perform quantitative analysis, two satisfaction questionnaires, with Likert scale response items, were administered to the students after each workshops session. Table 2 illustrates the experimental design with three factors, each having two levels: communication mode (F2F and CMC); requirements workshop (elicitation and negotiation); and role (client and developer). F2F workshops were held in a classroom while CMC workshops were run using the eConference tool [5], a text-based, distributed meeting system developed at University of Bari.

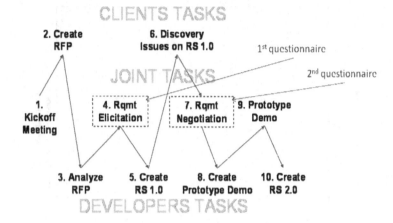

Fig. 14. Project workflow in [4]

The findings from the study were the following:

- during the requirements meetings, the subjects perceived a higher level of comfort with F2F communication mode than with CMC, while keeping an equal level of motivation to participate;
- compared to F2F requirements workshops, CMC workshops grant a higher opportunity to participate in a more structured, equal, and open discussion;
- being a customer or a developer has no effect;
- stakeholders significantly preferred F2F negotiation over F2F elicitation, and F2F negotiation over CMC negotiation;
- CMC elicitation is as good as F2F elicitation

These results suggest that, in order to reduce the negative effects of distance as well as the need and the number of collocated requirements workshops, synchronous text-based elicitations represent a better task-technology fit than synchronous text-based negotiations.

Table 2. Experimental design (adapted from [4])

Communication Mode	Requirements Workshop	Role	Subjects
F2F	elicitation	client	Gr1, Gr3, Gr5
CMC	elicitation	client	Gr2, Gr4, Gr6
F2F	negotiation	client	Gr2, Gr4, Gr6
CMC	negotiation	client	Gr1, Gr3, Gr5
F2F	elicitation	developer	Gr2, Gr4, Gr6
CMC	elicitation	developer	Gr1, Gr3, Gr5
F2F	negotiation	developer	Gr1, Gr3, Gr5
CMC	negotiation	developer	Gr2, Gr4, Gr6

6 Conclusions

Software development is an intense collaborative process where success depends on the ability to create, share and integrate information [37]. We presented a number of tools and collaborative development environments which are available to support distributed teams. We restricted our view to distributed teams of stakeholders when engaged in requirements elicitation and negotiation activities. Collaboration-intensive, these activities largely rely on face-to-face interactions of the project stakeholders and are thus greatly disrupted by distance.

Main media selection theories from the CSCW field assert that rich media alone do not provide the best performance to distributed teams and that switching between rich and lean media would smooth the progress of teamwork for complex activities. The CSCW body of knowledge about media selection, however, is mostly based on experiments which used generic, game-like tasks involving either idea generation or problem solving. Since our interest is in collaborative technologies for distributed development, we have presented our empirical software engineering studies about the effects of media usage on the execution of software engineering specific tasks such as distributed requirements workshops.

Current research in distributed development is very active in academia as well as in industry. Major ACM conferences, such as the International Conference on Software Engineering and the Conference on Computer Supported Cooperative Work, include technical papers and organize workshops about global software development. Further, the IEEE International Conference on Global Software Engineering, now at its third edition, has become the annual event for the community of researchers and practitioners interested in exploring how distributed teams work and how the problems can be solved. We hope that the state of the art and practice presented in this chapter will inspire young researchers to invest their effort into this challenging and interdisciplinary topic.

Acknowledgments

We are grateful to Fabio Calefato and Teresa Mallardo whose doctoral research contributed to the theoretical and empirical work reported in this chapter. I would also like to express my thanks to Daniela Damian who has been an invaluable partner in the research work here reported.

References

1. Agerfalk, P.J., Fitzgerald, B.: Flexible and Distributed Software Processes: Old Petunias in New Bowls? Communications of the ACM 49(10), 26–34 (2006)
2. Booch, G., Brown, A.W.: Collaborative Development Environments. In: Advances in Computers, vol. 59. Academic Press, London (2003)
3. Bugzilla Team: The Bugzilla Guide (2008), http://www.bugzilla.org/docs

4. Calefato, F., Damian, D., Lanubile, F.: An Empirical Investigation on Text-Based Communication in Distributed Requirements Workshops. In: Proc. of the Int. Conf. on Global Software Engineering, pp. 3–11. IEEE Computer Society, Washington (2007)
5. Calefato, F., Lanubile, F., Scalas, M.: Evolving a Text-Based Conferencing System: An Experience Report. In: Proc. of the 3rd Int. Conf. on Collaborative Computing: Networking, Applications and Worksharing. IEEE Computer Society, Washington (2007)
6. Carmel, E.: Global Software Teams. Prentice Hall, Upper Saddle River (1999)
7. Carmel, E., Agarwal, R.: Tactical Approaches for Alleviating Distance in Global Software Development. IEEE Software 18(2), 22–29 (2001)
8. Cheng, L., de Souza, C., Hupfer, S., Patterson, J., Ross, S.: Building Collaboration into IDEs. ACM Queue 1(9) (2003-2004)
9. Clark, H.H., Brennan, S.E.: Grounding in Communication. In: Perspectives on Socially Shared Cognition, American Psychological Association, Washington, DC, pp. 127–149 (1991)
10. Collaborative Development Group: Collab CDE (2008), http://cde.di.uniba.it/
11. CollabNet: SourceForge.net (2008), http://sourceforge.net/
12. CruiseControl (2008), http://cruisecontrol.sourceforge.net/
13. Daft, R.L., Lengel, R.H.: Organizational Information Requirements, Media Richness and Structural Design. Management Science 32(5), 554–571 (1986)
14. Damian, D., Lanubile, F., Mallardo, T.: On the Need for Mixed Media in Distributed Requirements Negotiations. IEEE Transactions on Software Engineering 34(1), 116–132 (2008)
15. De Lucia, A., Fasano, F., Oliveto, R., Tortora, G.: Recovering traceability links in software artifact management systems using information retrieval methods. ACM Trans. Softw. Eng. Methodol. 16(4), 13 (2007)
16. Dennis, A.R., Valacich, J.S.: Rethinking Media Richness: Towards a Theory of Media Synchronicity. In: Proc. of the 32nd Annual Hawaii Int. Conf. on System Sciences, p. 1017. IEEE Computer Society, Washington (1999)
17. Ebert, C., De Neve, P.: Surviving Global Software Development. IEEE Software 18(2), 62–69 (2001)
18. Edgewall Software: The Trac Project (2008), http://trac.edgewall.org/
19. Ellis, C.A., Gibbs, S.J., Rein, G.: Groupware: Some Issues and Experiences. Communications of the ACM 34(1), 39–58 (1991)
20. Erickson, T., Kellogg, W.A.: Social Translucence: An Approach to Designing Systems that Support Social Processes. ACM Transactions on Computer-Human Interaction 7(1), 59–83 (2000)
21. Espinosa, J.A., Nan, N., Carmel, E.: Do Gradations of Time Zone Separation Make a Difference in Performance? A First Laboratory Study. In: Int. Conf. on Global Software Engineering, pp. 12–22. IEEE Computer Society, Los Alamitos (2007)
22. Fowler, M., Foemmel, M.: Continuous Integration (2006), http://martinfowler.com/articles/continuousIntegration.html
23. Frost, R.: Jazz and the Eclipse Way of Collaboration. IEEE Software 24(6), 114–117 (2007)
24. GForge Group: GForge project, http://gforge.org/projects/gforge/
25. Glass, R.L.: Software Engineering: Facts and Fallacies. Addison-Wesley Longman Publishing Co., Inc., Amsterdam (2002)
26. Herbsleb, J.D., Moitra, D.: Global Software Development. IEEE Software 18(2), 16–20 (2001)

27. Herbsleb, J.D., Mockus, T.A.: An Empirical Study of Speed and Communication in Globally Distributed Software Development. IEEE Transactions on Software Engineering 29(6), 481–494 (2003)
28. Hupfer, S., Cheng, L., Ross, S., Patterson, J.: Introducing collaboration into an application development environment. In: Proc. of the ACM Conference on Computer Supported Cooperative Work, pp. 21–24. ACM, New York (2004)
29. Lanubile, F., Mallardo, T., Calefato, F.: Tool Support for Geographically Dispersed Inspection Teams. Software Process: Improvement and Practice 8(4), 217–231 (2003)
30. Louridas, P.: Using Wikis in Software Development. IEEE Software 23(2), 88–91 (2006)
31. McGrath, J.E., Hollingshead, A.B.: Groups Interacting with Technology: Ideas, Evidence, Issues and an Agenda. Sage, Thousand Oaks (1994)
32. Murugesan, S.: Understanding Web 2.0. IT Professional 9(4), 34–41 (2007)
33. Robert, L.P., Dennis, A.R.: Paradox of Richness: A Cognitive Model of Media Choice. IEEE Transactions on Professional Communication 48(1), 10–21 (2005)
34. Rus, I., Lindvall, M.: Knowledge Management in Software Engineering. IEEE Software 19(3), 26–38 (2002)
35. Sengupta, B., Chandra, S., Sinha, V.: A research agenda for distributed software development. In: Proc. of the 28th Int. Conf. on Software Engineering, pp. 731–740. ACM, New York (2006)
36. Short, J., Williams, E., Christie, B.: The Social Psychology of Telecommunications. John Wiley and Sons, London (1976)
37. Walz, D.B., Elam, J.J., Curtis, B.: Inside a Software Design Team: Knowledge Acquisition, Sharing, and Integration. Communications of the ACM 36(10), 63–77 (1993)
38. Whitehead, J.: Collaboration in Software Engineering: A Roadmap. In: Int. Conf. on Software Engineering, pp. 214–225. IEEE Computer Society, Washington (2007)

Web Cost Estimation and Productivity Benchmarking

Emilia Mendes

The University of Auckland, Private Bag 92019
Auckland, New Zealand, 0064 9 3737599 ext. 86137
emilia@cs.auckland.ac.nz

Abstract. Web cost estimation models and productivity analysis reports help project managers allocate resources more adequately, control costs, schedule and improve current practices, leading to projects that are finished on time and within budget. Therefore this chapter has two main objectives. The first is to introduce the concepts related to Web cost estimation & Web applications' sizing and present a case study where a real Web cost model is built; the second is to introduce the concepts of productivity measurement & benchmarking, and to also present a case study on productivity benchmarking.

Keywords: Web cost estimation, Effort accuracy, Multivariate Regression, Case-based reasoning, Classification and Regression Trees, Bayesian Networks, Web productivity measurement, Web productivity benchmarking.

1 Introduction

The distributed nature of the Web and the use of a simple hypertext-based mechanism and protocol allows for its use as a delivery platform for numerous types of Web applications, ranging from complex e-commerce solutions with large back-end databases to on-line personal static Web applications. Such flexibility led to a growing number of companies willing to have a Web presence, and as a consequence a growing number of Web companies bidding for as many Web projects as they can accommodate and often using technological solutions they are unfamiliar with. As usual, in order to win the bid, companies estimate unrealistic schedules, leading to applications that are rarely developed within time and budget.

Realistic effort estimates are fundamental for the successful management of software projects; the Web is no exception. Having realistic effort estimates at an early stage in a project's life cycle allows project managers and development organisations to manage their resources effectively. In addition, hand in hand with effort estimation is productivity assessment, which enables a company to benchmark its efficiency across its own projects, and also in comparison to projects developed by its competitors.

Prediction is a necessary part of an effective process, whether this process is authoring, design, testing, or Web development as a whole. In general a prediction process involves the following parts:

A. De Lucia and F. Ferrucci (Eds.): ISSSE 2006–2008, LNCS 5413, pp. 194–222, 2009.
© Springer-Verlag Berlin Heidelberg 2009

- The identification of application and project attributes (measures) (e.g. number of new Web pages, number of new images, team's previous experience, development tools used) that are believed to influence the effort required to develop a new Web application.
- The formulation of assumptions about the inter-relationship between the selected attributes and the effort required to develop a new Web application (e.g. the greater the number of new static Web pages, the greater the development effort for a new application, the greater the development team the greater the development effort).
- The capturing of historical data (e.g. number of new Web pages, actual effort) and/or expertise about past Web projects or even past development phases within the same project.
- The use of this historical data and/or expertise to build models, or as input to estimation techniques, for use in predicting effort for new Web projects.
- The assessment of how effective those effort estimation models/techniques are, i.e. the assessment of their prediction accuracy.

Cost and effort are often used interchangeably within the context of software and Web effort estimation (prediction) since effort is taken as the main component of project costs. However, given that project costs also take into account other factors such as contingency and profit [22] we will use the word "effort" and not "cost" throughout this chapter.

Numerous effort estimation techniques have been proposed and compared over the last 20 years. A classification and description of such techniques is introduced in Section 2 to help provide readers with a broader overview. One of the main predictors of effort is application size, so Section 3 discusses issues related to sizing Web applications. Section 4 briefly introduces a case study where real data on Web projects is used to build an effort estimation model. Once these three Sections are detailed, we move on to discuss productivity measurement. Section 5 introduces a productivity measurement method proposed by Kitchenham and Mendes [20], and detailed in [27], followed by Section 6 where a case study using the productivity measurement method is detailed. Finally, our conclusions are given in Section 7.

This Chapter uses reference material from a book on Web cost estimation written by this author [26] and a book on Web engineering, edited by this author and Dr. N. Mosley [28].

2 Effort Estimation Techniques

2.1 Overview

The prediction of the amount of effort necessary to produce a given deliverable is called effort estimation. This process requires as input data and/or knowledge of project characteristics that are believed to affect the amount of effort necessary to produce a deliverable. Note that a deliverable can be simple (e.g. a Web application's navigational model), or complex (e.g. a complete Web application). Project characteristics are the input to the estimation process (see Fig. 1), and estimated effort is the output of this process.

For example, a given Web company may find that in order to estimate the effort necessary to produce a new Web application w – the deliverable, it will need to estimate the following: estimated number of new Web pages the new application is likely to have, total number of developers who will help develop the new Web application, developers' average number of years of experience with the development tools employed, and the number of functions/features (e.g. shopping cart) to be offered by the new Web application. The effort estimation literature differentiates the input to an estimation process into two types: size and cost drivers. Size represents the attributes that characterise the size of the "problem" to be delivered. Typical size attributes (measures) are the number of new Web pages, number of new images, number of features/functions that the application will have. Conversely, cost drivers are any attributes that do not characterise the size of an application, such as developers' average Web development experience, number of tools employed in the development, development team size.

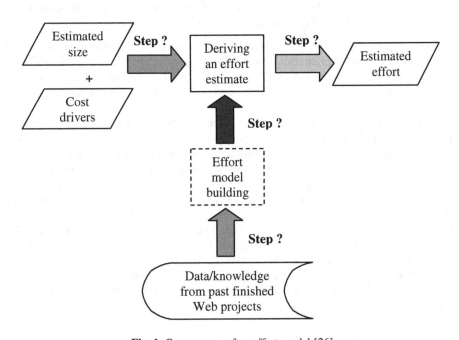

Fig. 1. Components of an effort model [26]

Fig. 1 shows that, in addition to the input attributes, data/knowledge from past finished Web projects can also be of use when estimating effort for a new project. However, the sequence in which they (input, data/knowledge from past projects) are used depends on the effort estimation technique being applied.

Several effort estimation techniques have been proposed over the past 30 years, falling into three general categories [43]: expert opinion, algorithmic techniques and artificial intelligence techniques. Each is going to be detailed next.

2.2 Expert Opinion

Expert opinion represents the process of estimating effort based on experts' judgment, and is often based on previous experience from developing/managing similar projects. Although this technique is still widely used by software and Web companies, it has a clear drawback: it is very difficult to quantify and to determine those attributes that have been used to derive an estimate, making it difficult to repeat.

However, studies show that this technique can be an effective estimating tool when used in combination with other less subjective techniques (e.g. algorithmic techniques) [11],[36],[37].

Fig. 2 shows a similar diagram to the one presented in Fig. 1, and outlines the sequence of steps used with expert opinion when estimating effort for a new project:

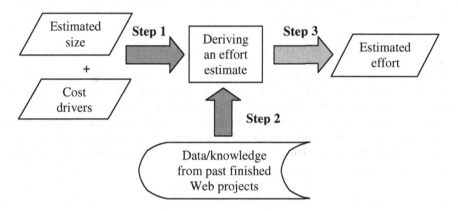

Fig. 2. Sequence used when estimating effort based on expert opinion [26]

Step 1) An expert estimates size and cost drivers related to a new Web application for which effort needs to be estimated.

Step 2) Based on the estimates obtained in Step 1, the expert uses his/her own knowledge from past finished similar projects and/or data on past finished projects for which actual effort is known.

Step 3) Based on the data/knowledge retrieved in Step 2, and the input from Step 1, the expert now subjectively estimates effort for the new project. Deriving an accurate effort estimate is more likely to occur when there are completed projects similar to the one having its effort estimated. The knowledge regarding the characteristics of a new project is necessary to retrieve, from memory and/or a database, knowledge/data on finished similar projects. Once this data/knowledge is retrieved, effort can be estimated.

2.3 Algorithmic Techniques

To date, the most popular techniques described in the effort estimation literature are algorithmic techniques. Such techniques attempt to formalise the relationship between effort and one or more project characteristics by creating an algorithmic model. This formalisation is often translated as an equation such as that shown by Equations 1 and 2.

Equations such as these are commonly obtained by applying regression analysis techniques [39] on datasets of past completed projects. Equation 1 assumes a linear relationship between effort and its size/cost drivers whereas Equation 2 assumes a non-linear relationship. In Equation 2, when the exponent is < 1 we have economies of scale, i.e., larger projects use less effort comparatively to smaller projects. The opposite situation (exponent > 1) gives diseconomies of scale, i.e. larger projects use more effort comparatively to smaller projects.

$$EstimatedEffort = C + a_0 EstSizeNewproj + a_1 CD_1 + \cdots + a_n CD_n \qquad (1)$$

$$EstimatedEffort = C\, EstSizeNewproj^{a_0}\, CD_1^{a_1} \cdots CD_n^{a_n} \qquad (2)$$

where:

C is a constant denoting the initial estimated effort (assuming size and cost drivers to be zero) derived from past data.

$a_0 \ldots a_n$ are parameters derived from past data.

$CD_1 \ldots CD_n$ are other project characteristics, other than size, that have an impact on effort.

Regression-based algorithmic models are most suitable to local circumstances such as "in-house" analysis as they are derived from past data that often represents projects from the company itself. Regression analysis, used to generate regression-based algorithmic models, provides a procedure for determining the "best" straight-line fit to a set of project data that represents the relationship between effort and project characteristics (e.g. size, experience, tools) [39]. The regression line (see Fig. 3) is

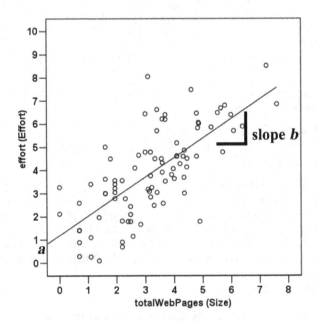

Fig. 3. Example of a Regression line [26]

represented as an equation, such as those given by Equations 1 and 2. The effort estimation model to be detailed in the case study falls into this category.

Regarding the regression analysis itself, two of the most widely used techniques are multiple regression (MR) and stepwise regression (SWR). The difference between both is that MR obtains a regression line using all the input variables (size measures and cost drivers) at the same time, whereas SWR is a technique that examines different combinations of input variables, looking for the best grouping to explain the greatest amount of variation in effort. Both use least squares regression, where the regression line selected is the one that minimises the sum of the squared errors. Errors are calculated as the difference between actual and estimated effort and are known as the residuals [39].

The Equation corresponding to the Regression line in Fig. 3 is shown below:

$$\text{Effort} = a + b \text{ totalWebPages} \qquad (3)$$

where a is called the intercept, obtained when b totalWebPages $= 0$; and b is called the slope of the regression line.

Fig. 4 shows the diagram presented in Fig. 1 and outlines the sequence of steps used with a regression-based algorithmic technique when estimating effort for a new project:

Step 1) Data on past finished projects is retrieved.
Step 2) The data retrieved in Step 1 is used to build a regression-based effort estimation Equation (model).
Step 3) The estimated size and cost drivers are used as input to the Equation built from Step 2)
Step 4) The output of the Equation is the estimated effort for the new Web project.

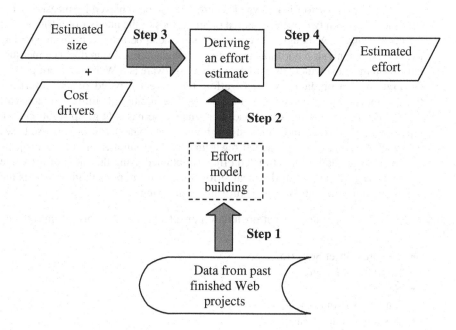

Fig. 4. Sequence used when estimating effort using an algorithmic technique [26]

A detailed description of regression analysis and how to build an effort estimation model using regression analysis is give in [26].

2.4 Artificial Intelligence Techniques

Artificial intelligence techniques have, in the last 12 to 13 years, been used as a complement to, or as an alternative to, the previous two categories. Examples include fuzzy logic [24], regression trees [40], neural networks [44], case-based reasoning [43], and Bayesian Networks [15]. We will briefly introduce case-based reasoning (CBR), regression trees (CART) and Bayesian Networks (BNs) in more detail as they are currently the most popular machine learning techniques employed for Web cost estimation. A useful summary of numerous machine learning techniques can also be found in [10].

Case-Based Reasoning

Case-based reasoning (CBR) provides estimates by comparing the current project to be estimated against a library of historical information from completed projects with a known effort (case base). It involves [1]:

i.   Characterising a new project p, for which an estimate is required, with attributes common to those completed projects stored in the case base. In terms of effort estimation, attributes represent size measures and cost drivers which have a bearing on effort. Attribute values are normally standardized (between 0 and 1) such that they have the same degree of influence on the result.

ii. Use of this characterisation as a basis for finding similar (analogous) completed projects, for which effort is known. This process can be achieved by measuring the "distance" between two projects, based on the values of the number of attributes (k) for these projects. Although numerous techniques can be used to measure similarity, nearest neighbour algorithms using the unweighted Euclidean distance measure have been the most widely used to date in both software and Web engineering.

iii. Generation of a predicted value of effort for project p based on the effort for those completed projects that are similar to p. The number of similar projects will depend on the size of the case base. For small case bases (e.g. up to 90 cases), typical values are 1, 2, and 3 closest neighbours (analogies). For larger case bases no conclusions have been reached regarding the best number of similar projects to use. The calculation of estimated effort is obtained using the same effort value as the closest neighbour, or the mean effort for two or more analogies. This is the common choice in both Web and software engineering.

When using CBR there are six parameters to consider, each to be briefly introduced below [41]:

- Feature Subset Selection
- Similarity Measure
- Scaling
- Number of Analogies
- Analogy Adaptation
- Adaptation Rules

Feature Subset Selection
Feature subset selection involves determining the optimum subset of attributes that yield the most accurate estimation. Some existing CBR tools, e.g. ANGEL [42] optionally offer this functionality using a brute force algorithm, searching for all possible feature subsets. Other CBR tools (e.g. CBR-Works) have no such functionality, and therefore to obtain estimated effort, we must use all of the known attributes of a project to retrieve the most similar cases.

Similarity Measure
The similarity measure measures the level of similarity between different cases, with several similarity measures proposed in the literature. The most popular similarity measure in the current Web/software engineering literature [1],[29],[41] is the unweighted Euclidean distance. Other similarity measures are presented in [1].

Unweighted Euclidean distance: The unweighted Euclidean distance measures the Euclidean (straight-line) distance d between the points (x_0, y_0) and (x_1, y_1), given by the equation:

$$d = \sqrt{(x_0 - x_1)^2 + (y_0 - y_1)^2} \tag{4}$$

Scaling
Scaling (also known as standardisation) represents the transformation of attribute values according to a defined rule, such that all attributes present values within the same range and hence have the same degree of influence on the results [1]. A common method of scaling is to assign zero to the minimum observed value and one to the maximum observed value [16].

Number of Analogies
The number of analogies refers to the number of most similar cases that will be used to generate the estimation. With small sets of data it is reasonable to consider only a small number of analogies [1]. Several studies have restricted their analysis to the closest analogy ($k = 1.0$) [3],[36], while others have used two and three analogies [1],[13],[14],[29],[30],[32],[38].

Analogy Adaptation
Once the similar cases have been selected the next step is to decide how to generate the estimation for project P_{new}. Choices of analogy adaptation techniques presented in the literature vary from the nearest neighbour [3],[14], the mean of the closest analogies [42], the median [1], inverse distance weighted mean and inverse rank weighted mean [16], to illustrate just a few. The adaptations used to date for Web engineering are the nearest neighbour, mean of the closest analogies [29],[30], and the inverse rank weighted mean [31],[32].

Adaptation Rules
Adaptation rules are used to adapt estimated effort, according to a given criterion, such that it reflects the characteristics of the target project more closely. For example, in the context of effort prediction, the estimated effort to develop an application would be adapted such that it would also take into consideration the application's size values.

Fig. 5 shows a similar diagram to that presented in Fig. 1, and outlines the sequence of steps used with the CBR technique when estimating effort for a new project:

Step 1) The estimated size and cost drivers relating to a new project are used to retrieve similar projects from the case base, for which actual effort is known.
Step 2) Using the input from Step 1) a suitable CBR tool retrieves similar projects to the one represented by the input.
Step 3) Once similar projects were retrieved, they are used to obtain the estimated effort for a new project.

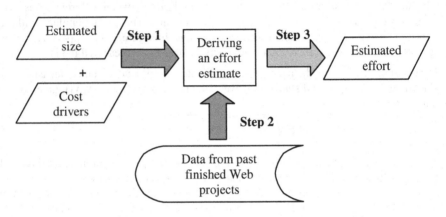

Fig. 5. Sequence used when estimating effort using CBR [26]

Classification and Regression Trees

The objective of a Classification and Regression Tree (CART) model within this context is to develop a simple binary tree-structured decision process for describing the distribution of values of effort given a set of size measures and cost drivers [5]. For example, assume the estimated effort to develop a Web application can be determined by an estimated number of pages (WP), number of images (IM), and number of functions (FN). A regression tree such as the one shown in Fig. 6 is generated from data obtained from past finished Web applications, taking into account their existing values of effort, WP, IM, and FN.

Once the tree has been built, it is used to estimate effort for a new project. So, to estimate effort for a new project where the estimated WP = 25, estimated IM = 15, and estimated FN = 4 we would navigate down the tree structure to find the estimated effort, which would be 45 person hours.

Whenever size and cost drivers are numerical the CART tree is called a *regression tree* and whenever size and cost drivers are categorical the CART tree is called a *classification tree*. Details on how CART models are built are found in [26].

Fig. 7 shows the diagram presented in Fig. 1 and outlines the sequence of steps used with a CART technique when estimating effort for a new project:

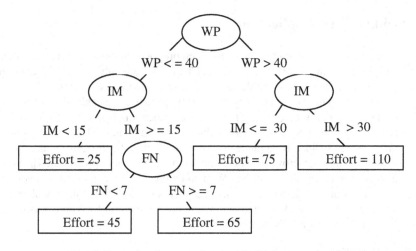

Fig. 6. Example of a regression tree for Web cost estimation

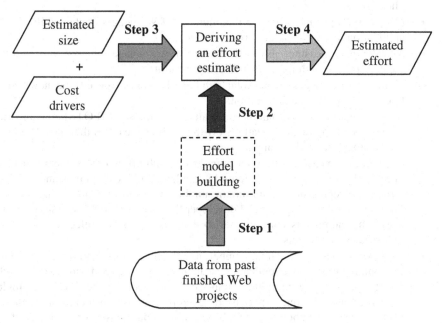

Fig. 7. Sequence used when estimating effort using CART [26]

Step 1) Past data is used to generate a CART model.

Step 2) A CART model is built using the past data obtained in Step 1).

Step 3) Estimates values for size and cost drivers are used to traverse the CART tree (model) built in Step 2).

Step 4) Estimated effort for a new project is obtained after traversing the model built in Step 2) using the estimated values from Step 3).

3 Sizing a Web Application

To date numerous Web size measures have been proposed in the literature, and a detailed survey is presented in [26]. However, in this Chapter we are only going to discuss one of these proposals, corresponding to the set of measures used in the Tukutuku Benchmarking project [34]. This is an ongoing project (http://www.cs.auckland.ac.nz/tukutuku), which collects data on Web projects, for the development of effort estimation models and to benchmark productivity across and within Web companies. The size measures and cost drivers were obtained from the results of a survey investigation, using data from 133 on-line Web forms that provided quotes on Web development projects [34][35]. They were also confirmed by an established Web company and a second survey involving 33 Web companies in New Zealand. Consequently, it is our belief that the variables identified are suitable for Web effort estimation, and are meaningful to Web companies. The set of Tukutuku size measures is detailed below:

Web application
- *Web Pages*: measures the total number of Web pages contained in a Web application.
- *New Web Pages*: measures the total number of Web pages contained in a Web application that were created from scratch.
- *New Images*: measures the total number of new images/photos/icons/buttons created from scratch for a given Web application.
- *Total Images*: measures the total number of images (reused and new) contained in a given Web application.
- *Fots*: measures the total number of features off-the-shelf (FOTS) contained in a given Web application. Features off-the-shelf are features that have been reused as they are, without any adaptation.
- *High FotsA*: measures the total number of High-effort FOTS contained in a Web application, which were reused and adapted to local circumstances. High effort here represents the minimum number of hours to adapt a single function/feature by one experienced developer that is considered high (above average). This number is currently set to 4 hours based on collected data from industrial Web projects.
- *High New*: measures the total number of new High-effort Feature / Functionality contained in a Web application, which were developed from scratch. High effort represents the minimum number of hours necessary to develop a single function/feature by one experienced developer that is considered high (above average). This number is currently set to 15 hours based on collected data from industrial Web projects.
- *FotsA*: measures the total number of Low-effort FOTS contained in a Web application, which were adapted to local circumstances.
- *New*: measures the total number of Low-effort Feature/Functionality contained in a Web application, which were developed from scratch.

Examples of feature/functionality are listed below:
- Auction/Bid utility
- Bulletin Boards

- Discussion Forum/Newsgroups
- Chat Rooms
- Database creation
- Database integration
- Other persistent storage integration (e.g. flat files)
- Credit Card Authorization
- Member login
- Online Secure Order Form
- Charts
- File upload/download
- Traffic Statistics
- Search Engine
- User Guest book
- Visitor statistics

The next Section will briefly introduce a case study where a regression-based algorithmic model was built and employed for effort estimation using data on 87 Web projects from the Tukutuku database. This case study is fully detailed in [28].

4 Web Effort Estimation Case Study

The case study briefly introduced in this Chapter provides an overview of the necessary steps required to build a regression-based effort estimation model. This model is built using data on industrial Web projects, developed by Web companies worldwide, from the Tukutuku database.

The dataset used in this chapter contains data on 87 Web projects: 34 and 13 are from 2 single Web companies respectively and the remaining 40 projects come from another 23 companies. The Tukutuku database uses 25 variables to store specifics about each company that volunteered projects, particulars about each project, and data about each Web application (see Table 1). Company data is obtained once, and both project and application data are gathered for each project a Web company volunteers.

All results presented were obtained using the statistical software package SPSS 12.0 for Windows produced and sold by SPSS Inc. Further details on the statistical methods used throughout this case study are given in [26]. Finally, all the statistical tests set the significance level at 95% ($\alpha = 0.05$).

The data analysis procedure presented herein is adapted from [25], and consists of:

1. Data validation
2. Variables and model selection
3. Model inspection
4. Extraction of effort equation
5. Model validation

Table 1. Variables for the Tukutuku database

NAME	DESCRIPTION
COMPANY DATA	
COUNTRY	Country company belongs to.
ESTABLISHED	Year when company was established.
SERVICES	Type of services company provides.
NPEOPLEWD	Number of people who work on Web design and development.
CLIENTIND	Industry representative of those clients to whom applications are provided.
PROJECT DATA	
TYPEPROJ	Type of project (new or enhancement).
LANGS	Implementation languages used.
DOCPROC	If project followed defined and documented process.
PROIMPR	If project team involved in a process improvement programme.
METRICS	If project team part of a software metrics programme.
DEVTEAM	Size of a project's development team.
TEAMEXP	Average team experience with the development language(s) employed.
TOTEFF	Actual total effort in person hours used to develop the Web application.
ESTEFF	Estimated total effort in person hours necessary to develop the Web application.
ACCURACY	Procedure used to record effort data.
WEB APPLICATION	
TYPEAPP	Type of Web application developed.
TOTWP	Total number of Web pages (new and reused).
NEWWP	Total number of new Web pages.
TOTIMG	Total number of images (new and reused).
NEWIMG	Total number of new images created.
FOTS	Number of reused features/functions without adaptation.
HFOTSA	Number of reused high-effort features/functions adapted.
HNEW	Number of new high-effort features/functions.
FOTSA	Number of reused low-effort features adapted.
NEW	Number of new low-effort features/functions.

Each of these steps is described below, and examples are given accordingly.

Data Validation

The Data validation (DV) step is used to perform the first screening of the data that has been collected. In general, this involves understanding what the variables are (e.g. their purpose, scale type) and also includes the use of descriptive statistics (e.g. mean, median, minimum, maximum) to help identify any missing or unusual cases.

Table 2 shows an example of descriptive statistics for some of the variables in the Tukutuku database (only the numerical variables). Here the objective is to check if there are any strange patterns in the data, which would require further investigation. For example, the maximum number of Web pages has a value of 2000 Web pages. Although it does not seem possible at first to have such large number of pages, we cannot simply assume this has been a data entry error. When a situation such as this one arises, the first step is to contact the company that provided the data and to confirm the data is correct. Unfortunately, in our case, we were unable to obtain confirmation from the source company. However, further investigation revealed that in relation to the Web project that contains 2000 Web pages, 1980 pages were developed from scratch, and numerous new functions/features (five high-effort and seven low-effort) were also implemented. In addition, the development team consisted of two people who had very little experience with the six programming languages used. The total effort was 947 person hours, which corresponds to a three-month project assuming both developers worked at the same time. If we only consider number of pages and effort, the ratio of number of minutes per page is 27:1, which seems reasonable given the lack of experience of the development team and the number of different languages they had to use [26].

Table 2. Descriptive statistics for numerical variables [26]

Variables	Minimum	Maximum	Mean	Median	Std. dev.
DEVTEAM	1	8	2.37	2	1.35
TEAMEXP	1	10	3.40	2	1.93
TOTWP	1	2000	92.40	25	273.09
NEWWP	0	1980	82.92	7	262.98
TOTIMG	0	1820	122.54	40	284.48
NEWIMG	0	800	51.90	0	143.25
HFOTSA	0	4	.29	0	.75
HNEW	0	10	1.24	0	2.35
FOTS	0	15	1.07	0	2.57
FOTSA	0	10	1.89	1	2.41
NEW	0	13	1.87	0	2.84
TOTEFF	1	5000	261.73	43	670.36

Table 3. Frequency table for type of project [26]

Type of project	Frequency	%	Cumulative %
New	39	44.8	44.8
Enhancement	48	55.2	100.0
Total	87	100.0	

Once we have checked the numerical variables, our next step is to check the categorical variables using their frequency tables as a tool. One example of a frequency table is shown in Table 3, and suggests that no unusual trends are apparent.

Once the data validation is complete, we are ready to move on to the next step, namely variables and model selection.

Variables and Model Selection
The second step part of the data analysis methodology is sub-divided into two separate and distinct phases: preliminary analysis and model building.

Preliminary analysis allows us to choose which variables to use, discard, modify, and, where necessary, sometimes create. Model building is used to construct an effort estimation model based on our data set and variables.

The Preliminary analysis phase is used to create new variables based on existing variables, discard unnecessary variables, and modify existing variables (e.g. joining categories). The net result of this phase is to obtain a set of variables that are ready to use in the next phase, model building. Since this phase will construct an effort model using stepwise regression we need to ensure that the variables comply with the assumptions underlying regression analysis, which are as follows [25][28][26]:

1. The input variables (size measures and cost drivers) are measured without error. If this cannot be guaranteed then these variables need to be normalised using a transformation.
2. The relationship between size measures & cost drivers and effort is linear.
3. No important input variables have been omitted. This ensures that there is no specification error associated with the dataset. The use of a prior assumption-based model justifying the choice of input variables ensures this assumption is not violated.
4. The variance of the residuals is the same for all combinations of input variables (i.e. the residuals are homoscedastic rather than heteroscedastic). A residual within the context of this book is the difference between actual and estimated effort.
5. The residuals must be normally distributed.
6. The residuals must be independent, i.e. not correlated.
7. The size measures & cost drivers are not linearly dependent, i.e. there are no linear dependencies between these variables.

The first task within the preliminary analysis phase is to examine the entire set of variables and check if there are any variables containing a significant amount of missing values (> 40%). If yes, they should be automatically discarded as they prohibit the use of imputation methods, which are methods used to replace missing values with estimated values, and will further prevent the identification of useful trends in the data.

Our next step is to look for symptoms (e.g. skewness, heteroscedasticity, and outliers) that may suggest the need for variables to be normalised, i.e. having their values transformed such that they more closely resemble a normal distribution. This step uses histograms, boxplots, and scatter plots.

Skewness measures to what extent the distribution of data values is symmetrical about a central value; heteroscedasticity represents unstable variance of values; finally, outliers are unusual values.

Histograms, or bar charts, provide a graphical display, where each bar summarises the frequency of a single value or range of values for a given variable. They are often used to check if a variable is normally distributed, in which case the bars are displayed in the shape of a bell-shaped curve. Some of the Histograms for the numerical variables are shown in Figure 8, and suggest that variables present skewed distributions, i.e. values not symmetrical about a central value.

Next, boxplots are used to check the existence of outliers.

The boxplots for some of the numerical variables (see Fig. 9) indicate that they present a large number of outliers and peaked distributions that are not symmetric. Whenever outliers are present they should be investigated further, since they may be a result of data entry error. In our analysis we looked at all cases, in particular in relation to projects that exhibited very large effort values, but did not find anything in the data to suggest they should be removed from the data set. Note that when there are doubts about the correctness of the data, the best solution is to contact the data source for confirmation. An assessment should only be based on consistency with other variables if the source is not available.

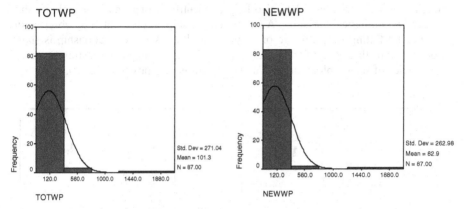

Fig. 8. Examples of Histograms [26]

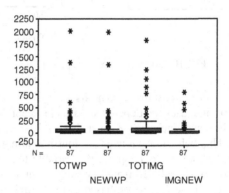

Fig. 9. Examples of Boxplots [26]

In terms of the Tukutuku data used in this Section, both histograms and boxplots indicated symptoms of skewness and outliers. When this situation arises it is common practice to normalise the data, i.e. to transform the data trying to approximate the values to a normal distribution. A common transformation is to take the natural log (ln), which makes larger values smaller and brings the data values closer to each other [25]. However, before transforming the data a statistical test can be used to confirm if the data is not normally distributed. If the dataset is small the test to use is the Shapiro-Wilk test of normality; otherwise it is the One-Sample Kolmogorov-Smirnov Test (K-S test). Both tests compare an observed distribution to a theoretical distribution. The K-S test found that none of the variables had distributions that matched the normal distribution. Therefore all variables had to be transformed. The transformation applied in our case to all numerical variables was the natural log transformation. For consistency, all variables with a value of zero had one added to their values prior to being transformed, as there is no natural log of zero.

The last part of the preliminary analysis is to check if the relationship between the effort and the size measures & cost drivers is linear. The tool used to check such relationships is a scatter plot. Scatter plots are used to explore possible relationships between numerical variables. They also help to identify strong and weak relationships between two numerical variables. A strong relationship is represented by observations (data points) falling very close to or on the trend line. A weak relationship is shown by observations that do not form a clear pattern, which in our case is a straight line.

Examples of scatter plots for the Tukutuku dataset are shown in Fig. 10.

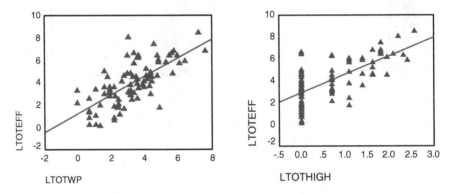

Fig. 10. Examples of Scatter plots [26]

Whenever a size measure or cost driver exhibits a large number of zero values (e.g. LTOTHIGH in Fig. 10), it causes the dependent variable to exhibit more variability at the zero point, i.e. when size measures & cost drivers have zero values, compared with non-zero values. This behaviour violates the fourth assumption underlying linear regression. Therefore, whenever this happens, the variable that exhibits a large number of zero values needs to be excluded from any subsequent analysis.

Our next step is to build the regression-based effort model using a two-step process. The first step is to use a manual stepwise regression based on residuals to select the categorical and numerical variables that jointly have a statistically significant effect on effort. The second step is to use these selected variables to build the final effort model using multivariate regression, which is a linear regression that uses more than one predictor variable.

Building the Model Using a Two-Step Process

The manual stepwise procedure uses data on the residuals to select the best predictor variables. This procedure, proposed by Kitchenham [19], enables the use of information on residuals to handle relationships amongst predictor variables (size measures and cost drivers). In addition, it only selects the input variables that jointly have a statistically significant effect on effort, thus avoiding any multi-collinearity problems. A detailed example explaining the use of this procedure is presented in [26]. Once the best predictor variables have been selected, the next step is to construct the full regression-based algorithmic effort estimation model, by applying a multivariate regression using only the variables that have been selected from the manual stepwise procedure.

At each stage of the stepwise process we also need to verify the stability of the model. This involves identifying if there are high–influence data points that could be responsible for driving all the observed patterns in the model. In addition, we also check if residuals are homoscedastic and normally distributed. Several types of plots (e.g. residual, leverage, probability) and statistics are available in most statistics tools to accomplish such tasks, and several examples are given in [26].

Based on the dataset used in this Chapter, the manual stepwise procedure selected the variables LNEWWP, LTOTHIGH and LDEVTEAM. When they are used together as input to a regression-based algorithmic technique (multivariate regression), they provide the results shown in Table 4. The model's adjusted R^2 is 0.765 suggesting that LNEWWP, LTOTHIGH and LDEVTEAM can explain 76.5% of the variation in LTOTEFF.

Table 4. Coefficients of the regression-based effort model [26]

Variable	Coeff.	Std. error	t	P>ltl	[95% conf. interval]	
(Constant)	1.544	0.185	8.368	0.000	1.177	1.912
LNEWWP	0.523	0.056	9.270	0.000	0.411	0.635
LTOTHIGH	0.797	0.157	5.076	0.000	0.485	1.110
LDEVTEAM	0.860	0.201	4.274	0.000	0.460	1.260

Extraction of the Effort Equation
The Equation obtained from Table 4 is shown to be:

$$LTOTEFF = 1.544 + 0.523 LNEWWP + 0.797 LTOTHIGH + 0.860 LDEVTEAM \quad (5)$$

This equation uses four variables that had been previously transformed; therefore we need to transform them back to their original states, which gives the following Equation:

$$TOTEFF = 4.683(NEWWP+1)^{0.523} (TOTHIGH+1)^{0.797} (DEVTEAM)^{0.860} \quad (6)$$

In Equation 6, the multiplicative value 4.683 can be interpreted as the effort required developing a single Web page.

Obtaining a model that has a good fit to the data and alone can explain a large degree of the variation in effort is not enough to assume this model will provide good effort predictions for new projects. To confirm this, this model also needs to be validated. This is the procedure explained in the next Section.

Model Validation
In order to validate an effort estimation model, we need to use data from completed Web projects as input to the model, in order to check, for each of the projects used as input, if the estimated effort suggested by the model matches the project's actual effort. To simulate this situation the following steps are followed:

1. The original dataset *d* is split into a training set *t* and a validation set *v*. Here we may use several training and validation sets; however within the context of this chapter we will only employ a single training & validation set.
2. Use *t* to produce an effort estimation model *te*.
3. Use *te* to predict effort for each of the projects in *v*, as if these projects were new projects for which effort was unknown.

This process is known as cross-validation. For an *n*-fold cross-validation, *n* different training/validation sets are used. In this section we will show the cross-validation procedure using a one-fold cross-validation, with a 66% split. This split means that 66% of our project data will be used as training set for model building, the remaining 34% to validate the model, i.e. the training set will have 66% of the total number of projects and the validation set will have the remaining 34%.

As previously mentioned the initial data set had 87 projects, which were split into training and validation sets containing 58 and 29 projects, respectively. Generally projects are allocated to training/validation sets randomly.

We created a regression-based algorithmic effort model using the 58 projects in the training set. Here we do not need to repeat the manual stepwise procedure. We simply use as predictor variables the only three variables that have been previously selected using the manual stepwise procedure: LNEWWP, LTOTHIGH and LDEVTEAM. The model's coefficients are presented in Table 5, and the transformed equation is presented as Equation 7. The model's adjusted R^2 was 0.668.

$$TOTEFF = 10.935\,(NEWWP+1)^{0.391}\,(TOTHIGH+1)^{0.714}(DEVTEAM)^{0.677} \quad (7)$$

Table 5. Coefficients of the regression-based training set effort model [26]

Variable	Coeff.	Std. error	t	P>|t|	[95% conf. interval]	
(Constant)	2.392	0.268	8.908	0.000	1.853	2.930
LNEWWP	0.391	0.069	5.677	0.000	0.253	0.529
LTOTHIGH	0.714	0.157	4.549	0.000	0.399	1.029
LDEVTEAM	0.677	0.225	3.013	0.004	0.227	1.127

To measure this model's prediction accuracy we used the following measures [6]:

*   Mean Magnitude of Relative Error (MMRE), which is the mean MRE.
*   Median Magnitude of Relative Error (MdMRE), which is the median MRE.
*   Prediction at 25% (Pred(25)), which measures the percentage of projects with MRE <= 0.25

MRE is the basis for calculating MMRE and MdMRE, and defined as:

$$MRE = \frac{|e - \hat{e}|}{e} \quad (8)$$

where *e* represents actual effort and *ê* estimated effort.

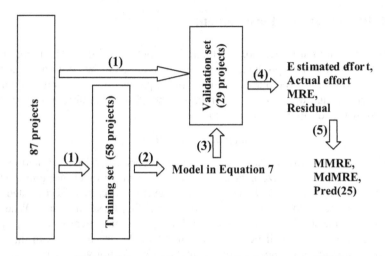

Fig. 11. Steps used in the cross-validation process [26]

Table 6. Accuracy of training set-based model [26]

Measure	%
MMRE	129
MdMRE	73
Pred(25)	17.24

MRE is gathered for each of the projects in the validation set (see Fig. 11)

How do we know if the prediction obtained for our model is reasonable?

If we were to use, instead of the effort model, the average actual effort (average = 261) or the median actual effort for the 58 projects (median = 43) as the estimated effort for each of the projects in the validation set, then prediction accuracy would be considerably worse (see Table 7). This means that, although the accuracy obtained using MMRE, MdMRE and Pred(25) does not seem wonderful, it would still be advantageous for a Web company to have used our effort model rather than to simply use as estimated effort the mean or median effort for past finished Web projects.

We suggest that a viable approach for a Web company would be to use the effort model described above to obtain an estimated effort, and to revisit the effort suggested by the model taking into account factors such as previous experience with similar projects and the skills of the developers. This means that the estimated effort provided by our model could still be calibrated to local circumstances, which would dictate the final estimate to be used for a new Web project.

Table 7. Prediction accuracy measures based on average and median effort [26]

	Average effort as estimated effort	Median effort as estimated effort
MMRE	4314%	663%
MdMRE	1413%	149%
Pred(25)	6.89%	3.44%

5 Web Productivity Measurement

Productivity is commonly measured as the ratio of output to input. The more output per unit of input, the more productive a project is assumed to be. Within the context of software development the output of the software production process is often taken to be product size and the input to the process to be effort. Therefore, productivity is represented by the following equation [20]:

$$Productivity = Size/Effort \tag{9}$$

Equation 9 can be used whenever product size is represented by a single dominant size measure (e.g. product size measured in lines of code or function points). However, there are circumstances when there are several different effort-related size measures and there is no standard model for aggregating these measures. When we have more than one size measure related to effort and no theoretical model for aggregating those measures, it is difficult to construct a single size measure. In these circumstances, Equation 9 cannot be used to measure productivity. This is exactly the problem we face when attempting to measure Web application productivity. The majority of studies published in the Web sizing literature have identified the need to use a variety of different measures to adequately characterise the size of a Web application, but there is no widely accepted method for aggregating the measures into a single size measure. In order to provide a solution to this problem, Kitchenham and Mendes [20] proposed a productivity measurement method that allows for the use of multiple effort-related size measures. It is based on the idea that any *size-based effort estimation model* constructed using the stepwise regression technique is *by definition* a function of effort-related size measures. Thus the *size-based effort estimation model* can be regarded as an *AdjustedSize measure*, and used in the following equation to represent productivity [20]:

$$Productivity = AdjustedSize/Effort \tag{10}$$

The *AdjustedSize* measure contains only size measures that *together* are strongly associated with effort. In addition, the relationship between these size measures and effort does not need to be linear.

The benefits of using this method for measuring productivity are as follows [20]:

- The standard value of productivity is one, since it is obtained using the ratio of estimated to actual effort.
- A productivity value greater than one suggests above-average productivity.
- A productivity value smaller than one suggests below-average productivity.
- The stepwise regression technique used to build a regression model that represents the *AdjustedSize* measure can also be employed to construct upper and lower bounds on the productivity measure. These bounds can be used to assess whether the productivity achieved by a specific project is significantly better or worse than expected.
- The productivity measure automatically allows for diseconomies (or economies) of scale before being used in a productivity analysis. This means that an investigation

of factors that affect productivity will only select factors that affect the productivity of all projects. If we ignore the impact of diseconomies (or economies) or scale, we run the risk of detecting factors that differ between large and small projects rather than factors that affect the productivity of all projects.

6   Web Productivity Measurement Case Study

The analysis presented in this Section was based on six datasets of Web projects from the Tukutuku database [35]. As shown in Table 8, the data comprises 111 Web projects contributed by six companies. These projects represent industrial Web applications developed by Web companies from four different countries. In Table 8 'Enh' means Enhancement projects; 'Co' means Company.

All single-company datasets available as part of the Tukutuku database were used in this study because the productivity method used automatically accounts for economies and diseconomies of scale, therefore contrasting application sizes and effort will not have a bearing upon the results of our productivity analysis.

Table 8 shows that all six companies presented similar team experience with the development languages employed in their projects, and provided carefully collected & validated data. Five companies follow a defined and documented process, and three have development teams that are involved in a process improvement programme & software metrics programmes. Four companies were formed over 10 years ago, and only one company does not follow a defined and documented development process. In terms of the amount of project data volunteered, except for Co-5, all companies volunteered a very similar number of projects.

Table 8. Comparison amongst companies' datasets

Criterion	Co-1	Co-2	Co-3	Co-4	Co-5	Co-6
Number of projects used	13	14	20	15	31	18
Average team experience (number of years) with the development language(s) employed	7	5	5	4	6	5
Average team size	3	3	2	7	1	1
Follows a defined and documented development process	Yes	Yes	No	Yes	Yes	Yes
Its development team is involved in a process improvement programme	Yes	Yes	No	Yes	No	Yes
Its development team is part of a software metrics programme	Yes	Yes	No	Yes	No	No
Type of projects	All New	13 Enh 1 New	All Enh	All New	All New	1 Enh 17 New
Was the data carefully collected and validated?	Yes	Yes	Yes	Yes	Yes	Yes
Company's age	>10 years	<10 years	<10 years	>10 years	>10 years	>10 years

AdjustedSize Models

For each of the six datasets the following steps were carried out to obtain the AdjustedSize Model:

The Manual Stepwise procedure proposed by Kitchenham [19] was used to identify the size variables that were strongly related with effort. While applying this procedure, we also verified the stability of each partial regression model generated. This involved identifying large residual and high-influence data points (i.e. projects), and also checking whether residuals were homoscedastic and normally distributed. Several types of plots (e.g. residual, leverage, probability) and statistics are available in most statistics tools to accomplish such task. The ones we have employed, all available in SPSS v15, were the following:

- A residual plot showing residuals vs. fitted values, to check if the residuals are random and normally distributed (data points distributed randomly about zero).
- A normal P–P plot (probability plots) for the residuals. Normal P–P plots are generally employed to verify whether the distribution of a variable is consistent with the normal distribution. If the distribution is Normal, the data points are close to linear.
- Cook's D statistic to identify projects that exhibited jointly a large influence and large residual. Any projects with D greater than $4/n$, where n represents the total number of projects, are considered to have high influence on the results. When there are high-influence projects the stability of the model needs to be tested by removing these projects, and observing the effect their removal has on the model. If the coefficients remain stable and the adjusted R^2 increases, this indicates that the high-influence projects are not destabilising the model and therefore do not need to be removed.

We also obtained upper and lower bounds of the *AdjustedSize* model to construct upper and lower bounds for the productivity values. This mechanism allows us to check the existence of productivity values significantly different from one (the baseline productivity). A detailed description on how to obtain upper and lower bounds is described in [28].

Once each size-based effort model, i.e. size-based effort Equation, was obtained, they were used as the *AdjustedSize* models, and, by applying Equation 10, productivity values were obtained for each of the six datasets used in this investigation. *AdjustedSize* models and corresponding adjusted R^2 are presented below:

AdjustedSize model for Co-1 (adjusted $R^2 = 0.540$)
$$TotEff = 2.307TotWP^{0.964} \tag{11}$$

AdjustedSize model for Co-2 (adjusted $R^2 = 0.376$)
$$TotEff = 9.944\,(Tot\,\mathrm{Im}\,g + 1)^{0.407} \tag{12}$$

AdjustedSize model for Co-3 (adjusted $R^2 = 0.467$)
$$TotEff = 2.529\,New\mathrm{Im}\,g^{1.124} \tag{13}$$

AdjustedSize model for Co-4 (adjusted $R^2 = 0.693$)
$$TotEff = 886.953 + 114.80Hnew \tag{14}$$

AdjustedSize model for Co-5 (adjusted $R^2 = 0.939$)

$$TotEff = 5.818(TotHigh + 1)^{0.939} \qquad (15)$$

AdjustedSize model for Co-6 (adjusted $R^2 = 0.694$)

$$TotEff = 12.244TotWP^{0.715} \qquad (16)$$

The adjusted R^2 is a measure that indicates what percentage of variation in the dependent variable is explained by the independent variable(s). The closer it is to 1, the higher the explanatory power of the independent variable(s) selected by the model. For example *TotHigh* + 1 (see Equation 15) explains 93.9% of the variation in *TotEff*, which is remarkable. A low adjusted R^2 suggests that there are other variables that may also contribute to explain the variation in the dependent variable. These variables are very likely environmental (e.g. team's experience), and removed from our analysis for not being size measures.

Productivity Comparison
Once the *AdjustedSize* models were obtained, our next step was to use Equation 10 to calculate productivity for each of the six datasets. Their descriptive statistics are shown in Table 9, where Co_1_p, Co_2_p, Co_3_p, Co_4_p, Co_5_p, and Co_6_p correspond to productivities for companies Co-1, Co-2, Co-3, Co-4, Co-5, and Co-6, respectively.

Table 9. Descriptive statistics for Productivity values

Statistics	Co_1_p	Co_2_p	Co_3_p	Co_4_p	Co_5_p	Co_6_p
Mean	1.37	1.34	0.42	1.04	0.81	1.01
Median	0.97	0.75	0.33	0.99	0.84	0.98
Std. Deviation	1.05	1.23	0.46	0.20	0.35	0.36
Minimum	0.11	0.44	0.00	0.82	0.30	0.40
Maximum	3.80	4.27	1.45	1.44	2.26	1.57

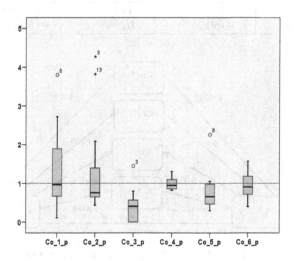

Fig. 12. Boxplots of productivity values for all six Companies

Table 9 shows that three companies (Co-6, Co-1, Co-4) had their median productivity very close to the productivity baseline of 1, indicating that half of their projects presented above average productivity and the other half presented below average productivity. Companies Co-5 and Co-2 presented median productivity slightly smaller than 1, indicating that more than half of their projects presented below average productivity. Finally, company Co-3 presented median productivity well below 1, thus indicating that most of its projects presented below average productivity. Companies Co-1 and Co-2 presented productivity values with a larger spread than the other companies, as indicated by their standard deviation.

A visual complement to descriptive statistics is boxplots of productivity values.

Fig. 12 shows boxplots of the productivity distributions for the six different companies. These boxplots suggest that the productivity values for companies Co_6, Co_1 and Co_4 are normally distributed, confirmed by the Shapiro-Wilk normality test ($\alpha = 0.05$). Company Co_4 presents a very peaked distribution showing that most of its productivity values lay around the baseline of 1; conversely, companies Co_1 and Co_2 present flatter distributions with a wider spread of values. Company Co_3 presented 19 of its productivity values below the baseline, indicating very poor productivity. The number of projects (and percentages) above 1, equal to 1 and below 1, per company, are detailed in Table 10.

Table 10. Productivity values $< 1, = 1, > 1$

Companies	Number and (Percentage) of Projects		
	Above 1	Equal to 1	Below 1
Co-1	6 (46%)	0 (0%)	7 (54%)
Co-2	6 (43%)	0 (0%)	8 (57%)
Co-3	3 (15%)	0 (0%)	17 (85%)
Co-4	7 (47%)	0 (0%)	8 (53%)
Co-5	5 (16%)	1 (3%)	25 (81%)
Co-6	9 (50%)	0 (0%)	9 (50%)

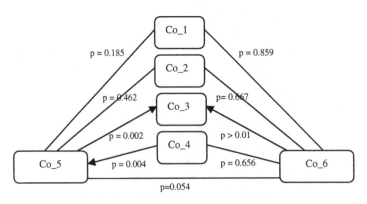

Fig. 13. Findings for the Statistical Significance test

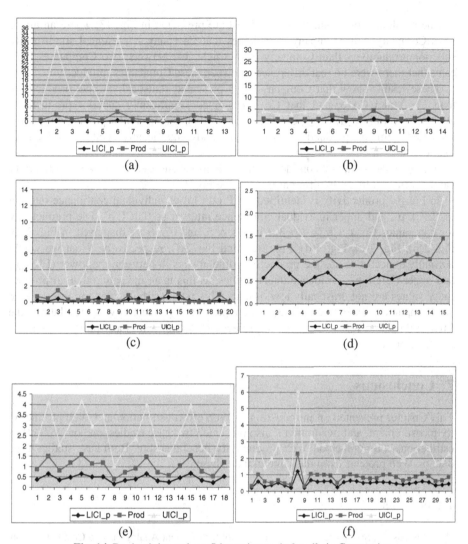

Fig. 14. Productivity and confidence intervals for all six Companies

These overall trends suggest that the companies that presented the best productivity were Co-6, followed by Co-4, Co-1 and Co-2. However, we still need to conduct a statistical significance test to ensure that the observed productivity differences between companies are legitimate, rather than having occurred due to chance. Statistical significance tests are used to check if different groups of data present similar distributions. If they do, this means that any observed differences between groups are due to chance alone. The statistical significance test used was the Mann-Whitney U test because the samples being compared were independent, and productivity values were not randomly distributed, confirmed using the Shapiro-Wilk normality test. Statistical significance was set at 95%.

The results of the Mann-Whitney U test are presented in Fig. 13, where an arrow from Company A to Company B indicates that Company A presented significantly superior productivity than Company B. A single line between two Companies indicates that there were no real differences between these Companies' productivity.

These results show that Company Co_3 presented statistically worse productivity than Co_5 and Co_6, and that Co_4 presented significantly superior productivity to Co_5. Overall Co_1, Co_2, Co_5 and Co_6 all presented similar productivity; Co_4 presented similar productivity to Co_6 and significantly better productivity than Co_5.

We have also obtained confidence intervals that were used to check if productivity values were significantly different from 1 (see Fig. 14).

In Fig. 14 productivity is identified as 'Prod', lower individual confidence interval as 'LICI_p', and upper individual confidence interval as 'UICI_p'. The productivity for companies Co_1, Co_2, Co_3, Co_4, Co_5, and Co_6 are displayed in Fig. 3(a), Fig. 3(b), Fig. 3(c), Fig. 3(d), Fig. 3(e), and Fig. 3(f), respectively. What we would normally expect is to see the productivity line always in between the lower (LICI_p) and upper (UICI_p) confidence interval lines, as this is an indication that all productivity values are not drastically low or high. This was clearly the pattern observed for all Companies, except for Co_3, which presented productivity values below the LICI_p threshold for seven of its 20 projects, indicating extremely poor productivity for those projects.

7 Conclusions

This Chapter presented an introduction to Web effort estimation and Web productivity measurement, and in addition it also presented two case studies, one on Web effort estimation, and another on Web productivity benchmarking. Both case studies used data on Web projects from the Tukutuku database.

References

[1] Angelis, L., Stamelos, I.: A Simulation Tool for Efficient Analogy Based Cost Estimation. Empirical Software Engineering 5, 35–68 (2000)
[2] Boehm, B.: Software Engineering Economics. Prentice-Hall, Englewood Cliffs (1981)
[3] Briand, L.C., El-Emam, K., Surmann, D., Wieczorek, I., Maxwell, K.D.: An Assessment and Comparison of Common Cost Estimation Modeling Techniques. In: Proceedings of ICSE 1999, Los Angeles, USA, pp. 313–322 (1999)
[4] Briand, L.C., Langley, T., Wieczorek, I.: A Replicated Assessment and Comparison of Common Software Cost Modeling Techniques. In: Proceedings of ICSE 2000, Limerick, Ireland, pp. 377–386 (2000)
[5] Brieman, L., Friedman, J., Olshen, R., Stone, C.: Classification and Regression Trees. Wadsworth, Belmont (1984)
[6] Conte, S., Dunsmore, H., Shen, V.: Software Engineering Metrics and Models. Benjamin/ Cummings, Menlo Park (1986)

[7] DeMarco, T.: Controlling Software Projects: Management, Measurement and Estimation. Yourdon, New York (1982)

[8] Finnie, G.R., Wittig, G.E., Desharnais, J.-M.: A Comparison of Software Effort Estimation Techniques: Using Function Points with Neural Networks, Case-Based Reasoning and Regression Models. Journal of Systems and Software 39, 281–289 (1997)

[9] Gray, A., MacDonell, S.: Applications of Fuzzy Logic to Software Metric Models for Development Effort Estimation. In: Proceedings of IEEE Annual Meeting of the North American Fuzzy Information Processing Society - NAFIPS, Syracuse, NY, USA, pp. 394–399 (1997)

[10] Gray, A., MacDonell, S.: A comparison of model building techniques to develop predictive equations for software metrics. Information and Software Technology 39, 425–437 (1997)

[11] Gray, R., MacDonell, S.G., Shepperd, M.J.: Factors Systematically associated with errors in subjective estimates of software development effort: the stability of expert judgement. In: Proceedings of the 6th IEEE Metrics Symposium (1999)

[12] Hughes, R.T.: An Empirical investigation into the estimation of software development effort. PhD thesis, Dept. of Computing, University of Brighton (1997)

[13] Jeffery, R., Ruhe, M., Wieczorek, I.: A Comparative study of two software development cost modelling techniques using multi-organizational and company-specific data. Information and Software Technology 42, 1009–1016 (2000)

[14] Jeffery, R., Ruhe, M., Wieczorek, I.: Using Public Domain Metrics to Estimate Software Development Effort. In: Proceedings of the 7th IEEE Metrics Symposium, London, UK, pp. 16–27 (2001)

[15] Jensen, F.V.: An introduction to Bayesian networks. UCL Press, London (1996)

[16] Kadoda, G., Cartwright, M., Chen, L., Shepperd, M.J.: Experiences Using Case-Based Reasoning to Predict Software Project Effort. In: Proceedings of the EASE 2000 Conference, Keele, UK (2000)

[17] Kemerer, C.F.: An Empirical Validation of Software Cost Estimation Models. Communications of the ACM 30(5), 416–429 (1987)

[18] Kirsopp, C., Shepperd, M.J.: Making Inferences with Small Numbers of Training Sets, January, TR02-01, Bournemouth University (2001)

[19] Kitchenham, B.A.: A Procedure for Analyzing Unbalanced Datasets. IEEE Transactions on Software Engineering 24(4), 278–301 (1998)

[20] Kitchenham, B.A., Mendes, E.: Software Productivity Measurement Using Multiple Size Measures. IEEE Transactions on Software Engineering 30(12), 1023–1035 (2004)

[21] Kitchenham, B.A., MacDonell, S.G., Pickard, L.M., Shepperd, M.J.: What accuracy statistics really measure. IEEE Proceedings Software 148(3), 81–85 (2001)

[22] Kitchenham, B.A., Pickard, L.M., Linkman, S., Jones, P.: Modelling Software Bidding Risks. IEEE Transactions on Software Engineering 29(6), 54–554 (2003)

[23] Kok, P., Kitchenham, B.A., Kirakowski, J.: The MERMAID Approach to software cost estimation. In: Proceedings of the ESPRIT Annual Conference, Brussels, pp. 296–314 (1990)

[24] Kumar, S., Krishna, B.A., Satsangi, P.S.: Fuzzy systems and neural networks in software engineering project management. Journal of Applied Intelligence 4, 31–52 (1994)

[25] Maxwell, K.: Applied Statistics for Software Managers. Prentice Hall PTR, Englewood Cliffs (2002)

[26] Mendes, E.: Cost Estimation Techniques for Web Projects. IGI Publishing (2007)

[27] Mendes, E., Kitchenham, B.A.: Web Productivity Measurement and Benchmarking. In: Mendes, E., Mosley, N. (eds.) Web Engineering, pp. 75–105. Springer, Heidelberg (2005)

[28] Mendes, E., Mosley, N. (eds.): Web Engineering. Springer, Heidelberg (2005)

[29] Mendes, E., Counsell, S., Mosley, N.: Measurement and Effort Prediction of Web Applications. In: Murugesan, S., Desphande, Y. (eds.) Web Engineering. LNCS, vol. 2016, pp. 57–74. Springer, Heidelberg (2001)

[30] Mendes, E., Mosley, N., Counsell, S.: Web Metrics – Estimating Design and Authoring Effort. IEEE Multimedia, Special Issue on Web Engineering, 50–57 (January/March 2001)

[31] Mendes, E., Mosley, N., Counsell, S.: The Application of Case-Based Reasoning to Early Web Project Cost Estimation. In: Proceedings of COMPSAC 2002, Oxford, UK (2002)

[32] Mendes, E., Mosley, N., Counsell, S.: Do Adaptation Rules Improve Web Cost Estimation? In: Proceedings of the ACM Hypertext conference 2003, Nottingham, UK (2003)

[33] Mendes, E., Mosley, N., Counsell, S.: A Replicated Assessment of the Use of Adaptation Rules to Improve Web Cost Estimation. In: Proceedings of the ACM and IEEE International Symposium on Empirical Software Engineering, Rome, Italy, pp. 100–109 (2003)

[34] Mendes, E., Mosley, N., Counsell, S.: Early Web Size Measures and Effort Prediction for Web Costimation. In: Proceedings of the IEEE Metrics Symposium, Sydney, Australia, pp. 18–29 (September 2003)

[35] Mendes, E., Mosley, N., Counsell, S.: Investigating Web Size Metrics for Early Web Cost Estimation. Journal of Systems and Software 77(2), 157–172 (2005)

[36] Myrtveit, I., Stensrud, E.: A Controlled Experiment to Assess the Benefits of Estimating with Analogy and Regression Models. IEEE Transactions on Software Engineering 25(4), 510–525 (1999)

[37] Ruhe, M., Jeffery, R., Wieczorek, I.: Cost Estimation for Web Applications. In: Proceedings of ICSE 2003, Portland, USA (2003)

[38] Schofield, C.: An empirical investigation into software estimation by analogy. PhD thesis, Dept. of Computing, Bournemouth University (1998)

[39] Schroeder, L., Sjoquist, D., Stephan, P.: Understanding Regression Analysis: An Introductory Guide, No. 57. In: Quantitative Applications in the Social Sciences. Sage Publications, Newbury Park (1986)

[40] Selby, R.W., Porter, A.A.: Learning from examples: generation and evaluation of decision trees for software resource analysis. IEEE Transactions on Software Engineering 14, 1743–1757 (1998)

[41] Shepperd, M.J., Kadoda, G.: Using Simulation to Evaluate Prediction Techniques. In: Proceedings of the IEEE 7th International Software Metrics Symposium, London, UK, pp. 349–358 (2001)

[42] Shepperd, M.J., Schofield, C.: Estimating Software Project Effort Using Analogies. IEEE Transactions on Software Engineering 23(11), 736–743 (1997)

[43] Shepperd, M.J., Schofield, C., Kitchenham, B.: Effort Estimation Using Analogy. In: Proceedings of ICSE-18, Berlin (1996)

[44] Srinivasan, K., Fisher, D.: Machine Learning approaches to estimating software development effort. IEEE Transactions on Software Engineering 21, 126–137 (1995)

[45] Stensrud, E., Foss, T., Kitchenham, B.A., Myrtveit, I.: An Empirical validation of the relationship between the magnitude of relative error and project size. In: Proceedings of the IEEE 8th Metrics Symposium, Ottawa, pp. 3–12 (2002)

Knowledge Base and Experience Factory for Empowering Competitiveness

Giuseppe Visaggio

Dipartimento di Informatica
SER& Practices s.r.l.- Spin off-
UNIVERSITA' DI BARI
visaggio@di.uniba.it

Abstract. As it is well-known, knowledge exploitation is becoming the focus of the economy for the competitiveness of both organizations and countries. In this chapter some models that enable enterprises towards the knowledge society are presented. An Experience Factory is suggested as support to such behavioral models. It collects empirical experiences as Experience-Knowledge Packages. The most relevant innovation of the chapter is represented by the contents and structure of the packages which are different from ones in the literature. The changes made to the structure aim to convince potential addressees to use the contents of the packages and favor their adoption independently from the author(s) of the package. Consequently, the proposed structure allows to produce packages incrementally and cooperatively. The proposed changes derive from the lessons learnt in previous experiences of technology transfer. The chapter presents the PROMETHEUS platform which implements all the requirements for collecting and distributing Knowledge-Experience Packages.

Keywords: Experience Factory, knowledge transfer, experience base; knowledge management.

1 Introduction

The competitive pressure for organizations and countries has moved the focus of economy from material to immaterial assets. Acquiring competitiveness in terms of immaterial factors requires empowering the capabilities for managing the immaterial assets through the knowledge chain. The comparative advantage of a public *administration*, of an enterprise or of a physical person (all referred to as *organism* in the rest of the chapter) based on immaterial factors is more enduring than the one based on material ones. Indeed, it is difficult to fill the knowledge gap that represents the benefit. The knowledge cycle for improving the competitive advantage is the basis of any *knowledge society* and of the development of new economic, technological and scientific paradigms related to it. It is characterized by an exploitation of knowledge as predominant factor for generating profit [16].

Given the space limitations of this chapter and in order to assure proper readability and comprehension, only part of the ample context of knowledge economy will be considered. Consequently, this chapter considers the economical aspects of knowledge

A. De Lucia and F. Ferrucci (Eds.): ISSSE 2006–2008, LNCS 5413, pp. 223–256, 2009.
© Springer-Verlag Berlin Heidelberg 2009

from an enterprise perspective and according to the Information Technology (IT) production and user enterprises. The chapter faces topics in a general way so that most of the concepts and technologies illustrated can be applied to any intensive knowledge business, but the chapter puts specific attention to Small to Medium Enterprises (SME) because they have the most difficulties in moving towards a knowledge economy and must therefore be supported. Moreover, in the IT sector they represent not less than 90% of the enterprises world wide [18].

Among the factors that favour an efficient use of knowledge, this chapter refers to the acquisition and enforcement of technological capabilities that characterize the excellence and diversity of an organism within a business domain [17]. Indeed, diversity provides a competitive benefit; excellence transforms such benefit into market opportunities. In order to develop and preserve the comparative advantage and to transform it into economical benefits, the behavioural models of the interested organisms can be different and not exclusive one from another.

Due to the dynamism of markets, both in the demand and offer, these capabilities must be continuously adapted through innovation that must consequently be frequent and rapid. Frequent innovation requires for an organism to dispose of original research results in its business domain, be able to quickly transform them in technological innovation to adapt in its business processes and socialize the new knowledge produced in order to preserve excellent and distinctive capabilities. Many investments are needed to achieve these goals. As so, an organism tends to limit the number of capabilities to invest on, in order to enhance excellence and diversity. The extension of the enterprise capabilities for each organism can be regulated according to the capabilities of investments and to the number of human resources of the organism itself. A minor extension of the enterprise capabilities corresponds to a lower request of human and financial resources, needed to support the acquisition, maintenance and continuous update of competences it is based on.

Research results are produced by unpredictable processes in terms of time and investments. Their transformation into innovation is also difficult to predict. Furthermore, specialised competences developed within an organism, through research and socialization of research results, create further risk for turnover; and make research and development investments highly risky. For example, the loss of a researcher implies the loss of the tacit knowledge assets that he/she has acquired during the research and development processes. Also, the unpredictability of research processes make the risk of wrong investment predictions and time needed for achieving satisfactory results important. So, it is important to go from a *Closed Innovation* towards an *Open Innovation* model [11]. In the *Closed Innovation* model the entire knowledge chain, from research to innovation, is carried out within the organism. On the other hand, in the *Open Innovation*, each organism provides research results or technologies produced during internally financed research and development projects that it is unable to use in a short term, but uses results made available by other organisms to create the innovations it needs, according to its strategic goals. Forwarding the knowledge produced by an organism's research to others allows for a quicker return of investments. Having the need to formalize research results, the organism must pay attention to the knowledge acquired during the job (near-the-job learning). Furthermore, exchanging knowledge with other organisms increases the number of knowledge providers, and reduces the risk of knowledge assets loss.

In spite of the incomes achievable with *Open Innovation*, the acquisition and enforcement of excellence capabilities is costly. This affects the costs of resources that support such capabilities, and therefore the project costs that the resources are involved in. To support competition, the project costs must decrease. As so, activities with low added value are distributed and transferred to enterprises with lower staff costs (off shoring or outsourcing), while the activities requesting excellence capabilities with high added value tend to be kept within the organism. This behavioural model, *distributed production*, allows speeding up the production and maintenance processes and facing time to market issues which inevitably have to cope with small time spaces. To adopt this approach the organisms must have good project planning and monitoring capabilities. Also, they must dispose of instruments for evaluating supplier and their own capabilities. Finally, in distributed projects, the risk of turnover of human resources increases, as so, the adoption of this model requires the ability to rapidly recover the lack of competences.

In some cases, the organism in charge of the project may not have all the excellence capabilities required for the project execution. In these cases it must cooperate with other organisms and make up the *Digital Business Ecosystem* (DBE) [15]. In such a situation, the organism in charge of the project is the customer and the other cooperating organisms are the suppliers. It is obvious that the customer organism in a DBE must have capabilities for managing distributed projects. For completeness, large enterprises use an alternative paradigm to DBE, without excluding it, for acquiring complementary excellence capabilities through Merge & Acquisition processes.

In the previous behavioural models, the common denominator that this chapter intends to analyze is knowledge management. Currently, the Experience Factory (EF) model that collects empirical knowledge in an Experience Base (EB) repository is well known [10]. The EF aims to understand, plan, predict, control, verify and improve business processes. The collection of empirical knowledge in an Experience Package (EP) aims to reduce the consequences of knowledge loss due to staff turnover that tacitly detain the knowledge, improve products and processes, and assure near-the-job learning for improving the quality of tasks to carry out.

This chapter proposes a model for systematically structuring the content of a *Package* particularly oriented to explicit practices for adopting knowledge (acquisition and exploitation) in a business process of a productive organism. The organism we refer to can be a research one, or a service/product production one. Different types of contents are expressed in a same Package such as: research results, experience, tools, and innovative technologies. The structure of the package can be adapted to different types of contents. The package has a modular structure and expresses the relation between the state of art the package refers to, and the package contents: the research results, the practices, and the experience for adoption in a business process. Explicit experience is able to convince the potential users of the values deriving from the adoption of the Package. The structure of the package has components that guide user organisms in adopting it. The knowledge expressed according to this structure is called from here on *Knowledge-Experience Package* (KEP). The repository that contains the KEP is called, *Knowledge-Experience Base* (KEB).

The proposal in this chapter is innovative with respect to current literature and to other existing knowledge bases, for the contents and the structure of the KEP along with its components that derive from lessons learned during knowledge management and exploitation in business processes. Indeed, the chapter shows that thanks to the outlined structure, the proposed KEP, together with conventional activities of EF, is a good support for any organism operating within knowledge economy with behavioural models expressed in the previous paragraphs.

The remaining part of the chapter is organized as follows: section 2 provides a rigorous definition of data, information, knowledge and experience according to the perspective of this chapter. Section 3 describes the state of art about the EB and EF. Section 4 describes the author's proposal for extending the EB and KEB and increases its efficacy given the aim of the chapter. Section 5 describes the PROMETHEUS platform that is an experimental prototype of the KEB with the characteristics presented in the previous paragraph. Section 6 describes the guidelines for producing and evolving KEB contents. Next, section 7 analyzes the value of PROMETHEUS for stakeholders as support to how the KEB can contribute to satisfy the requirements of relational and business models as factors of knowledge economy. Finally, conclusions are drawn. References are provided for further details on the topics faced in the chapter.

2 Data, Information, Knowledge and Experience

In order to better understand the contents of the chapter, it is important to have suitable definitions of data, information, knowledge and experience. In literature there are many definitions of these concepts that are adapted to the context they are applied to, but they are not effective for the aims of this chapter. As so, it is necessary to provide rigorous definitions appropriate to the context of application considering that they are different from the meaning attributed to them in literature and in everyday language.

Knowledge of IT in most cases derives from empirical induction. As so, it is important that the definition of *data* should indicate the value of one of the attributes required to describe a Fact (F); each attribute corresponds to one aspect of a fact and is relevant to the point of view from which it is being considered. Formally, a fact is described by a set of data that can be expressed as in (1) where: K is the number of attributes, generic d_{ij} is a data that represents the j-th attribute of the i-th fact.

$$F_i = (< d_{i1}, d_{i2}, d_{i3}, \dots d_{iK}>) . \tag{1}$$

For example, table 1 shows the data that describe facts: Maintenance requests, sorted by date, for a software system S. Each fact is described by a set of attributes <# Maintenance Request, Maintenance Type, Effort Spent, Components Involved>.

Information is a concept that assumes many meanings. In common language it describes something material (i.e. a product, a tool) or immaterial (i.e. historical, television, radio event); this type of information can be defined as *Descriptive Information*. In many scientific contexts information is contained and coded in a message transferred by a source (i.e. codes from electronic transmissions, genes of a DNA, data inserted into an information system, etc), it can be classified as *Entropic*

Table 1. Example of Data

#Maintenance Request for S	Maintenance Type	Effort Spent (Man/days)	Components Involved
1	C (Corrective)	2	1
2	A (Adaptive)	4	35
3	C	4	7
4	C	4	8
5	C	5	10
6	C	6	8
7	P (Perfective)	15	43
8	C	2	2
...	...	...	...
29	C	6	8

Information. Some times this concept is used to identify data classification models used to confirm or reject elements useful for someone or something (i.e. surveys, exit pool, and so on). These can be identified as *Notion Information.*

Since the aim of the chapter is empirical induction, we are interested in information that can be extracted from data that describe facts. It will be called *Information Mining* to distinguish it from other types of information described previously. The generic term of *Information* (INF) in the context of this chapter refers to this type of definition. It is the interpretation of a set of facts or relations. The information reveals the underlying meaning of facts and makes it useful for the users who perform tasks and make decisions. Formally, this can be represented as a function M (Mining) applied on a set of facts:

$$INF_l = M_l\{F_1, F_2, F_3, \ldots, F_n\} = M_l (\{d_{ij}\}: i = 1, \ldots N; J = 1, \ldots, K(i)) \qquad (2)$$

M_l is a function that points out and interprets data patterns that describe facts, classified in the best way to extract useful information.

For example, some information mined from the facts in table 1, with different M functions to classify, extract patterns and interpret them, are listed as follows. To ease reading, codes have been used instead of generic INF_l.

$\underline{E_c}$: <u>effort for corrective maintenance increases over time</u> as it appears from Fig. 1 that graphically illustrates the effort spent over the course of time to satisfy each corrective maintenance request. If a longer series of facts were available it would be possible to extract other information from the set of data, such as the prediction model for the trend of number of maintenance requests and for the effort needed to fulfil them.

$\underline{N_a}$: adaptive maintenance requests are less frequent than corrective or perfective ones;

$\underline{E_a}$: <u>the effort required to make the software evolve tends to increase in time, and it is greater than for corrective maintenance;</u>

$\underline{N_p}$: <u>requests for perfective maintenance are less frequent than corrective ones but more frequent than adaptive ones.</u>

$\underline{E_p}$: the effort required for perfective maintenance is generally greater than corrective and lower than effort for adaptive maintenance;

$\underline{R_a}$: after an adaptive maintenance request, the number of requests for corrective maintenance increases

$\underline{R_p}$: after perfective maintenance, the number of corrective maintenance requests decreases.

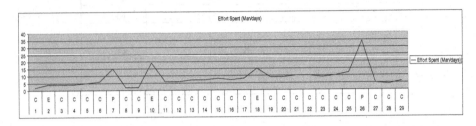

Fig. 1. Effort spent vs Maintenance Requests

A further Mining of the facts presented in table 1 showing the number of components involved in each request for maintenance, is presented in Fig. 2 Other information can be extracted.

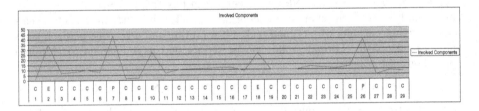

Fig. 2. Maintenance Request vs Components Involved

$\underline{C_a}$. The corrective and adaptive maintenance changes gradually increase the number of components involved.

$\underline{C_p}$. The perfective maintenance changes reduce the number of software components involved.

The concept of *knowledge* in everyday life, as well as in literature is defined as one or more relations between notions, extracted from what data and facts describe.

In order to favour empirical induction, it is important to provide a definition that points out the concept of knowledge as induced from information and that requires formalization so that it can be used independently from who has generated it. As so, we define *Mined Knowledge* as broader than data and information, which requires understanding of information along with the relations between information mined by the data. To make the definition clearer, we assume that: the relations between information elements are complex. Consequently, they can be interpreted from a view point that reduces the relevant aspects of the relation. Such view point is expressed by a *problem that knowledge application must contribute to solve*, usually identified as P_i.

For clearness, a problem, in the remaining part of this chapter, is a question, simple or complex, of relevant interest for a knowledge domain having difficulties and that may lead to inconveniences. Its solution is made up of notion information known in certain circumstances. According to the scope of the question, a *Problem* can be classified as: *decisional* if the solution supports decisions for overcoming negative effects that occur or may occur during process execution; *transcendental* if it requires deductive reasoning, even formal based on proven theories.

For Pi the contents of a set of information items:

$$\{INF\}:\{ < INF_1, INF_2, INF_3,.... INF_i>\} \tag{3}$$

and the relationships among information items are needed:

$$\{R(\{INF\})\}:\{ R_1\{ INF_1\}; R_2\{ INF_2\} R_3\{ INF_3\}... R_l\{ INF_l\}\} \tag{4}$$

In these formulas (3 and 4), each $\{ INF_k\}$ is a combination of elements in $\{INF\}$. In the rest of the chapter *Mined Knowledge* will be referred to as *Knowledge* (KW).

Formally, KW can be represented by a function G (Generates):

$$KW_i = G_i(P_i, \{R(\{INF\})\}) \tag{5}$$

Function G_i selects the information components and the relations, among the ones available from the data and M functions, and generalizes the interpretation of the information and of the relations. The generic G_i function is produced by a competent organism that is able to identify which information and which relations, among the available ones, are effective to provide a solution to problem P_i, and interpret and generalize such relations. Once the generic KW_i is expressed, it can be used by all organisms in spite of the knowledge producer.

For example: suppose to have a problem P <how can software quality degradation be reduced during maintenance?>. The problem domain is software maintenance. The information that describes the context where the maintenance process is executed has been extracted from table 1. The essential relations, among the extractable ones, to solve the problem are: after corrective or adaptive maintenance the number of components impacted (C_a) increases, this implies that corrective maintenance tends to increase the internal cohesion of a system. Consequently, perfective maintenance should be carried out to mitigate such complexity (R_p); following to perfective maintenance, the number of corrective maintenance requests is less (C_p), this reduces the trend of quality degradation. Consequently, in this case the application of formula (5) gives the following result:

KW = < to reduce quality degradation of a software system, when quality of a system decays following to corrective and adaptive maintenance, perfective maintenance is advisable > = G (P, R(C_e, R_p, C_p)).

Experience in everyday contexts as well as in literature is tacit, it is closed in the mind of who has acquired it by continuously applying knowledge and abilities. Experience can also have various classifications. For example, Common Experience, Critical Experience, Religious Experience and so on.

This chapter refers to *Empirical Experience* (EXP), acquired by applying knowledge in various contexts and by extracting data and facts from its application that confirm or deny the previous extracted knowledge. Application of knowledge can be required by a project, or by a laboratory experiment replicated in a controlled context to confirm or deny a conjecture or a principle.

Project is intended as the execution of a set of correlated processes that use knowledge or technology to validate their efficacy in practice. In this chapter, a controlled experiment, carried out in a laboratory context to prove the efficacy of the innovation when adopted and applied to a process, is also intended as a project.

Applications of interest of this chapter are the *acquisition* and *exploitation* of knowledge in order to improve business process goals along with the quality of its products and services; *performances*, execution speed, costs, conformity, stability, capability. The application of knowledge requires proper indicators that allow to make a cost-benefit analysis following to each acquisition or exploitation. Such indicators must be empirically validated in different contexts. The more the replications of experiments, the more confident managers and researchers will be in acquiring and exploiting knowledge.

EXP is critical for the scope of this chapter. Indeed, acquired or exploited knowledge in a business process goes from the state of art to the state of practice and then becomes a technology that supports continuous improvements in process performances. If the knowledge that is transformed into technology is a set of research results, this transformation carries out an *innovation* and, normally, it increases the competitive benefit of who uses it. Moreover, if the research result is used to improve the product of the business process, it is defined as *product innovation*, if it refers to an improvement of the performances, then it is defined as *process innovation*.

Formally, an EXP is a function EE (Empirical Evidence) of a chunk of knowledge used in Acquisition or Exploitation projects (A/E) from where a set of process or performance indicators (I) are extracted.

$$\text{EXP}(KW_i) = \text{EE}\ (KW_i,\ \{ A/E_{i1},\{I_{i1}\},\ A/E_{i2},\{I_{i2}\},\ A/Ei_3,\{I_{i3}\},\ldots,\ A/E_{iN},\{I_{iN}\}\}) \quad (6)$$

KW_i is the knowledge to require. It can be descriptive and/or formally expressed, as defined above;

A/E_{ij}, describes the project where KW_i was applied the j-th time;

$\{I_{ij}\}$ is the set of indicators measured on the business process during the application of the j-th chunk of KW_i knowledge.

The number of N applications varies in time because the application of KW_i may be replicated in an increasing number of projects in the package life time.

The set of $\{I_{ij}\}$ indicators can be different from the set $\{I_{ik}\}$ because the k previous experiences may have led to decisions for validating the efficacy of KW_i by adding or modifying indicators.

EE is a function that abstracts the main results after applying KW_i. For example, suppose to have a problem P < improve the maintainability of a software system > and a KW <the maintainability of a software system can be improved by a Reverse engineering (RE) and Renewal process; Renewal is guided by software quality indicators>. KW would also include a formal description of the process, the techniques and the tools used for its description. For space reasons we have omitted it.

Table 2. Example of EXP

N	Acquisition				Last trimester without RE					First trimester without RE				
	T	Staff	EA	C	MU	E	ER	IM	IR	MU	E	ER	IM	IR
1	20	IH, DK	600	630	60	2520	92	7	85	42	1272	22	2	15
2	12	IH	280	336	72	2870	91	6.3	83	45	1356	5	2	8

Legend

T= time needed to acquire RE in working days.

Staff = competences that the enterprise does not have and that must be identified externally

EA = effort for acquisition in man hrs. This includes the effort for transferring and the effort for acquiring and eventually the effort for training.

C = cost in thousands of Euros

MU = number of Maintenance Unit (MU) carried out. A MU is a set of maintenance requests that are assigned to an individual developer. It is expected that they require about 30 man hrs of effort to be satisfied. This time includes the changes to software documentation;

E = average effort in man hrs spent for carrying out MU;

ER = Effort Risk in percentage = N_i/M.U. *100 where N_i is the number of MU having E > (30 ± 0,05*30);

IM = average number of components impacted by the MU carried out;

IR = Impact Risk in percentage = N_i/U.M. *100 where N_i is the number of MU having IM > ($IM_{expected}$ ± 0,05*30).

IH = knowledge of Information Hiding and of the practices needed to develop it

DK = knowledge of the application domain

In order to measure the efficacy of RE, a set of measures has been set. In the example, they correspond to {MU, E, ER, IM, IR}. Other measures that express the contexts in which projects are carried out have been collected {T, EA, Staff, IM, IR}. Note that the indicators, the projects and the measurement values are fictitious and are only used for explanatory reasons for clearing the concepts of EXP. The two projects we have applied RE to, shown in table 2, refer to different contexts, with different competences. The second project already has the IH competence, the dimensions of the problem are different because the second project has more UM and the software is more maintainable. Applying RE generates the following EE < RE makes the system more maintainable by reducing the impact of changes and the risk of incorrect predictions; increases software quality by reducing maintenance requests along with MU; reduces Effort and its prediction risks making the maintenance process more stable and assuring that costs return in reasonable time spans>

3 State of Art on EB and EF

3.1 Aim and Representation of the EB

The aim of the EB is to support enterprise competitiveness. Indeed, in order to win competition it is important to dispose of a well defined set of products able to satisfy customer needs. As so, the EB must contain *product models* and how their characteristics relate with the expectations of a specific market sector. It must also contain *process models* that continuously improve products and services included in the enterprise assets. Finally it must contain process and product quality models that allow evaluating the enterprise placement with respect to strategic goals. In this case the models must also specify improvement actions in case the measures collected are far from the expected values.

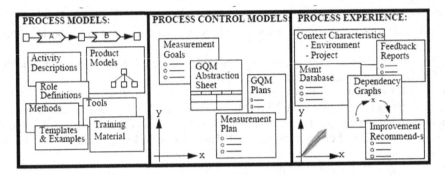

Fig. 3. Experience Package

Fig. 3 shows the representation of the contents of an Experience Package (EP) as known in the literature the author refers to [8]. It represents the process, product and quality models along with the details needed for adopting the package. This component may also contain training material for learning how to use the knowledge to apply. The second view covers the Process Control Model, i.e. models for how to evaluate the quality of process goals and performances before and after applying the Knowledge Package. The third view covers the empirical experience of how to use the Knowledge Package. The essential elements for building an Experience Package according to [8] are: the Goal Question Metrics paradigm for measuring and controlling quality; the Quality Improvement Paradigm (QIP) and the Experience Factory.

3.2 Aim and Representation of the Experience Factory

The EF represents a continuous cycle that allows learning from experience collected in the EB during project execution. The learning process starts from a quality control and assurance cycle. The first consists in collecting measures, according to specific quality models, evaluating their achievement with respect to the project in execution, and identifying improvement actions. The second consists in collecting information from executed projects and improving the EP in order to assure that their adoption reduces the gap between project goals and strategic enterprise ones.

The control cycle relies on the Goal Question Metrics (GQM) paradigm, while the quality assurance one uses the Quality Improvement Paradigm (QIP).

GQM is a paradigm for building goal oriented, and therefore flexible, quality models. It is a systematic approach for specializing goals according to specific project and organization needs, process or product models, quality values [24]. GQM produces operational results of quality model measurements in a systematic manner. In other words, a same combination of measurement values is associated to an interpretation that is independent from who carries it out and when it is carried out. The GQM schema is represented in Fig. 4.

Fig. 4. GQM Model Representation

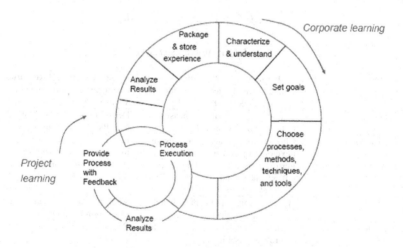

Fig. 5. Quality Improvement Paradigm

The Quality Improvement Paradigm is the underlying methodological framework for systematic improvement [8]. As such, it guides the activities and goals of the continuous improvement oriented organizations. QIP is essentially based on an appropriate characterization of the environment. The paradigm provides a context for goal definition and is essentially based on the systematic reuse of obtained experiences by packaging them in structured knowledge. The improvement process due to QIP is defined as an iterative process that repeatedly performs a sequence of basic activities. QIP includes two different cycles. One cycle can be seen as a step towards project related improvement (project level). Simultaneously, it is a step

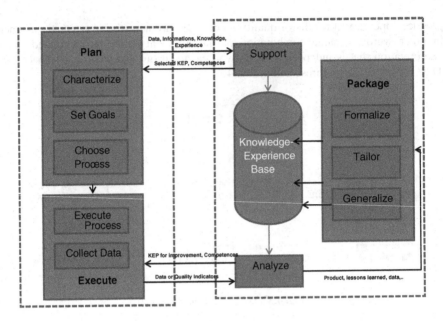

Fig. 6. Experience Factory Model

Table 3. QIP Activities Description

QIP Step	Project Level Activities	Strategic Level Activities
Characterize	Characterize Project and identify relevant models to be reused.	Characterize organizations and identify future trends.
Set Goals	Define project goals in measurable terms and derive related metrics.	Define improvement goals and add hypothesis in measurable terms.
Choose Models	Choose appropriate processes and develop project plan.	Identify projects or pilots for investigating the hypothesis.
Execute	Perform project according to plan, collect data, and provide on line feedback for project guidance.	Perform projects or pilots and collect data.
Analyze	Analyze project and collect data and suggest improvements.	Analyze project and pilots and evaluation hypotheses.
Package	Package analysis results into improved reusable models.	Package experiences for use in future projects.

towards long-term learning and improvement in an organization (strategic level). The QIP process is summarized in Fig. 4. The project level improvement process is integrated into the strategic-level improvement process, because achieving a long term improvement goal is typically done by means of improvement in multiple projects or pilot studies.

During the last 25 years, the topic of knowledge transferring, reuse and storing has largely been discussed in literature. In 1989, evolving research previously conducted by Rombach [8], was extended by Basili with the Experience Factory (EF) [23]. The EF concept was developed in research and industrial context and refined (http://www.esernet.org), surveyed [17], taught [19], specialized to different domains

Table 4. EB characterization

Name	Organization	Goal	Contents	Users
CeBase	National Science Foundation (NSF): Centre for Empirically Based Software Engineering	Collect empirical models in order to provide validated guidelines for selecting techniques and models, for research, and for supporting software engineering education.	A variety of empirical data on topics such as COTS or reading techniques: - FAQs - Lessons learned - publications/ papers	Empirical researchers
Acquisition Best Practices Clearinghouse	US Department of Defence (DoD)	To provide a centralized repository of validated, actionable practice information that have been approved and deemed useful	descriptions/ characterization of practices : - applicable context descriptions; - cost/benefit information - validity information - empirical studies about the practices - contacts to experts and discussion groups	DoD workforce and government contractors
VSEK	German BMBF (Ministry for Education and Research) developed by a consortium of research organizations	Exchange experience to engineer increasingly complex software via web-portal, presentations and workshops, and project collaboration.	Software Engineering topics: - Software Engineering Body of Knowledge SWEBOK; - application domains systems; - extensive glossary of terms	Open Community
ESERNET	Fraunhofer IESE	Information extracted from empirical studies and their packaging so they can be reused across company boundaries. Fraunhofer provides training and coaching people to support experience extraction via empirical studies. It thereby establishes a world-leading network of excellence in Experimental Software Engineering (ESE).	Current topic areas of interest are: - Inspections and Testing - Object-oriented design and implementation - Component-based software engineering Agile Software Development	European software intensive organizations.

Table 4. (*Continued*)

The MIT Process Handbook	MIT	Online libraries for sharing and managing many kinds of knowledge about business.	The area of interest is - Process model - Process activities - Process elements - Process Example - Process Applications	Researcher and Business people
HPCBugBase	Experimental Software Engineering Group (ESEG) at the University of Maryland	Accumulate empirical knowledge about commonly occurring defects in HPC codes using an incremental approach.	Patterns of: - functional bugs - performance bottlenecks - portability problems - bad practices	Practitioners and programmers
Software Program Managers Networks	Assistant Secretary of the Navy	To identify proven industry and government software best practices and convey them to managers of large-scale software-intensive acquisition programs.	- Best practices - Best practices acquisition models	Organization, managers and subject matter experts interested in improving the practice of managing software development and maintenance programs.

[1], [2], [11], [12], [16], [22], [23], and implemented [17]. EF is a logical organization, which may have a separate physical implementation [23].

The EF interacts with business processes as shown in Fig. 5.

3.3 Interrelationship between QIP and EF

The literature analysis and study of QIP and Experience Factory issues are strictly linked to practices and applications. Indeed, QIP and EF emerge as consequence to the collaboration of research and industrial communities (http://bpch.dau.mil; http://ccs.mit.edu/ph/).

With refer to Fig. 6, at a strategic level the cycle abstracts and packages empirical experience extracted during the project level cycle. The latter uses experience collected in the EB to eliminate or at least mitigate the shifting between the goals expected for each project and the ones carried out during project execution.

More precisely, table 3 describes the activities carried out according to the QIP paradigm and how they fill the EF.

3.4 EB and EF in Industrial Contexts

Many EF and EB are developed in industrial contexts. An important reference for analysis is the website http://ccs.mit.edu/ph. It contains a list of developed and experimented EB. Table 4 lists the most common and used EB. The analysis of the EB listed in the table shows that EB contents, goals and stakeholders are very different. None of them is able to fulfil the motivations and the goals of this chapter, outlined in the introduction.

As so, the author has defined the structure and the contents of an EB according to the aims of the chapter.

4 Implementation of the EB in KEB

The aim of the KEB is, as for the EB, to support enterprise competitiveness. KEB considers the fact that enterprises move towards knowledge economy and in doing so, they use the behavioural models described in the introduction. Consequently, the contents of the KEB are oriented to explicit the practices for adopting *research results* or *innovation*. Furthermore, the KEB adds all the useful components to the EB that can guide an organism in adopting the KEP. From this point on, KEP will generically identify either: a package only containing knowledge, or one containing knowledge and experience.

The relations between KEB and GQM, QIP and EF are the same as described for EB.

4.1 Types of KEP

KEP can be classified by their content. In the following, a set of types are listed. They are not to be intended as a check list because experience can point out the need to define other KEP.

Product. Descriptive information of tools, software tools of any abstraction level that can be used in one or more activities of a software process in order to improve them. The KEP must contain information that expresses how to specialize them in the various contexts, how and when to use or reuse them and the experiences collected as they are adopted in various projects.

Process. Paradigms or models of process parts; details of procedures, techniques or algorithms to use in development processes to improve them. The experience collected in development projects following to their enactment.

Relations. Relations among observable process or product characteristics and specific quality goals. They may also contain relations among competences (knowledge and abilities) and the enterprise capabilities to develop, and between the competences and the tests for evaluating them. Finally, they contain the empirical evidence of their validity collected during the projects they were used in.

Management. Useful knowledge for managing co-located and distributed projects. In particular, the knowledge needed to monitor and mitigate project risks that use different process paradigms (i.e. product line development, component development including COTS, OSS development; service development). The experiences connected contain indicators for evaluating the efficacy of the application of knowledge in real projects.

Intelligence. Knowledge derived from the statistical analysis of collected data for various scopes. For example, logs of tools or software usage, semantic extraction of messages collected by tools assisting users on a product or service. Essentially, this type of package explicates stakeholder knowledge of a process or product. The experiences connected are needed to confirm or deny the same knowledge in different contexts and in different projects.

It is the case to recall that a KEP can be a hybrid, in other words, its content can be made up of pieces belonging to different types of packages. In each case, the readability and *comprehensibility* of the KEP should be guaranteed. To comprehend a KEP in the meaning of the chapter, one must be able to understand the semantics of its contents and learn the practices to adopt it.

4.2 Structure of the Contents of a KEP

The presentation of information and of the relations that represent the knowledge and the indicators that express their application or knowledge exploitation can be done through Formal Reports or Narrative Stories [14]. The first are cheap to produce and minimize the ambiguities in the description of contents, but they are complex to *comprehend.* The second ones require relevant effort to be produced and can have many ambiguities, although they are easier to *comprehend.*

The first innovation introduced by the author's proposal consists in using a structured form of presentation using various types of expression, according to the contents to represent: graphs, algorithms, mechanisms to package experience (such as decision tables, dynamic prediction models), and text. The schema of the contents is represented in Fig. 7.

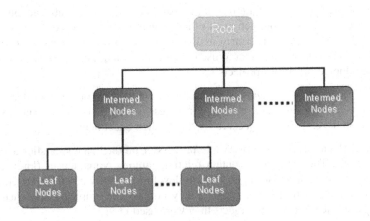

Fig. 7. Hierarchical schema of the KEP

The description is logically organized as a tree. The contents of each node must be adapted to a screen so it remains easy to read. The root node describes the problems the KEP refers to. It contains a reasoned index of the overall structure and explains the reader which part of the solution is expressed in each of the underlying nodes. In case of a complex problem, sub problems can be identified each focusing on a specific section of the KEP. The intermediate nodes describe a sub problem or an aspect of the solution they refer to and contain the index of the underlying levels of nodes. The intermediate nodes contain the information and the relations among them. If there are nodes relating to knowledge, extracted following to the acquisition or to the exploitation of knowledge in projects, the package is a KEP. The leaf nodes contain details of the knowledge or of the experience that the intermediate node refers to. In particular, they contain the information and the relations that make up the described knowledge. It is the case to point out that the index contained in the node allows the reader to select the parts he/she is interested in, or decide the sequence for reading the contents. This structure generally improves the readability of the KEP [6].

To assure readability it is advisable that a node does not depend from more than eight other ones. Also, the tree underlying a KEP should not have more than three levels. In case the description needs more levels of detail, the KEP should be divided into multiple KEP connected one to another. The division can be made according to sub-problems, acquisition experience, knowledge exploitation, or according to a combination of the previous elements. The choice is left to the author of the KEP.

4.3 Contents of a KEP

The second innovation of the author concerns the KEP content [6]. A KEP must contain problems one intends answering. As so, the information derives from research results or previous projects together with the relations that are able to provide an answer to the problem.

The specific contents of knowledge can be left to literature and to other conventional sources, while the content of the KEP must pay attention to expressing the relations between research results and extracted knowledge used to answer the problem. Furthermore, the KEP must express how the knowledge is transformed in practice, i.e. the processes and the activities that it must innovate and how it should be applied to provide an efficacious answer to the problems. In order to promote the reuse of a KEP its specific contents should indicate the knowledge that users should have to adopt it. In this sense, a set of indications is reported. It can be improved as a KEP is adopted and new knowledge is developed.

The requirements for acquiring and for efficiently using the research or innovation results proposed by the KEP include: enterprise capabilities, competences, economical and instrumental resources. It is also the case to point out the adoption risks of the KEP. Among these, the experts of the problem domain faced by the KEP should identify the barriers that they expect to overcome with the solutions. Without this correspondence they will most likely discard the KEP and not consider it relevant for the problem domain [5], [13], [20]. Improvement initiatives should be enacted for each risk so that users become confident in overcoming possible barriers in adopting the KEP and are sure to achieve the expected goals [5], [20]. Another aspect to point out is the plan for adopting the experience package. It must point out the activities, times, resources and the competences needed. The plan should provide all the information for evaluating adoption costs. In order to make a precise cost-benefit analysis the impact on processes and products connected to the involved knowledge should be pointed out. The description of the impact should possibly be formal, or at least rigorous to allow for a cost-benefit analysis of the adoption and exploitation of the knowledge in the

KEP. All stakeholders should participate to this process to favour KEP adoption. Also, to induce this participation all the values that adoption generates should be pointed out and classified by each stakeholder [2], [14], [20].

Among the experiences that have to be added to knowledge, it is important to consider the ones showing that the application of KEP is efficacious in one or more projects. GQM can be used to point out the goals that evaluate the efficacy of adoption in previous projects, monitor the adoption process, and describe the metrics model. The metrics model should evaluate each business aspect and therefore set perspectives of interest, from the stakeholders' point of view. As so, it must quantitatively express the values for stakeholders. Furthermore, it must express the statistical indicators that show the validity of results achieved with the reuse of KEP. The indicators expected by the metrics model should be used to enforce and support the empirical validity of KEP reuse. In particular, they must point out the success or failure of reusing the KEP with respect to the aspects of interest: goals predicted and achieved enactment of financial and economical returns, risk control and mitigation, appropriateness of improvement initiatives. KEP should be continuously improved, as so the QIP paradigm can be used.

The history of a KEP should be reported in order to point out the maturity of the package, track the evolutions and the motivations for change, along with the decisions made during each change. Decisions should be supported by empirical evidence, extracted after reusing KEP in projects. It must describe the initiatives carried out for improving KEP, the acquisition processes, the corresponding metrics model, and possible failures that arise during the adoption process. To better point out the history of the KEP its content can be divided into two sections: the current KEP and the history of its evolution with all the decisions adopted. The improvement must concern KEP components, described in the next section.

The content of the KEP must be adaptable to various contexts [5], [8], [20]. As so, its presentation must specify how it can be tailored to each context. In detail, the author of the KEP should describe an invariant and variant part of the acquisition process that describes the portability, scalability and usability in various contexts.

If a KEP is complex, its acquisition is incremental [20]. For this reason, in case of a complex KEP (i.e. with a long acquisition process, with high costs, a high number of risks and expensive improvement actions) the author should break it down into simpler KEP connected one to another that can be acquired by following a specific sequence.

4.4 Components of the KEP

The components of a KEP aim, in the author's proposal, to quickly improve *comprehension* of the KEP. The rapidity of acquiring a KEP in research or production processes is favoured by tools that automate repetitive process acquisition activities [3], [5]. So, it is the case to adopt tools that support KEP reuse and training courses that speed up learning. Furthermore, it is important to include competence producers that are able to support researchers and practitioners in acquiring and exploiting a KEP. The projects that have adopted a KEP should also be described and contain the context, the specializations carried out on the KEP to tailor it to the context, the values of the measures carried out to monitor the project. These can be used to verify

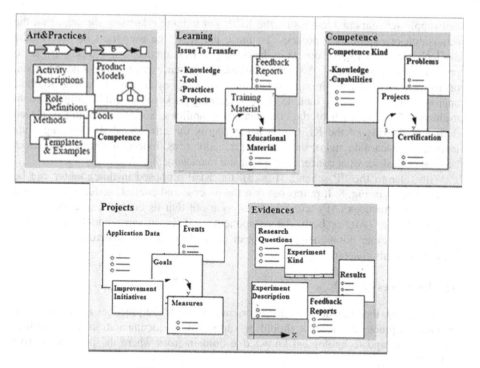

Fig. 8. Knowledge-Experience Package

the efficacy of the KEP according to the metric model described in the KEP and to collect other observations that may be useful for improving the KEP in any of its components.

The details of the project may not be available, for privacy restrictions of the organism. In each case, it is important to know the characteristics of the investigation that has been carried out with the project details and the results used for proving the cause-effect relation between the application of the KEP and the values expressed in the indicators that characterize the KEP [5], [20]. Such information makes up the contents of the evidences component.

In projects and in evidences, the data must be controlled to increase the confidence level for potential users of the KEP [20]. As so, the contents of the two components should describe the process and the instruments for controlling data and the result of their application during process execution. Project descriptions should also refer to tools and resources used during their execution. The relation between competences, tools, projects and evidences assures the appropriateness of tools and of available competences for the KEP. Given the incremental adoption of KEP, the time needed to complete this process tends to increase [20]. To mitigate the risk of resources volatility when adopting a KEP, which increases as the process time increases, it is advisable to have a consistent number of knowledge suppliers in the competences component.

A good comprehension of a KEP favours the consent among stakeholders in terms of its application [20]. This leads to enriching a KEP with instructive e-learning courses that supply seminars and lessons on the KEP, and training e-learning for details on the acquisition or exploitation process. To reuse the KEP, the user must be sure of the available resources [5]. Resources in the competences component should be certified to prove their appropriateness. Also, the available competences within the same organism, or formed and trained through e-learning must be evaluated according to their appropriateness. To satisfy such need, the e-learning packages should be complete with evaluation tests for each of the components or abilities. Specific attention is placed during monitoring of the KEP for what concerns the efficacy of the learning units included in e-learning and of the relative evaluation tests. Indeed, the human resources become critical for what concerns adoption and management of KEP.

With refer to the EP schema (Fig. 3), the KEP proposed in this chapter can be represented as in Fig. 8. It points out that the process and control model is substituted by the Art&Practices (AP) component to point out that its content can express only research results (Art) or both, the components and the process models (Practices). Furthermore, other components have been pointed out by the structure of the KEP presented in this chapter.

4.5 Resources of KEP

As mentioned, the content of a KEP is oriented towards the practices for its adoption in business processes, as so it should be supported by documentation that describes the scientific and technological knowledge domain from where the practices derive [13], [20].

In spite of the interest towards rigour of each author, a KEP can contain ambiguities and incomplete parts that a user may want to clear. It is therefore important to have contacts with KEP knowledge suppliers.

4.6 Metadata

In a public or private KEB the number of collected KEP tend to increase. As so, the KEB should be supported by search tools for quickly searching candidate solutions and to evaluate its appropriateness. In particular, researchers must find all the available research results in the KEB that can favour achieving expected goals [20]. Practitioners must find the available solutions to give a consistent and convincing solution to the problems that they face in projects [14].

Practitioners that do not find available KEP, tend to face problems that arise during project execution according to their own experience. Such experience is most likely tacit and therefore costly to apply and scarce in terms of quality. Novice practitioners are more conformant to the contents of a KEP. Otherwise they are disoriented, do not assure a good quality level, and end up making many attempts before reaching a satisfactory goal [14].

To facilitate the search of KEP and KEB, metadata are used. The author's proposal consists in using two sets of metadata. The first set answers the question: *does the KEB provide at least a solution that can be used for a specific problem?* This set contains: the type of KEP, the knowledge domain area that for a software engineer can be: techniques, methods, processes, quality models, empirical validation, keywords, problems that a KEP can answer. The second set answers the question:

among the available KEB, which have the most appropriate contents? This second set of metadata contains a synthetic description of contents like requirements, risks, plan, balance, value and history.

5 PROMETHEUS

Practices pROcess and Methods Evolution Through Experience Unfolded Systematically (PROMETHEUS) is a platform developed in the Software Engineering Research LABoratory (SERLAB) of the University of Bari. It is made up of a framework that specializes the KEB with the components and the relations between components, adaptable to the needs of the organization using the platform. As so, it can assume different configurations.

PROMETHEUS has been conceived as a public platform because its aim is to support knowledge transfer among all the organisms that can contribute to accumulate transferable knowledge within business process as innovation, and accumulate experience that increases the confidence of the efficacy of available knowledge. Nevertheless, PROMETHEUS limits the access of deposited knowledge. Indeed, a public or private organization, user of PROMETHEUS, can make part of its KEP public and restrict access to another part of it.

In the following the platform with all the components and relations described in the chapter is outlined. The KEB is made up of different sections, one for each component of the KEP. The decomposition in sections of the KEB allows incremental publishing of a KEP and eases its consultation. The KEB schema is reported in Fig. 9. All the components have contents structured as a tree (Fig. 7) to express knowledge. The metadata described previously are those associated to the AP component which is the main one of the KEP. The other components have metadata that answer the same questions, but their attributes are generally different. The relations between the KEB components represent all the paths that a user can follow in the platform. For example: a user can search for a Knowledge Experience Content and after reading it he/she may want to know about other tools cited in the contents and/or the competences that can be used as support to KEP adoption.

Each section of the KEP can be populated independently from the others. So the KEB can be enriched incrementally. For example, a practitioner may introduce his profile in CM though he is not the author of a KEP, but if he has the competences for adopting a KEP in a business process he can be connected to it. Also, if he has certified competences in a set of projects described in PR its profile can be connected to these projects. Tools can also be presented in TO as support to the adoption of a KEP. Evidences are described in EV and show the positive effects that arise in the project due to its use.

The consultation interface of each section contains connections to resources and to relations of other components of the KEP. Through the e-learning link, seminars, courses, and or details can be consulted. The *Relations* connect the KEP section to analogous sections of other KEP that are in some way connected with the one being consulted. This is particularly interesting in that the author has divided the KEP to make it less complex. The *Attachments* contain papers, books, reports or other forms of conventional sources that detail the motivations of the KEP with respect to a

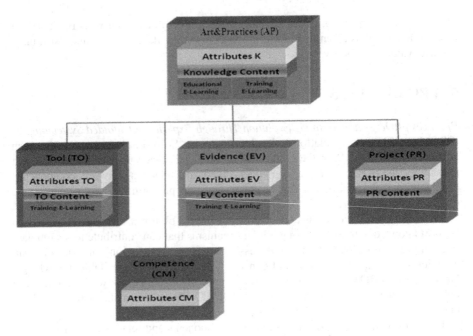

Fig. 9. Schema of Prometheus Art and Practices Component

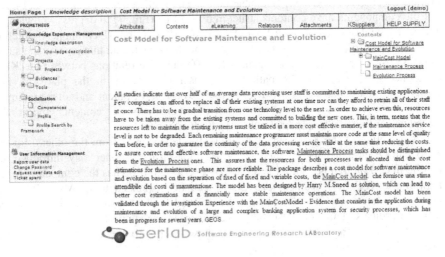

Fig. 10. Example of content for AP

specific section. The *Help Supply* communicates with the authors of a KEP to ask for clarifications or make observations on the KEP; or with the administrators of PROMETHEUS to make observations, claims and other types of communication concerning usability and the level of satisfaction of the platform. The left side refers to a tree that lists all the other sections of the KEP that is being consulted.

The Art and Practices Component (AP) is the central one. An example of its content is shown in Fig. 10; it is possible to note a root node and the pointers to intermediate nodes. Fig. 11 shows the metadata related to the KEP which are the ones expressed in the main component, AP.

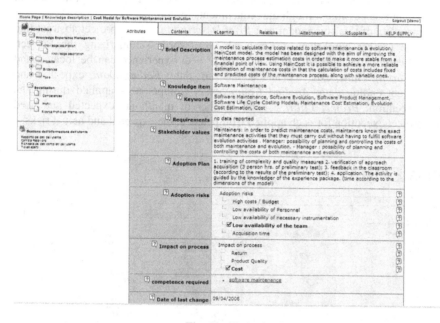

Fig. 11. AP Attributes

5.1 Project Component

Project Components contain all the information useful for Project characterization: Project description and Project contest description; Project used resources; Project results; Events occurred during the project execution.

Many factors characterize the contexts. A tentative list for software engineering is the following:

- *human factors*: number of people, level of competence with refer to one or more standards, propensity towards group work, integration of groups in projects, experience on problems that arise during projects, experience on process resources, techniques and tools to use;
- *problem characterization*: application domain, novelty with respect to the state of art, problem restrictions
- *product characterization*: development and exploitation machines, available time and budget, existing software.

Each project should include the metrics model used for monitoring and therefore the values collected by the measures. Of particular interest are the economical indexes: *expected cost of the planned work*; *actual costs of the work carried out*, *predicted cost of the work carried out*.

A project may contain the detailed data if the organization does not consider it critical. The organism providing the data can decide to make it available to the platform but allow access only to those having specific access credentials. Detailed data in the platform can be used to extract empirical experiences different from the collected ones, and therefore represent an important source for producing information. Detailed data is accessible through the Attachments button.

The metadata of this component are: *Brief Description*, a brief project abstract that contain the project aim; *Project Keywords*, key words summarizing the Project; *Project Domain*; thematic area in which the project experience can be located and applied; *Starting Data*, expected and actual start date; *Ending Data*, expected and actual project ending data; *Applied Competence*, Competences applied during the project execution; *Project Effort*,   Total number of man/hours expected and used during project execution for each applied Competence, the expected and actual risks.

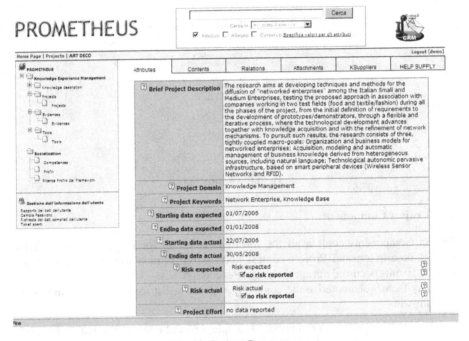

Fig. 12. Project Component

5.2 Tool Component

This component contains a short description of the tool, and the knowledge that can convince possible users to adopt it. Consequently, as for AP, it is important to describe the problems that the tool allows to overcome and answer and which problems it is appropriate for. The competences needed should be outlined, along with the adoption risks and mitigation initiatives. To speed up adoption, stakeholders should be involved. Finally, the tool maturity should be pointed out explicating the number of versions released, the motivations that have led to change version and the changes carried out. Training courses should also be planned.

The metadata are: *short description, technical domain* area covered by the tool, *keywords, date of first release, adoption requirements; competences* and *adoption risks, plan for adoption,* classification *values* for type of stakeholder, number of *versions* and *history.*

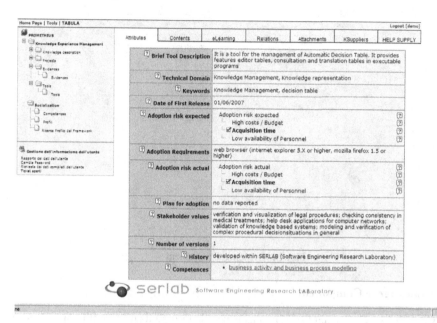

Fig. 13. Tool Component

5.3 Evidence of Components

The EV contains the description of all the empirical investigations that validate the cause-effect relation between research results the innovations proposed and the answers to the problems. In particular this component should describe the data used, the controls carried out on them to assure their accuracy and the mechanisms needed to carry them out, the experimental design, the statistical analysis and the results obtained.

In some cases it may be necessary to produce material to prepare the experimental subjects for the investigation or the instrumentation to use during the investigation itself. In this case the instrumentation can be stored in a repository and be accessible via the *attachments* button. Some times the process can also be supported by training. The EV should express the empirical evidences of all the changes carried out in the KEP and in all its components.

The description of the investigation should be supported by details able to convince the reader of their accuracy and allow for replications. It is obvious that in both cases the PROMETHEUS community expects that these replications be registered in the platform to enforce evidence. A possible guide for outlining a replicable experimental investigation is [7].

The contents of EV are closely related to PR and AP Components. The metadata are: *Brief Evidence Description, brief abstract synthesizing the Evidence Content*; *Evidence Kind, Empirical evidence, Industrial context.*

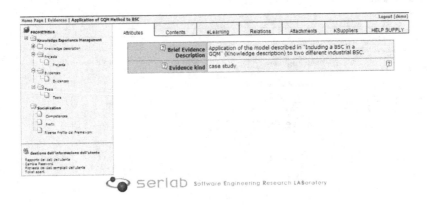

Fig. 14. Evidence Component

5.4 Competence Component

The Competence Component (CM) collects people or organizations with competences in the first case, and capabilities in the second that support the adoption of a KEP or of a Tool. Each subject referring to this component is characterized by a description of the combination of knowledge, skills and behaviours that are part of the professional assets. In CM a subject can be explicitly referred to or use a fictitious name according to his preferences.

Each subject has a portfolio of experience that certifies his professional profile. Often it includes projects, which should be described in the PR component as well. In case it is not possible, a synthesis of the project can be provided in CM. Details like application domain, total hrs implied in the project, professional profiles necessary and included in CM.

The e-learning connected to this component allows for details on the components, and skills, along with tests for each knowledge item and skill. This is important for validating competences that do not have any other type of certification. In the continuous improvement plan for a KEB the contents of the courses and of tests are improved. The improvement is enacted each time a competence prepared with the available course or certified with the available tests, ends up not being perfectly adequate to the projects it is used in.

The metadata for this competence are made up by the list of professional profiles according to the standards used. PROMETHEUS provides the following syllabus for defining competences: EUCIP (EUropean Certification of Informatics Professionals http://www.cepis.org), SFIA (Skills For the Information Age http://www.sfia.org.uk), CIGREF (Nomenclature of ICT Job Profiles http://www.cigref.fr), AITTS (Advanced IT Training System http://www.kibnet.org).

The curriculum vitae and/or other certification of competences that a person wants to provide can be consulted through the attachments button.

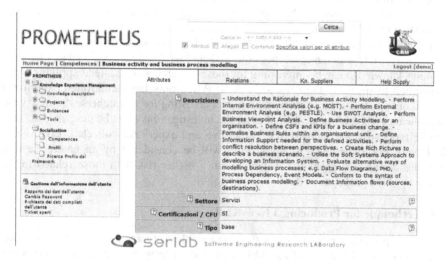

Fig. 15. Competence Component

6   Guidelines for Production

6.1   Production and Publication

First of all the structure of the KEP allows to continuously improve PROMETHEUS. Indeed, if all the community surrounding the platform uses the same standard for contents, a single model can be used to evaluate if they satisfy all the KEP.

The contents of a KEP require relevant effort to be produced and often a long time to be completed. The effort for production is due to the high amount of knowledge that must be formalized in the KEP. The production time results to be long because experience must be collected as knowledge is applied. To mitigate the first problem, a KEP can be produced incrementally. When part of the knowledge is available for AP, a first version of KEP can be published on the platform. As so it can evolve in time and lead to further versions. The other components of the KEP can be produced in other moments. It is recommended that the production of other parts of KEP be planned so that interested people know when they will be available. The components of the KEP may also be planned according to the requests of users. This is indeed one of the secondary effects of an open community, in that it promotes the production of KEP parts according to the interest or the need of a specific period.

For what concerns the empirical evidence of the experience of KEP, it can be collected as the KEP is adopted in executed projects in various contexts. The collection of experiences is clearly another effect of the community that relies on PROMETHEUS and of the cooperation that is enacted among its members.

The empirical investigation that produced evidence related to a KEP should be rigorously described so that it is clearly comparable to all the other investigations carried out with the same KEP. Moreover, they must make up a family of experiments [9].

In case of a production project, the essential data should be extracted from all the available data to describe the empirical investigation and express the evidences supporting the KEP.

It should be clear to the author of a KEP that a package published with partial contents restricts the range of possible stakeholders. Indeed, a package that only contains knowledge can be interesting for those researchers that intend applying Open Innovation to speed up their research. A KEP that only has a controlled experiment carried out on students as experience can be interesting for researchers who may want to replicate the experiment. In this case, the investigations must be described so they can be replicated and increase the knowledge and experience collected. Likewise, a KEP with low experience of application will be considered by an enterprise if it provides answers to problems that represent a higher risk than those related to the adoption of the package itself.

6.2 Technique for Producing a New KEP

In order to produce a new AP the author must synthesize large amounts of information and knowledge. The author of the KEP must find the most accredited information and knowledge from other sources. So, the first task is to identify the sources to consult. A possible set of sources for a software engineer can be: IEEExplore, ACM Digital Library, Google Scholar (http://scholar.google.com), Citeseer Library (http://citeseerx. ist.psu.edu/), Inspec (http://www.theiet.org/publishing/), Science Direct (www. sciencedirect.com), EI Compendex (www.engineeringvillage2.org/Controller/Servlet/ AthensService/). In case of industrial knowledge sources of implicit or explicit knowledge can be consulted such as: developers, market analysts, salesmen, support, reports, users, customers.

Literature can be synthesized through Systematic Literature Review [21]. It is made up of three main phases: Planning, Conducting and Documenting. During the planning phase, the motivation of the study is pointed out, along with the strategy, and research questions related to the problems that a KEP intends to answer. The protocol is described and it is then verified and validated. The sources used for extracting the literature are then subject to quality assurance criteria which allows to select and filter the documents. When conducting the review, information is extracted according to the data extraction tables defined in the protocol and the answers to the research questions are formalized. During the documentation phase, the AP component is produced.

During the synthesis carried out to produce AP, the author identifies if there are empirical evidences on the application of the knowledge being extracted. They produce the EV component. The same can be said for training material that produces e-learning resources of one or more components.

The synthesis process identifies possible knowledge suppliers of the KEP being produced. If appropriately authorized by the knowledge suppliers, the author could produce part of the CM component.

6.3 Identification Expressions

The nodes underlying the displayed node in a KEP component are indicated as links within the package. Internal links are distinguished from links to other packages with the following standard: [Name of Link]-[Type of component]. [Name of Link] is chosen by the author of the package and identifies the element it points to. [Type of Component] relates to the component the link refers to. So: [Type of component] ∈ {Art&Practices, Learning, Tool, Evidence, Project, Competence}.

6.4 Verification and Validation of Packages

The author of the KEP is in charge of its verification. Currently, the check list used for verification is the following:

I.   the names of the components must not contain synonyms;
II.   all the links of a node must be reachable;
III.   no loop links must be defined;
IV.   contents of the components are traceable with the knowledge contained in the component according to the guidelines of the PROMETHEUS platform.

It can me improved with experience as KEP are produced and improved. Validation is carried out mainly with the use and application of KEP on behalf of users. More so, the validation will be carried out in different moments than when the KEP is published and will be more accurate as the KEP is applied. The users will validate the KEP and communicate their satisfaction/dissatisfaction and their motivations through the Help Supply.

6.5 Evolution of KEP

During verification and validation of KEP one or more elements concerning completeness, correctness, ambiguity of KEP may be pointed out. In this case the package is subject to *corrective changes*. These changes do not have to be motivated.

Thanks to the application of QIP in the EF, failures in the indicators characterizing the KEP can be pointed out along with failures in any of the KEP components. In this case *perfective changes* are carried out. They require explicating decisions that relate to the changes. KP must contain a new version of the updated contents and a new element of its history.

By interacting with users, the author of a KEP can receive suggestions for changes that improve the comprehension and attractiveness of a KEP. In this case, *adaptive changes* arise. As for the previous ones, they must be motivated, and decisions for changes must be described and registered in a new history element of the KEP-

The set of decisions and versions prove the maturity of the package.

6.6 Cooperation for Development

Production organizations provide knowledge to a KEB concerning: models (resources, quality, product and process), product or process components and data that can be used to extract experience from the application of knowledge.

Knowledge and experience are extracted from the KEB to support projects in execution or planned. They transfer the innovations contained in the KEP to business processes and collect further experiences that enrich the KEB.

The research organizations or single researchers internal or external to the organization provide research results even without the experience component. They produce technological innovation from research results collected by different sources. This is a way to confirm or deny the knowledge contained in the KEP through various types of empirical investigations.

The organisms that have validated capabilities through projects they have been involved in, can explicit them in the CM component. The same information can be attributed to the KEB on behalf of single persons that have competences explicable in CM and that can be validated in PR. If parts of these competences are also useful for adopting a KEP, they can be related to them. The organisms looking for specialised competences, for a project or the adoption of a KEP, can find the available ones in the KEB with the requested certification. When the competences are included in other projects by other organisms that have chosen them, their certification is enforced.

The training and research organisms provide training and education material along with tests for evaluating the useful competences for adopting the KEP and the decision models used to plan the training courses and improvement initiatives for overcoming competence gaps. The organisms using competences that have been prepared and validated through e-learning and tests can evaluate the appropriateness of the competences themselves.

7   Values of PROMETHEUS

To attract subjects that can make up one or more stakeholder communities of PROMETHEUS it is the case to list the benefits that being part of the community provides to stakeholders. The following is a tentative list. Some of the values listed are typical of knowledge bases and others are specific for PROMETHEUS for the services that distinguish this platform from the concurrent ones.

7.1   Physical Subjects

The physical subjects are knowledge workers external to the organizations. They can be practitioners or researchers according to the scope of their work: carry out productive goals or create new knowledge or diffuse technological innovation. They can use PROMETHEUS to collect knowledge or available practices and can provide experience to the platform and contribute to its improvement. Furthermore, they can provide their time and competences to other stakeholders. In this case PROMETHEUS represents a marketplace for them extended to the entire globe.

A knowledge supplier has economical returns not from his knowledge but from the application of his knowledge to the production goals. Furthermore, unexpressed knowledge is lost due to the volatility of tacit knowledge. As so, it is important for a knowledge supplier to explicit the practices for its application. Explicated knowledge that is published in PROMETHEUS increases the reputation of suppliers, and therefore the chance of being selected to be included in other projects by other stakeholders.

The subjects in PROMETHEUS can certify their competences through projects they have been part of and through the KEP they produce and publish. Furthermore, they can increase their reputation by being part of the online support for stakeholders of PROMETHEUS. This interaction allows subjects to communicate with others by exchanging information, knowledge and experiences [14].

The importance of rigorously defining KEP contents, used in PROMETHEUS, allows for standard contents and therefore improves KEP *comprehension*. This eases acquisition and minimizes the need for tailoring the KEP. To collect evidence on this statement, a first experiment has been carried out to show how a KEP is a more efficient and effective means than conventional sources for transferring knowledge and practices for application. For space reasons, this experiment has not been described in this chapter but it can be consulted in [4].

7.2 Organizations

The organizations are a structured set of knowledge workers. They are interested in enforcing the services and intensifying the relation and cooperation between subjects. Particular attention is given to relations and cooperation based on the use of PROMETHEUS and consists in exchanging knowledge between subjects of the organization. According to the PROMETHEUS perspective, the interacting organizations act as a single organism. Productive organizations can be distinguished from research ones. The first put particular attention to increase business, the second to increase knowledge by innovating and transferring it to business processes.

The possibility of using and specializing a KEB for a specific context of the user organizations preserves their identity in spite of the collaboration with a community based on a KEB [5].

The knowledge that makes up the KEP represents problems from different perspectives for a same package. Furthermore due to the structure of the model, described in this chapter, they are divided and located in the various components of the KEP. The structure of the contents allows the reader to define a reading navigation path according to his level of knowledge and experience.

The user organisms find research results in the KEB that can be used to rapidly reach the goals or to answer problems arisen during the innovation process. The KEP also contains the adoption process, the risks presented from the process and the ways for overcoming them. All this allows the adopting organism to have an important benchmark that favours the adoption on behalf of the knowledge-workers internal to an organism, along with a rapid socialization of the KEP which produces new knowledge and innovates business processes.

The EF allows collecting data from executed projects and transforming them in empirical evidence for validating the KEP. This analysis continuously improves the KEP in all its components with the knowledge acquired during job learning which gives more confidence in using the KEP on behalf of interested organisms.

KEP explicit the knowledge that is tacitly collected during work and that tend to remain in the mind of the project manager or expressed in various documents distributed within the organism. As so it is difficult to localize. If the contents of a

KEP refer to project management problems, the acquisition of knowledge improves project management.

In managing cooperation, the socialization of a KEP can be used to harmonize the competences between the cooperating organisms. PROMETHEUS offers resources for empirically validating the capabilities of organisms that are candidates to cooperation. In case of turnover of human resources, PROMETHEUS identifies subjects with the competences searched. In delocalizing the production, PROMETHEUS offers resources for searching available organisms for empirical validation. Also, it provides resources for evaluating competences of the organisms for outsourcing or off shoring along with the training material.

The organizations that are part of the PROMETHEUS community, and exchange knowledge, minimize the costs and production risks of knowledge and experience contained in the KEB. These minimizations represent a return which increases as the use of the KEP increases. In synthesis, PROMETHEUS promotes scale economy in the market within the community.

The organization that makes knowledge and experience available defines all the circumstances for making them available, according to a personal business model. The acquiring organization has the research results immediately available with defined costs. As so, the market within the community that surrounds PROMETHEUS is able o create scale economy for its suppliers and provide it to the users of the KEP.

8 Conclusions

This chapter has proposed definitions of knowledge and experiences oriented towards the adoption of research results in business processes or research projects that use it as starting point to carry out new research goals. These definitions are based on problems that knowledge intends answering and on the empirical evidence that the research results want to provide to the problem.

From these definitions and keeping in mind the lessons learnt, both known in literature and learnt by the author, a structure of Knowledge-Experience Package has been suggested. It allows or contributes to overcome the barriers that arise in adopting a new knowledge in business processes and in exchanging research results. The content of the KEP is complementary to knowledge which can be collected by conventional sources. Thanks to the structure the KEP has a high level of readability and comprehensibility although its production requires high effort. For this reason it is advisable for it to be incremental and defined in collaboration with other stakeholders of the KEP.

The chapter also describes a platform, PROMETHEUS, which manages the KEB and collects KEP that are available to the community around PROMETHEUS. In the analysis of the values produced by PROMETHEUS for different types of stakeholders the contribution for supporting user organisms is important for moving towards knowledge economy. In particular, it is important for supporting behavioural models: diversity and competitive advantage based on high level technological competences; open innovation, distributed production, digital business ecosystems.

Many of the assertions made in this chapter need empirical evidence to become universally accredited or recognized. As so, much work must still be done to produce such empirical evidence. This work can be seen as a proposal of the author who invites all researchers and practitioners and organisms interested in these topics to collaborate by joining the PROMETHEUS community.

References

1. Aamodt, A., Nygard, M.: Different roles and mutual dKEPendencies of data, information and knowledge - An AI perspective on their integration. Data and Knowledge Engineering 16, 191–222 (1995)
2. Althoff, K., Decker, B., Hartkopf, S., Jedlitschka, A.: Experience Management: The Fraunhofer IESE Experience Factory. In: Perner, P. (ed.) Proc. Industrial Conference Data Mining, Institute for Computer Vision and applied Computer Sciences, Leipzig, Germany, July 24-25, 2001, pp. 12–29 (2001)
3. Ardimento, P., Baldassarre, M.T., Caivano, D., Visaggio, G.: Innovation Diffusion through Empirical Studies. In: 17th International conference on Software Engineering and Knowledge Engineering (SEKE), Taipei China, pp. 701–706 (July 2005)
4. Ardimento, P., Caivano, D., Cimitile, M., Visaggio, G.: Empirical Investigation of the Efficacy and Efficiency of tools for transferring software engineering knowledge. Journal of Information & Knowledge Management (submitted, 2007)
5. Ardimento, P., Baldassarre, M.T., Caivano, D., Cimitile, M., Visaggio, G.: Controlled Experiment on Search Engine Knowledge Extraction Capabilities. In: 3rd International Conference on Software and Data Technologies (ICSOFT), 5-8 July, pp. 388–395. INSTIC Press, Porto Portugal (2008)
6. Ardimento, P., Baldassarre, M.T., Cimitile, M., Visaggio, G.: Empirical Validation of Knowledge Packages as Facilitators for Knowledge Transfer. Knowledge and Information Systems, an International Journal (submitted)
7. Baldassarre, M.T., Visaggio, G.: Report on Empirical Investigations. White paper, http://serlab.di.uniba.it/about_us_it/people_it/ TBaldassarre_it/
8. Basili, V.R., Caldiera, C., Rombach, H.D.: Experience Factory. In: Encyclopedia of Software Engineering, vol. 2, pp. 469–476. John Wiley &Sons, Chichester (1994)
9. Basili, V., Shull, F., Lanubile, F.: Building Knowledge through Families of Experiments. IEEE Transactions on Software Engineering 25, 456–473 (1999)
10. Basili, V.R., Caldiera, C., Rombach, H.D.: Experience Factory Concepts as a Set of Experiences Bases. In: 13th Conference on Software Engineering and Knowledge engineering (SEKE), Buenos Aires, Argentina, pp. 102–109 (June 2001)
11. Chesbourg, H.: Open innovation. Harvard Business School Press, Harvard (2002)
12. Chesbrough, H.: Open Platform Innovation: Creating Value from Internal and External Innovation. Intel. Technology Journal 7, 5–9 (2003)
13. Reidar, C., Torgeir, D.: Software Experience Bases: A Consolidated Evaluation and Status Report. In: Bomarius, F., Oivo, M. (eds.) PROFES 2000. LNCS, vol. 1840, pp. 391–406. Springer, Heidelberg (2000)
14. Desouza, K.C., Awazu, Y., Baloh, P.: Managing Knowledge in Global Software Development Efforts: Issues and Practices. IEEE Software 23, 30–37 (2006)
15. Dini, P., Darking, M., Rathbone, N., Vidal, M., Hernandez, P., Ferronato, P., Briscoe, G., Hendryx, S.: The Digital Ecosystems Research Vision: 2010 and Beyond. Creative Commons, Stanford, California (2005), http://www.digital-ecosystems.org/ events/2005.05/de_position_paper_vf.pdf

16. Department of Trade and Industry (DTI), Competitive Futures: Building the Knowledge Driven Economy, DTI, London (1998)
17. Economic and Social Research Council, Annual Report, 2004-2005 Published by The Stationery Office (TSO),
    http://www.official-documents.gov.uk/document/hc0506/hc00/0092/0092.asp
18. Kemp, R.G.M., Mosselman, M., Blees, J., Maas, J.: Barriers to Entry, EIM (Research report / EIM, Business & Policy Research H200301), p. 153 (2003)
19. Foray, D.: The Economics of Knowledge. MIT, Cambridge (2006)
20. Gorschek, T., Wohlin, C., Garre, P., Larsson, S.: A Model For Technology Transfer in Practice. IEEE Software 23, 88–95 (2006)
21. Kitchenham, B.: Guidelines for Performing Systematic Literature Reviews in Software Engineering. EBSE Technical Report (2007)
22. Reifer, D.J.: Is the Software Engineering State of the Practice Getting Closer to the State of the Art? IEEE Software 20, 78–83 (2003)
23. Schneider, K., Schwinn, T.: Maturing Experience Base ConcKEPts at DaimlerChrysler. Software Process Improvement and Practice 6, 85–96 (2001)
24. Solingen, R.V., Berghout, E.: The Goal/Question/Metric Method: a Practical Guide for Quality Improvement of Software Development. McGraw Hill, London (1999)

Author Index

Printed in the United States
By Bookmasters